# Around
# Our Table for Two

## PAM WERLEY

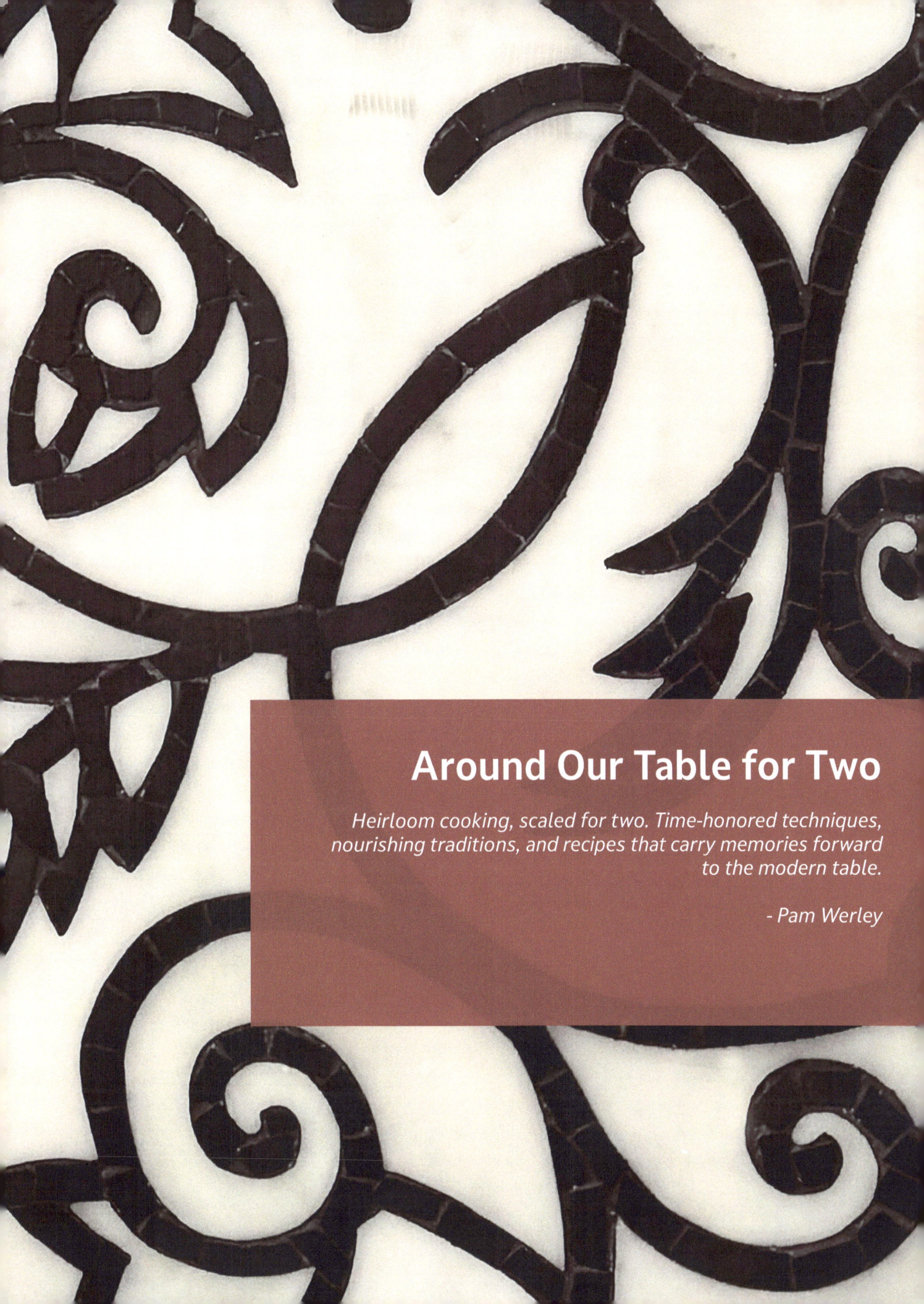

# Around Our Table for Two

*Heirloom cooking, scaled for two. Time-honored techniques, nourishing traditions, and recipes that carry memories forward to the modern table.*

*- Pam Werley*

**Art & Design Director:** *Kurt Mueller*

**Designer:** *Pam Werley*

**Cover Design:** *Kurt Mueller*

**Copy Editors:** *Mark Werley and a few dear friends*

**Proof Readers:** *Julia Ponder, Laura Johnson, Camie Donohue & Kim Pinkham*

**Recipe Testers:** *Vicki Brunsvold, Hannah Brown, Kelsey Griffin, Beth Grund, Betty Ford, Sherri Erickson, Lisa Helminiak (and Ben), Daniela Morgan, Kim Pinkham, Greg Pomerantz, Julia Ponder, Lisa Ramsden, Jill Sagehorn, Nina Sexton, Betsy Werley, Michael Werley, Zach Werley, Kay Whaley*

Copyright © 2025 by Our Table 4 2, LLC

Photographs copyright © 2025 by Pam Werley

All rights reserved.

Published and printed in the United States of America. No part of this book may be used or reproduced in any manner whatsoever without written permission except in the case of brief quotations embodied in articles and reviews.

For more information, please contact pam@ourtable42.com

ISBN: 979-8-9938035-0-0

**DEDICATION**

To my sons, who inherited the spirit of curiosity and adventure that makes every meal an exploration—thank you for always being ready to try something new, even when it was one of my "happy accidents."

And to my husband, who has encouraged me to reach higher in the kitchen and who, with steady patience, has always taken on cleanup duty with love.

# Contents

Introduction: Around Our Table for Two.............9
My Manifesto........................................................12
Smart Strategies when Cooking for Two...........15

## GATHER 'ROUND STARTERS

Pan Con Tomate.................................................21
North Shore Taleggio Fondue............................23
Mediterranean Crostini.....................................24
Cheesy Mexican Street Corn Dip......................25
Traditional Hummus..........................................26
Balsamic Pear, Pistachio Pesto Tartine............28
Baba Ghanoush..................................................31
Rosemary Ricotta Toast with Figs....................32
Bourbon-Glazed Salmon Bites..........................35

## TOASTING TRADITIONS

Minnesota Bootlegger........................................39
Limoncello Sorbet Spritz...................................41
Blackberry Mojito...............................................41
Watermelon Lime Mocktail................................42
Twist on a Dirty Martini.....................................42
Dr. Werley Whiskey Sour...................................43
Blood Red Orange Margarita............................45
Slope-side Hot Chocolate..................................46

## SOUPS TO SAVOR

Tomato and Fennel Soup...................................50
Roasted Carrot Soup..........................................53
Fall Farmer's Market Soup................................54
Baked Onion Soup..............................................57
Soupe Au Pistou.................................................58
Roasted Red Pepper Soup.................................60
Asparagus, Leek & Edamame Soup.................62
Leftover Roasted Chicken Noodle Soup..........65
Kim's Award Winning White Chicken Chili......66
Icelandic Fish Stew............................................68
Heirloom Tomato Gazpacho..............................72
Cantaloupe and Sweet Corn Gazpacho...........72
Peach and Cucumber Gazpacho......................73
Strawberry Gazpacho........................................74

## HANDHELD HEIRLOOMS

Philly Cheesesteaks...........................................79
Aunt Sherril's Runza..........................................80
Short Rib Burger................................................82
Crispy Lamb Pita................................................83
Grilled Portobello Burger..................................84
Tuna Cheese Melt..............................................86
Smashed Chicken Sandwich.............................87
Croque Monsieur Sandwich..............................88

## BUTCHER'S FAVORITES, COOKS PRIDE

Beef Wellington..................................................93
Spiedies..............................................................95
Glazed Ham........................................................97
Passover Brisket.................................................99
Greek Baked Ziti...............................................100
Pear and Prosciutto Stuffed Pork Loin..........103
Fruitcake Stuffed Pork Loin............................104
Hollace's Family Bolognese Recipe...............107
Leftover Bolognese Lasgana..........................108
Adobo Flank Steak...........................................110
Asian Flat Iron Steak.......................................112
Sausage and Fennel Rigatoni.........................113
Perfect Pot Roast.............................................114
Sunday Supper Pork Ragu..............................115
Hachis Parmentier...........................................116
Wine Braised Short Ribs.................................119
Prime Rib Roast...............................................120

## GATHERED FROM FARM & WATER

Apricot Harissa-Glazed Chicken....................125
California Fish Tacos.......................................126
Pasta Diavola...................................................127
Sheet Pan Chicken Thighs..............................128
Low Country Boil..............................................130
Can Pepi Fried Chicken...................................131
Baked Chicken Parmesan Meatballs.............132

Rhode Island-Style Calamari ..................................133
Supper Club Cordon Bleu..........................................134
Tuna Poke Bowl.............................................................136
Harissa Baked Fish.......................................................139
Baked Halibut en Pappillote....................................140
Chicken, Leek & Tarragon Pot Pie .........................142
Spring Lasagna .............................................................145
Chicken Marsala ...........................................................146
Baked Salmon ...............................................................147
Six-Minute Seared Ahi Tuna Steaks .....................148
Turkey Breast.................................................................149

## THE SUPPORTING CAST

Parmesan-Crusted Salmon Caesar Salad...................155
Supperclub Creamed Spinach Casserole....................157
Apple Kohlrabi and Manchego Slaw.............................158
Roasted Beets.......................................................................158
Chive Popovers....................................................................159
Roasted Vegetable Platter...............................................160
Bookclub Quinoa Chicken Salad....................................163
Spicy Cucumber Salad......................................................165
Artichoke and Ricotta Flan...............................................166
Lagoon Chicken Wild Rice Salad....................................167
Deviled Egg Salad...............................................................168
Maple Roasted Carrots.....................................................170
Supper Club Wedge Salad...............................................171
Roasted Celery Root .........................................................172
Apple and Winter Squash Salad....................................173
Skillet Scalloped Potatoes...............................................174

## MORNING GATHERINGS FOR TWO

Herb-Pot and Gruyere Souffles......................................179
Lemon Blueberry French Toast .....................................181
Chilaquiles with Mushrooms..........................................182
Eggs in Purgatory ...............................................................183
Easy Sausage and Spinach Egg Bake............................184
Acai Bowls .............................................................................186
Blueberry Yogurt Smoothie ............................................187
Mango Lassi Smoothie .....................................................187
Mango Green Tea ...............................................................187

Maple Granola .....................................................................188
Citrus-Cured Gravlax......................................................... 189
Parsnip and Potato Latke .................................................191
Avocado Toast with Sweet & Spicy Tomatoes...........192

## TWO SPOONS, PLEASE

Lemon-Blackberry Fool .....................................................197
Panna cotta Dessert Cups ...............................................199
Molten Lava Cakes .............................................................200
Tiramisu Icebox Cake ........................................................201
Salted Shortbread Chocolate Chip Cookies ..............202
Chocolate Mouse................................................................204
Grandma's 4th of July Ice Cream ..................................205
Upside Down Peach Cake ................................................206
Stout Chocolate Bundt Cake ..........................................207
Fudgy Brownies ..................................................................210
Layered Pumpkin Cake .....................................................213

## LITTLE EXTRAS

Mediterranean Relish ........................................................218
Fruit Compote...................................................................... 220
Horseradish Sauce .............................................................220
My "Keeper" Risotto ..........................................................221
Homemade Gravy ..............................................................221
Homemade Chicken Stock ..............................................222
Mint Mojo Sauce .................................................................222
Roasted Rhubarb Agrodolce ..........................................223
Hot Fudge .............................................................................223
Green Salad and Jam Vinaigrette ..................................224
Tuscan Salt ...........................................................................225
Lemon Tahini Sauce ..........................................................226
Creamy Green Peppercorn Sauce .................................227
Oven-Dried Tomatoes ......................................................227
Garlic Confit .........................................................................229

*"Cooking is one of
the great gifts you can
give to those you love."*
— **Ina Garten**

# Welcome to Around Our Table for Two

Come on in. Pour yourself a cup of coffee or a glass of wine and settle in with me around the table. This cookbook is a celebration of heirloom cooking—timeless recipes passed down through generations, lovingly adapted for a table of two. Whether you're cooking for yourself and someone you love, or simply savoring the joy of a well-made meal, you're in the right place.

My summers growing up were spent in the warm, bustling kitchens of my grandmothers on their Nebraska farms. I remember the rhythm of those days—shelling peas on the porch, helping stir a bubbling pot, the hum of conversation as meals came together. Cooking wasn't just about getting food on the table, it was an act of caring and connection. Meals were how my grandmother and aunt's showed love. And in that crowded kitchen filled with laughter, cousins and casseroles, I found my place.

Around Our Table for Two is my way of honoring those memories while recognizing the way life shifts. For years, my dinner table was filled with the voices of my two sons, Michael (now in Colorado) and Zach (in Washington, DC). These days, it's often just my husband Mark and me. But the kitchen? It's still the heart of our home—a place of creativity, comfort and conversation.

> *"Food brings people together on many different levels. It's nourishment of the soul and body; it's truly love."*
> *– Giada De Laurentiis*

Scaling down cherished family recipes to serve two is no small feat. These dishes were originally crafted to feed large families or entire communities, so resizing them means more than simply cutting the quantities in half. It takes careful attention to timing, texture and balance to preserve the soul of the recipe. That's the work I've done here. Through trial, error and lots of taste tests, making sure every dish still earns its place as a "keeper."

Many of the recipes in this book, like a small-batch version of my aunt's farm-style runzas or a comforting bolognese passed down through my friend Hollace's Sicilian family, are rooted in the kitchens of my past. Others, like a downsized Icelandic fish stew or a Supperclub-style Chicken Cordon Bleu with mushrooms, leeks, and prosciutto, were born out of travel and curiosity.

My cooking continues to evolve with where I live and what is in season. After more than 40 years in Minnesota, I have become a passionate advocate for eating local. I'm a longtime member of our food co-op and CSA (community supported agriculture) community and I believe deeply in supporting local growers and producers. Food just tastes better when it comes from people you know.

You'll see that reflected throughout these pages. I've added notes to many recipes, offering ideas for incorporating market finds like fresh heirloom tomatoes, farm eggs, or locally made cheese into the dishes you make at home.

Cooking heirloom recipes with local flair is one way we nourish both body and community. It supports sustainability, strengthens local food systems and brings more flavor to the plate. It also gives new life to the recipes we hold dear, reminding us that heirloom cooking isn't static. It's a living tradition that adapts to time, place and the people around the table.

Whether you're making my twist on Grandma Lois's chocolate chip cookies (I always snuck them from the freezer and ate them while still frozen!) or my version of Grandma Maxine's homemade ice cream (you can make it right in your blender!), I hope these recipes bring a little joy to your home.

Of course, these are my updated versions because no matter what my aunts say, it's basically the recipe off the Nestlé Toll House® package! But we all know our grandmothers didn't follow recipes exactly. While I can't quite replicate the exact taste of the cookies or the ice cream I remember, I've tried to infuse what I learned in their kitchens into the best version I can share now. These recipes carry their spirit, their care and a little bit of my own twist.

So welcome to my kitchen, my memories, and my modern-day table for two. I'm so glad you're here. Let's cook, share and celebrate the stories that live on in every bite.

Join me around our table,

Pam

*"I'm just someone who likes cooking and for whom sharing food is a form of expression."*
**– Maya Angelou**

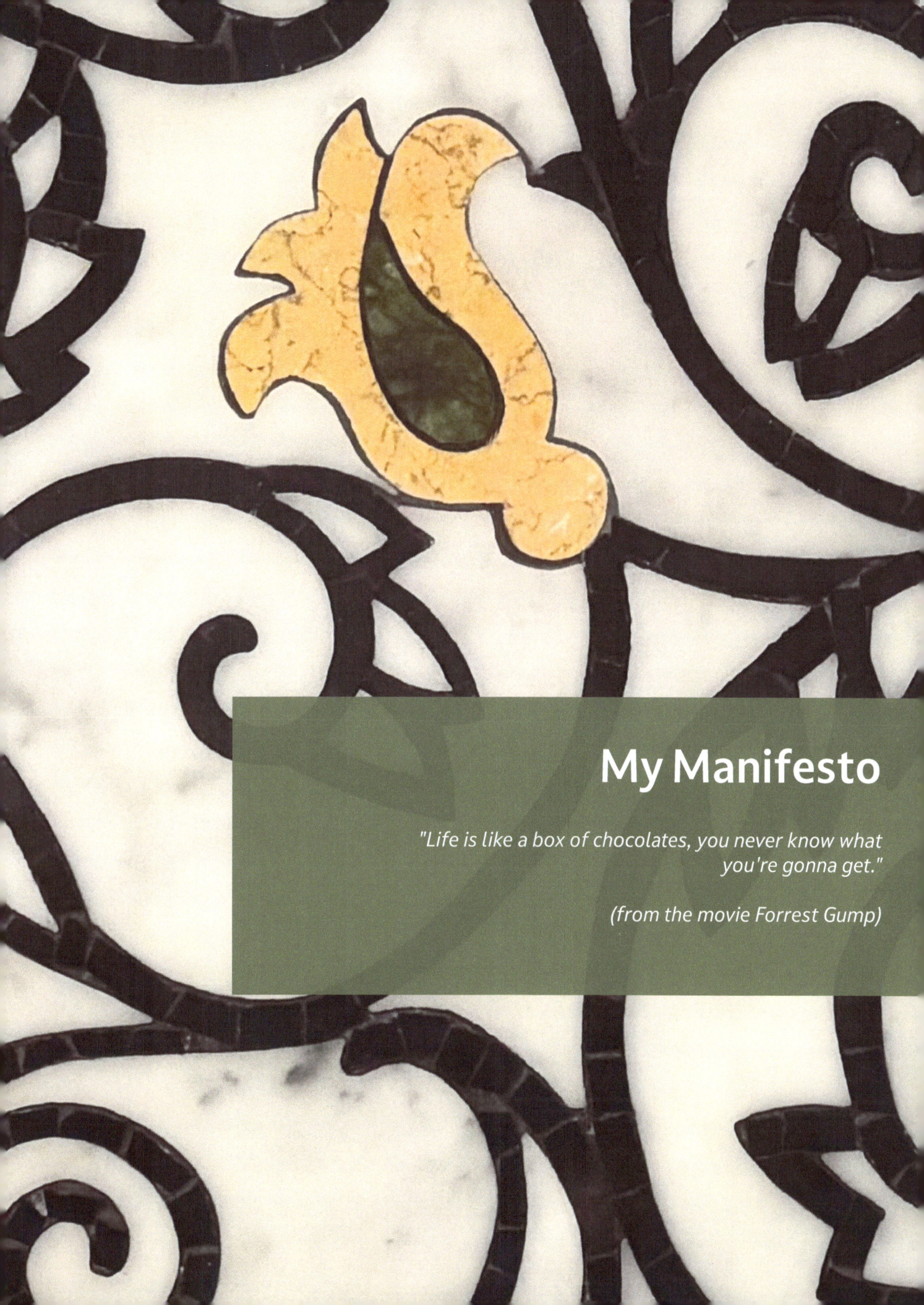

# My Manifesto

"Life is like a box of chocolates, you never know what you're gonna get."

(from the movie Forrest Gump)

# My Manifesto

My childhood summers were spent in the farm kitchens of my grandmothers where the rhythm of the day revolved around what was growing in the garden and what was simmering on the stove. Meals weren't just made; they were tended to, cared for, and shared. I can still picture their aprons, the hum of conversation, and the smell of something comforting in the oven. Food was how they showed love.

To me, heirloom cooking is rooted in those memories. It is not about strict recipes or perfect technique. It's about cooking with intention, with heart and with a deep respect for the people and places that shaped you. It's about honoring dishes passed down through generations and re-imagining them with what's fresh and local today, cooking them in a way that feels right for your life now, even if your table seats just two.

This manifesto is a collection of the values and lessons I carry into my own kitchen. Some come from the women who raised me, others from farmers, chefs or conversations at the market. All of them are reminders that cooking is more than a task—it's a way of staying connected to your story.

**1. Be proud of your roots.** Be proud of your home, your family, your culture—that is your inspiration. Your history is not something to overcome, it's something to cook from.

**2. Cook as if your grandmother were watching.** Or better yet, cook alongside her. Learn from those who came before you. Ask questions. Capture the details. Write down the stories as much as the measurement they are part of the recipe.

**3. Respect your ingredients.** And the people who grow, raise, or make them. A tomato tastes better when you've shaken hands with the farmer who picked it that morning.

**4. Shop with intention.** Make the farmers' market part of your weekly rhythm. Use it as a guide for your meals. Let your food basket reflect your values—choose what's in season, what's close to home, and what brings joy.

**5. Grow something—anything.** A pot of basil on the windowsill. A tomato plant in a bucket. A backyard herb garden. The connection you feel to your food when you've helped it grow is priceless and the flavor is better, too.

**6. Cook in a clean space.** Not because it looks pretty, but because it keeps your mind focused and your creativity shine. Clean as you go. It's not fussy, it's freeing.

**7. Let vegetables lead the way.** Taste them raw. Are they sweet? Earthy? Starchy? Let their natural character inspire how you cook them. A vegetable can teach you more than a recipe ever could.

**8. Make vegetables the main event sometimes.** A well-cooked vegetable—caramelized, roasted, grilled, or braised—can be just as satisfying as a piece of slow-cooked meat. Let them take center stage.

**9. Stay flexible.** Don't let a missing ingredient or a change in plans derail your dinner. If the peaches aren't ripe or the herbs are wilted, pivot. Let go of perfection. Improvise. Some of the best meals come from a little kitchen serendipity.

**10. Think in sauces and accents.** If you see a beautiful bottle of pomegranate molasses or local maple syrup, ask yourself: where could I use this? Could it brighten Grandma's old broccoli salad in place of the heavy mayo? Could it glaze carrots or sweeten a pan sauce? Let little ingredients spark big ideas.

**11. Learn by going too far.** Over season something with salt or lemon just once and you will know what "too much" really tastes like. Once you understand the line you will walk it confidently.

**12. Taste. Season. Taste again**. There's no shortcut. Your tongue is your most important tool. Trust it.

**13. Keep a kitchen notebook.** Jot down notes in your cookbooks. Write what you loved, what you would change, what you would try next time. Capture creative sparks and accidental genius. That's how heirloom recipes begin.

**14. Stretch your meals.** If a dish takes effort, let it reward you more than once. A roasted turkey breast can become sandwiches the next day. That pot of bolognese can become a layered lasagna for two. Cook smart. Make the most of it.

**15. If it's not bringing you joy, take a break.** Cooking should make you happy. If it starts to frustrate you, stop. Go out to eat. Order takeout. Let someone else do the work for a night. Then come back, figure out what went sideways, and try again tomorrow. That's how we learn.

**16. Stay curious.** Ask questions—of yourself, your family, even your server. Most home cooks love to talk about the dishes they cherish. Behind every beloved meal is a story; when it was first made, why it's still made, what it means. Food opens the door to culture, memory, and connection. Curiosity is the ingredient that keeps cooking alive.

*"Cooking is love made visible."*

— **Anonymous**

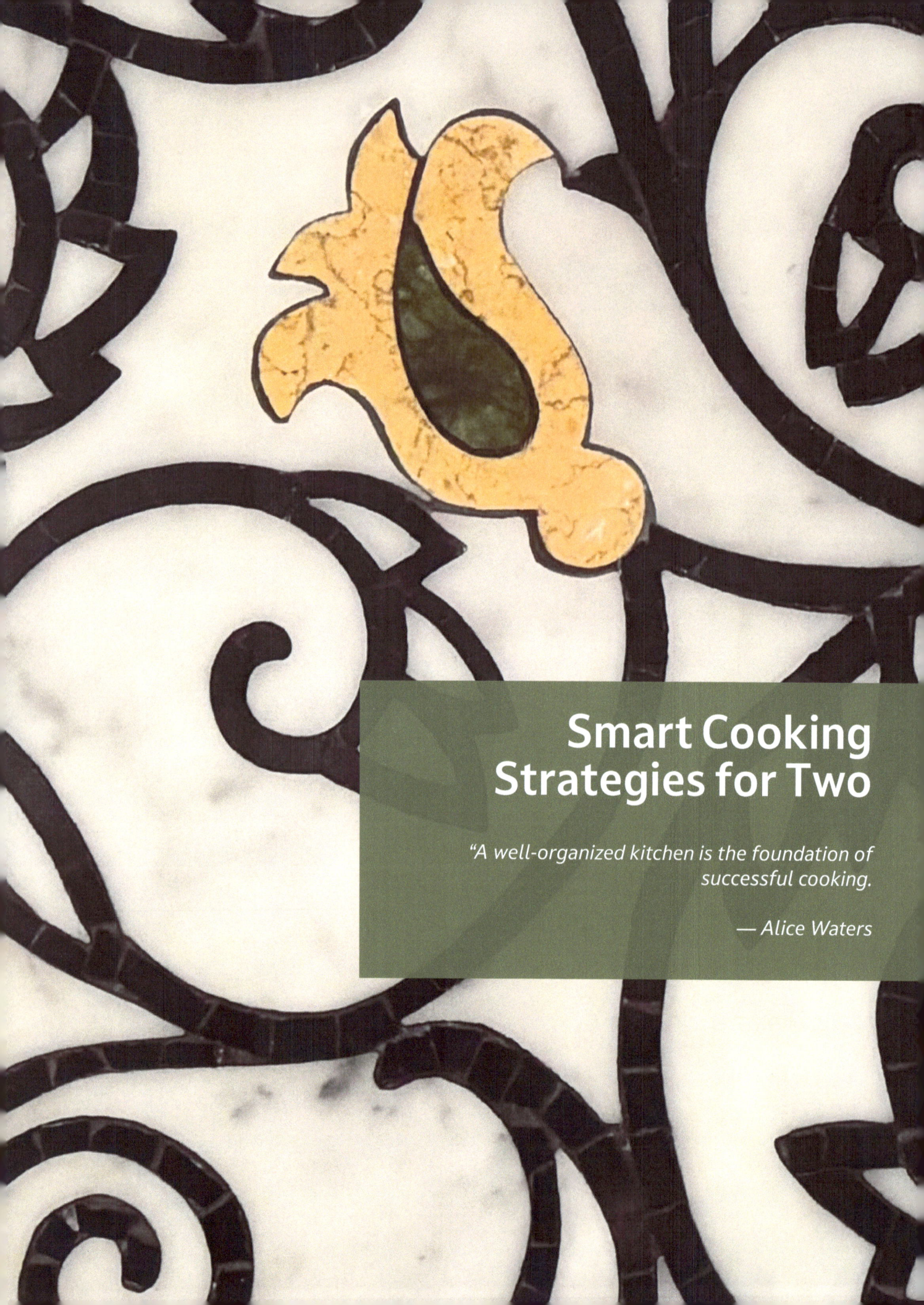

# Smart Cooking Strategies for Two

"A well-organized kitchen is the foundation of successful cooking.

— Alice Waters

# Smart Strategies
## when Cooking for Two

Cooking for two requires a different approach than cooking for a crowd. Grocery stores, packaging, and even standard cookware tend to cater to families or large households. But with a few simple tricks, you can avoid waste, shop wisely, store smartly, and equip your kitchen for meals that are just the right size.

## Shopping Smarter

Grocery stores are designed to encourage you to buy more—think "family-size" packs, buy-one-get-one deals and discounts for bulk purchases. But when you're cooking for two, those deals can lead to food waste and cluttered pantries.

Here are some of my favorite strategies for buying just what you need:

### *Get creative in the produce section*

Produce can be the trickiest to buy in small amounts. A whole head of lettuce, a giant bag of carrots, or a two pound bag of cherries may be more than you'll use. Try these ideas:

- Head to the organic section, where items are often sold loose by weight.
- Visit your local farmers market or food cooperative for smaller quantities and fresher selections.
- Make use of the grocery store salad bar—a great option if you need just half a pepper or a handful of greens.
- Don't forget frozen produce! Individually quick-frozen peas, corn, and berries are often fresher than what's in the produce section. I learned that as a former market researcher for Green Giant!

### *Shop the meat counter*

If your grocery store has a butcher or meat counter, take advantage of it. You can buy exactly what you need—say, two chicken breasts or half a pound of ground beef.

If you find a great deal on bulk meat, portion it into smaller amounts before freezing. I freeze ground meat in half-pound containers and chicken breasts individually in zip-top freezer bags.

And when it comes to shrimp, go frozen! Most "fresh" shrimp has already been frozen and thawed. Buy frozen and defrost just what you need under cold running water.

### *Use the bulk bins*

Dry goods like flour, rice, beans, lentils, and even spices are often cheaper and fresher when purchased in bulk. Buying only what you need means less waste—especially for spices. I keep just enough dried thyme or chili flakes for a few recipes. (Natural food stores and co-ops are especially good for this.)

### *Pay more per pound—and save money*

While it may feel counterintuitive, buying a smaller package at a higher per-pound price can actually save you money. Six eggs instead of a dozen, an eight ounce container of sour cream instead of 16, or just two pork chops instead of a family pack can lead to less waste and less money in the trash.

### *Look for individually packaged items*

Single-serving containers of yogurt, applesauce, or even milk can help you avoid spoilage. For my pies and breads that require only ½ can of puree, I find exactly what I need in the baby food aisle.

## Ingenious Ingredients for Two

Many recipes call for just a splash of broth or a tablespoon of wine—what do you do with the rest? Here are a few small-sized ingredient heroes I love:

### Bouillon or broth concentrates

No need to open a whole carton of broth for just half a cup. Better Than Bouillon ®, a broth concentrate, or similar broth concentrate products, mixes easily with water, keeps in the fridge for months and saves space and waste.

### Boxed wine or mini bottles

Boxed wine lasts for weeks once opened, thanks to its vacuum-sealed bag. And those tiny airplane-sized liquor bottles? Perfect for recipes that call for just a splash of vodka, rum, or whiskey. I've even found single-serve cans of sparkling wine, for occasions when you need just a bit for a champagne sauce.

### Shallots

Large onions often go unused in small-batch recipes. Shallots offer that same sweet-savory flavor but in a much smaller package. One shallot is just the right amount for most recipes.

## Storing Smarter

Learning how to store ingredients efficiently is key to cooking for two. Here are my go-to techniques:

### Freeze bacon in single portions

Roll up individual slices into tight cylinders, freeze in a zip-top bag and pull out what you need—no more wrestling with frozen blocks of bacon.

### Wash and prep berries properly

To prevent mold, rinse berries in a solution of 3 parts water to 1 part vinegar. Rinse again, dry thoroughly (a salad spinner works wonders) and store in a paper towel–lined container with a loose-fitting lid.

### Portion and freeze meat smartly

Separate portions within a single zip-top freezer bag by folding the bag between pieces. This keeps portions from sticking together and speeds up defrosting.

### Freeze soup in 24-ounce glass jars

I love freezing leftovers of my Tomato and Fennel Soup (pg.50) in wide-mouth jars. They seal tight to prevent freezer burn, stack neatly, and you can always see what's inside. Just label the lid with the name and date.

## Surprising Things You Can Freeze

Freezing helps extend the life of small leftovers that might otherwise go bad. Here are a few of my favorites:

1. **Bananas** – Peel, freeze, and use for banana bread or smoothies.

2. **Butter** – Keeps longer in the freezer. To soften quickly, cut into small pieces or pound in a bag.

3. **Chipotle chilies in adobo** – Spoon individual portions onto parchment, freeze, then store in a bag.

4. **Cheese** – Hard cheeses freeze well. Wrap tightly and defrost in the fridge.

5. **Citrus** - The zest of any citrus can be frozen in an airtight container, then break off a piece when you ready to use it. Squeeze the juice into ice cube trays and freeze. Pop cubes into a freezer bag and take out as needed.

6. **Ginger** - Frozen ginger is much easier to grate than the fresh stuff, so it makes sense to keep it in the freezer. Wrap it in plastic (either whole or in 1-inch pieces, if desired) and place in

a freezer bag. Pop it out, grate the amount you need and place back in freezer.

**7. Herbs** – Freeze chopped herbs in ice cube trays with water or olive oil.

**8. Nuts** – Prevent rancidity by storing in the freezer. Use directly from freezer.

**9. Tomato paste** - Portion it onto a plastic-lined cookie sheet by tablespoons and freeze. Once frozen, wrap in plastic and place in a freezer bag. (Do not freeze tomato paste in the can.)

**10. Wine** – Freeze in tablespoon-sized portions using an ice cube tray.

# Handy Equipment for Two

Cooking for two often calls for smaller cookware and clever substitutions. Here are the tools I reach for again and again, with recipes from this book to prove it:

### Small oven-safe skillets

Perfect for game-day dips or scalloped potatoes. My 10-inch All-Clad and 8-inch cast iron skillets are always in use.

- » Cheesy Mexican Street Corn Dip (pg. 25)
- » Skillet Scalloped Potatoes for Two (pg.174)
- » Turkey Breast with Grandma's Stuffing (pg.148)

### 3-quart Dutch oven

Great for soups, stews, braises or reheating leftovers.

- » Fall Farmer's Market Soup (pg. 54)
- » Pot Roast for Two (pg. 114)
- » Harissa Baked Fish in Tomato Fennel Ragu (pg.139)

### Loaf pans

Sided baking dishes help baked pastas, lasagnas and baked desserts brown evenly.

- » Spring Lasagna (pg.145)
- » Greek Baked Ziti (pg.100)
- » Easy Sausage and Spinach Egg Bake (pg.184)

> *"Every women should have a blow torch"*
> **- Julia Child**

### Ramekins (various sizes)

Handy for flans, soufflés and individual desserts.

- » Artichoke and Ricotta Flan (pg.166)
- » Herb-Pot and Gruyere Soufflés (pg.179)
- » Panna Cotta Dessert Cups (pg.199)

### 6-inch cake pans

Make a petite layer cake or perfectly scaled upside down cake.

- » Layered Pumpkin Cake with Browned Butter Cream Cheese Frosting and Caramel (pg.213)
- » Upside-Down Peach Cake with St. Cecilia Sauce (pg.206)

### 6-inch pie plates and bundt pans

Essential for sweet or savory pies and elegant, small Bundt cakes.

- » Chicken, Leek & Tarragon Pot Pie (pg.142),
- » Stout Chocolate Bundt Cake with Bailey's Cream Filling (pg.207).

### Slow cooker tip for two

If your slow cooker is too big, place an oven-safe bowl (like Pyrex or two ramekins) inside the cooker to make smaller portions. This helps avoid burning and overcooking. Always cook with the lid on and resist the urge to peek!

- » Caramelized onions for Baked Onion Soup (pg.57)

**Pan Con Tomate**
Pg.21

**Mexican Street Corn Dip**
Pg.25

**Bourbon-Glazed Salmon Bites**
Pg.35

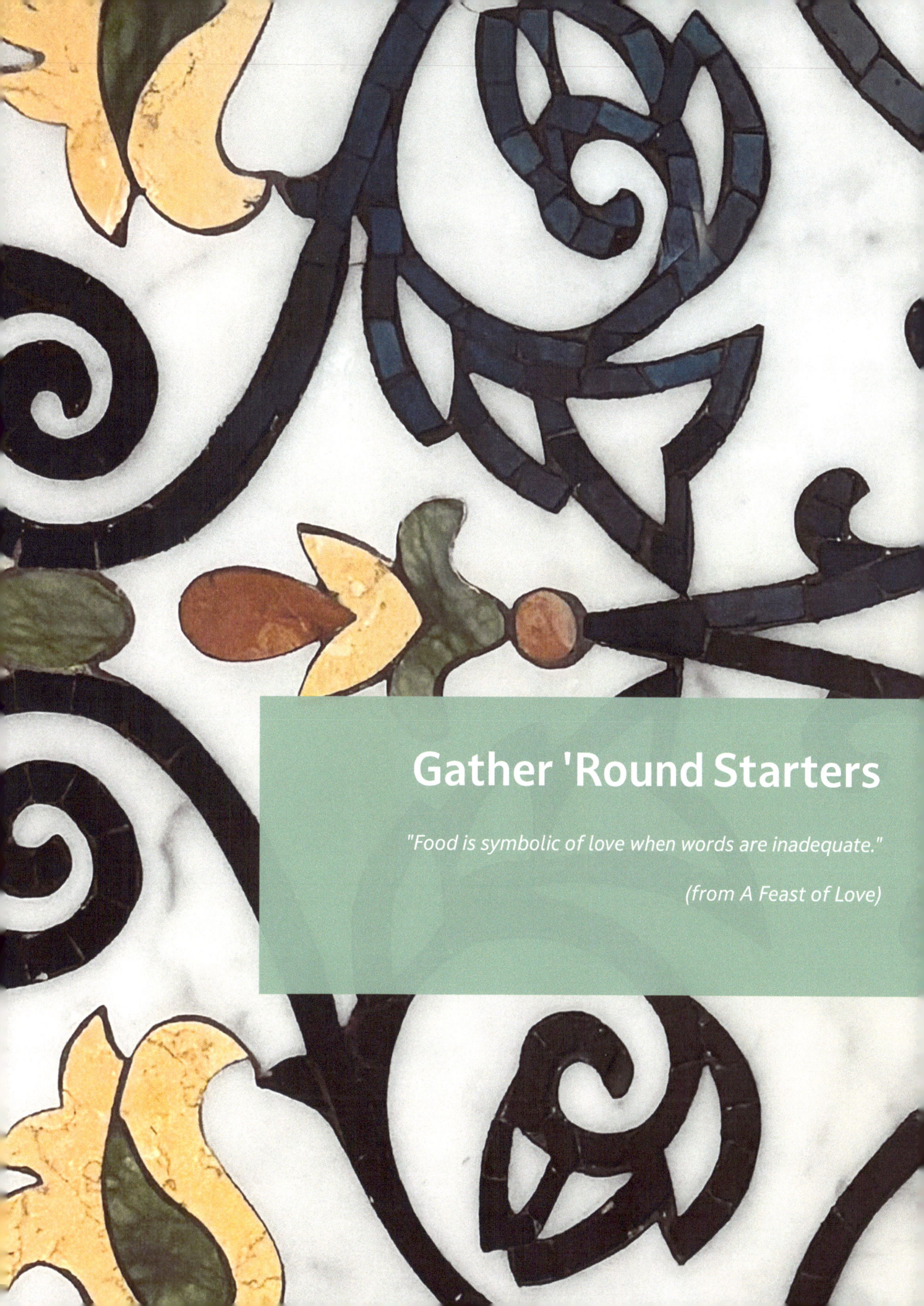

# Gather 'Round Starters

*"Food is symbolic of love when words are inadequate."*

(from A Feast of Love)

# Pan Con Tomate
## (Spanish Tomato Bread)

Think of this as Spain's answer to tomatoes on toast—but make it fun, interactive and totally summer-worthy. I first fell for Pan Con Tomate while wandering (and snacking) my way through Barcelona, where crusty breads are rubbed with garlic, juicy tomatoes and olive oil. That's it — and it's perfect.

### What you need:

2 to 3 very ripe medium tomatoes

1 pint cherry tomatoes, about 6 oz / 170 g

2 to 3 large slices sturdy sourdough bread, about ½-inch thick (1.3 cm)

2 to 3 garlic cloves, peeled

Freshly ground black pepper

Extra-virgin olive oil

Basil leaves, for garnish (optional)

Black salt or flaked sea salt

1. **Grate a tomato:** Grab one ripe tomato and slice in half horizontally. Hold the cut side against the coarse holes of a box grater and grate into a shallow bowl. You'll end up with about ¾ cup of juicy, rustic tomato purée. Toss the skins—they've done their part.

2. **Slice and dice the rest:** Take remaining tomatoes (whatever variety you fancy!) and slice the larger ones into ¼-inch rounds. Halve those cute cherry tomatoes. Set aside.

3. **Toast your bread:** Toast thick slices of your favorite crusty bread until golden and crisp. If you have a charcoal grill handy, give the bread some smoky vibes. Otherwise, your trusty toaster or broiler work just as well.

4. **Go big on the garlic:** Take a peeled garlic clove, cut in half and rub cut side across the top of each toast. Want just a whisper of garlic? Press gently. Want a garlic punch? Go all in.

5. **Layer on the tomatoes:** Place toasts on a pretty platter or straight onto plates. Spread a generous spoonful of the tomato purée over each slice. Now scatter your tomato slices and cherry halves on top and sprinkle on some black pepper. Drizzle with olive oil and garnish with basil and flaked salt.

NOTES FOR NEXT TIME:

**TABLE TALK TIPS:** When I serve this at home, I make it a build-your-own situation. Toast the bread and rub it with garlic ahead of time, then set out bowls of grated tomato and the sliced and cherry tomatoes. Guests get to do the fun part: swipe on the purée, pile on the tomatoes, drizzle generously with olive oil, and finish with a pinch of salt. Flaky salt, Tuscan Salt (pg.225 ), or dramatic black sea salt—any of them make this a total showstopper.

North Shore Taleggio Fondue | 23

24 | Mediterranean Crostini

Cheesy Mexican Street Corn Dip | 25

26 | Traditional Hummus

# North Shore Taleggio Fondue
## with Cranberry Walnut and Sourdough Croutons

Skiing has always been part of our family rhythm, with Zach racing competitively from the age of eight. There were always a couple winter weekends that found us on Minnesota's North Shore, either for a family trip or a race, driving Highway 61 toward Two Harbors. Just outside of town sits the New Scenic Café, a cozy spot where we'd often stop for dinner on our way to or from the slopes. One of our earliest visits introduced us to their unforgettable cheese fondue, served with in-house-made croutons. The boys loved the ritual of dipping warm bread into molten cheese and it quickly became a family craving. After a few failed attempts to recreate it, I finally called the Café's sous chef, who graciously shared the secret: two parts Taleggio cheese to three parts really good cream. Now it's the one dish the boys always request when they're home.

**What you need:**

7 oz (200 g) Taleggio cheese, rind removed, cut into large cubes

1 ¼ cups (300 ml) heavy whipping cream

3 to 4 slices cranberry walnut loaf, sourdough, or a mix, cut into dippable-sized cubes (¾-inch / 2 cm)

1 tablespoon olive oil

Slices of apple for dipping (optional)

NOTES FOR NEXT TIME:

1. **Prepare croutons:** Preheat your oven to 350°F (175°C) and position the oven rack in the middle. Line a baking sheet with parchment paper and scatter bread cubes across it. Drizzle with olive oil and give them a good toss, right on the baking sheet so they're all nicely coated. Spread the cubes out and pop the sheet in the oven.

2. **Bake croutons:** Place in oven for 15–20 minutes, until the croutons are just starting to take on some color: we want them soft in the middle to allow easy placement on the fondue fork without breaking apart.

3. **Make fondue:** Grab a Dutch oven or a heavy-bottomed saucepan and pour in the cream. Warm it over medium heat until it just starts to simmer, until it's very hot to the touch but not boiling. Lower your temperature to medium-low.

4. **Add the taleggio cheese:** Add cheese in batches, whisking constantly until each addition is fully melted before adding the next. Keep whisking until the fondue is smooth and creamy. Transfer to a warm fondue pot or a large ramekin, and serve immediately with your crispy croutons and sliced apples for dipping.

**TABLE TALK TIPS:** When it's just the two of you, skip buying a whole loaf. Pick up a sourdough roll and a cranberry walnut roll (or another favorite artisan flavor) from the bakery. You'll have just the right amount for dipping—fresh, flavorful and no extra bread going stale on the counter.

If you want to prep ahead, this fondue can be stored in an air tight container and refrigerated overnight. Reheat gently on the stovetop over low heat until it's warm and melty again.

# Mediterranean Crostini
## with Whipped Feta

I fell in love with this relish during a week-long farm-to-table cooking class at the Culinary Institute of America, where fresh, simple ingredients took center stage. The secret is oven-dried roma tomatoes (pg. 227)—their deep, concentrated flavor makes all the difference. Here, that bright, savory relish meets creamy whipped feta. For a fun appetizer twist: toast slices of baguette until golden, spread generously with whipped feta, then spoon on this amazing relish. It's a beautiful bite that's just as perfect for a casual night in as it is for an elegant starter.

**Whipped Feta:**

*6 oz (170 g) feta*

*3 oz (85 g) cream cheese*

*3 tablespoons olive oil*

*1 tablespoon lemon juice, about ½ a large lemon*

*½ teaspoon salt*

*¼ teaspoon freshly ground black pepper*

**Crostini:**

*6 ½-inch (1.3 cm) thick diagonal baguette slices, toasted*

*⅓ cup (80 ml) Mediterranean relish (pg. 218)*

*Basil, for garnish (optional)*

NOTES FOR NEXT TIME:

1. **Whipped feta:** Place the feta and cream cheese in the bowl of a food processor fitted with the steel blade. Pulse until the cheeses are mixed. Add the olive oil, lemon juice, ½ teaspoon salt, and ¼ teaspoon pepper and process until smooth.

2. **Assemble the crostini:** Spread each slice of bread with a generous amount of whipped feta. With a slotted spoon, place Mediterranean relish on top. Put the crostini on plates and sprinkle with basil. Serve immediately.

**TABLE TALK TIPS:** For an interactive, make-your-own appetizer, set out a basket of toasted crostini, a bowl of the Mediterranean relish, and a bowl of whipped feta. Guests can build their own bites, keeping the bread perfectly crisp and letting everyone customize each piece to their taste.

# Cheesy Mexican Street Corn Dip

Perfect for game day, this small-batch dip is a cheesy, melty riff on Mexican street corn—loaded with cotija, pepper jack cheese and a generous sprinkle of Tajín® for that signature chili-lime kick. Inspired by esquites, this cast iron skillet version lets you char the corn for extra flavor and keeps the dip warm and gooey straight through serving.

**What you need:**

- 2–3 ears of corn, about 2 cups / 320 g kernels, divided (fresh is best, but you can sub thawed frozen—just pat it dry before cooking!)
- 1 tablespoon vegetable oil, divided
- ½ teaspoon table salt, divided
- 1 garlic clove, minced
- 2 scallions, thinly sliced, divided
- 4 oz (115 g) cream cheese, cut into 4 pieces and softened
- 4 oz (115 g) pepper jack cheese, shredded, divided
- ¼ cup (60 g) mayonnaise
- ¼ cup (60 g) sour cream
- 1 serrano chile, stemmed, seeded, and sliced thin (want more heat? Keep the seeds!)
- 2 tablespoons lime juice, plus lime wedges for serving
- 1 teaspoon Tajín® seasoning (that chili-lime magic! Look for it in the hispanic aisle)
- 2 tablespoons cotija cheese, crumbled
- 2 tablespoons chopped fresh cilantro
- Fritos® or tortilla chips for scoop'n

1. **Charring the corn:** First, set oven rack about 6 inches from the broiler and turn on the broiler—it'll be ready when we need it. Now, grab an 8-inch cast-iron skillet and heat ½ tablespoon oil over medium-high heat until it's just smoking. Toss in half the corn and ¼ teaspoon of salt, then spread it out in an even layer. Let it sit! No stirring for about 3–5 minutes while it gets that beautiful char. Transfer the corn to a bowl and repeat with remaining oil, corn, and salt. When the second batch is just starting to char, stir garlic and half of the scallions, and cook for about 1 more minute—just until fragrant. Then, remove skillet from heat.

2. **Making It cheesy:** Time to bring it all together! Add that first batch of corn back into the skillet with the warm corn-scallion mixture. Stir in the cream cheese, ¾ cup of pepper jack cheese, mayonnaise, sour cream, serranos, lime juice, and Tajín®. Give it a good mix until everything is combined—the cheese will start melting into the dip already. Spread it all out into an even layer, then sprinkle the top with the last ¼ cup of pepper jack cheese.

3. **Broil to perfection:** Pop the skillet under the broiler for about 2 minutes, just until the cheese is melty and starting to get golden brown in spots. Keep an eye on it—you don't want it to burn!

4. **Finishing touches & serving:** Let the dip cool for 5 minutes (if you can wait!). Then, sprinkle on the cotija, cilantro, and the rest of the scallions. Serve it straight from the skillet with Fritos® and lime wedges on the side for that final citrusy punch.

 **NOTES FOR NEXT TIME:**

**TABLE TALK TIPS:** I adapted these flavors into a hot, gooey, and delicious dip served in the cast-iron skillet the dish was made in. The skillet was key for getting good char on the corn kernels. It also kept the dip hot during serving.

# Traditional Hummus
## with Garlic Confit and Tahini Sauce

If you've ever thought, "Why doesn't my hummus taste like the creamy, velvety spread from my favorite restaurant?", this recipe is here to change the game. It starts with the hero of the dish: dried chickpeas. Head to your local food co-op and scoop them from the bulk bins or grab a packaged bag (they might be labeled garbanzo beans, but don't worry, it's the same thing). Using dried chickpeas might sound fussy, but the payoff is huge: better texture, fresher flavor and total control over the cooking process. And here's the best part—this recipe shaves cooking time down to just 20 to 40 minutes, thanks to a brilliant trick involving baking soda. But hey, canned chickpeas work in a pinch.

**What you need:**

1 cup (200 g) dried chickpeas or 2 cans (800 g) chickpeas, drained

1¼ teaspoon baking soda (if using dried chickpeas), divided

1 pinch ground cumin

½ to ⅔ cup (120–150 g) tahini, divided

1 garlic clove, crushed , more to taste

1½ tablespoons lemon juice . plus more to taste

Salt

2–3 tablespoons Garlic Confit (pg.229)

¼ cup (60 ml) Lemon Tahini Sauce (pg.226)

1. **Make the garlic confit:** Set aside. Now make the Lemon Tahini Sauce and refrigerate until ready to garnish the hummus.

2. **Prepare the dried chickpeas (if using, otherwise skip to step 4):** Soak your dried chickpeas overnight in plenty of water and ¾ teaspoon baking soda. **The next day,** rinse and drain them well, tossing them into a medium saucepan with ½ teaspoon baking soda (this helps soften the chickpeas) and enough water to cover by about 4 inches. Bring to a simmer over medium-high heat, skimming off any foam that bubbles to the surface. Lower the heat to medium-low, cover and simmer for 30-50 minutes. (Pro tip: Start checking at 20 minutes. Depending on the age of the chickpeas, cooking times can vary!) In the last 15 minutes of cooking, add about a teaspoon of salt to the water and sprinkle in a pinch of cumin. Cook until chickpeas are so soft.

3. **Skin the chickpeas (optional, but worth it):** Use a slotted spoon to gently stir the cooked chickpeas in the pot. You'll notice the skins start floating to the top. Scoop them out and discard. While it is a bit tedious, it will give you a silky-smooth hummus. Don't stress if you don't get them all. Skip to Step 5.

4. **Quick prep for canned chickpeas (if using):** Spread canned chickpeas between two tea towels. Rub the towels together vigorously, but not too hard; we are peeling, not smashing! Check under the top towel and discard the loosened skins. Put peeled chickpeas into a saucepan, cover with water and add 1 teaspoon salt and a pinch of cumin. Simmer for 15 minutes to soften.

5. **Blend the hummus:** Drain chickpeas (save that water!) and transfer to a food processor. Add ½ cup tahini, fresh garlic cloves, a good squeeze of lemon juice, a couple of ice cubes (about 2 tablespoons worth), 2 tablespoons of reserved chickpea water, and a pinch of salt. Blitz until smooth-ish. Taste and adjust. More tahini? Garlic? Lemon? Don't hold back—make it yours. Add extra chickpea water if needed; it will thicken as it sits.

6. **Serve it up:** Spread hummus in a shallow bowl and create a little well in the center. Drizzle generously with olive oil. Now for the fun part: toppings! Pour tahini sauce into the well. Drizzle edges with garlic confit oil and arrange some of the garlic, a sprig of thyme, and the pepper from the oil on the top.

 **NOTES FOR NEXT TIME:**

**TABLE TALK TIPS:** Other toppings to consider if you choose not to make the garlic confit: sprinkle on herbs, toasted nuts, a dollop of rose harissa or whatever strikes your fancy. Hummus is your blank canvas.

**Store (if you can resist):** If not serving right away, transfer to a sealed container and store in the fridge for up to two days. But let's be honest, it probably won't last that long.

# Balsamic Pear, Pistachio Pesto Tartine
## with a Whipped Honey Ricotta

When pears and fresh greens start popping up at the market, I can't help but whip up this simple, light dish. It's one of those recipes that's hard to categorize—am I making an appetizer or is this an open-faced sandwich that pairs perfectly with a warm cup of soup or a cold gazpacho? Either way, it's a winner.

**Balsamic Mayonnaise**

1 tablespoon good-quality balsamic vinegar of Modena PGI

2 tablespoons mayonnaise

**Pistachio Pesto**

¼ cup (30 g) pistachios

1 small garlic clove

Pinch of salt

¼ cup (15 g) flat-leaf parsley leaves (packed)

¼ cup (10 g) baby arugula leaves (packed)

1 tablespoon Parmesan cheese

2 tablespoons plus 2 teaspoons extra-virgin olive oil

2 tablespoons water

1½ teaspoons lemon juice

Salt, to taste

Freshly ground black pepper, to taste

**Whipped Ricotta**

3 oz (85 g) whole milk ricotta

1½ teaspoons honey

**Marinated Pears**

2 tablespoons balsamic vinegar of Modena PGI

2 tablespoons extra-virgin olive oil

Salt, to taste

Freshly ground black pepper, to taste

1 Anjou pear, peeled and cut into eighths

½ red onion, cut into thin wedges

**Glaze**

2 tablespoons balsamic vinegar of Modena PGI

2 tablespoons honey

**For Serving**

2 thick slices ciabatta or other rustic bread

1 tablespoon extra-virgin olive oil

1 bunch baby arugula

4 slices prosciutto (optional)

1. **Balsamic mayonnaise:** In a small bowl, mix together the balsamic vinegar and mayonnaise. Set aside for later.
2. **Pistachio pesto:** In a food processor, pulse pistachios, garlic and pinch of salt until it's finely chopped. Then add in parsley, arugula, and Parmesan, and pulse again until everything is chopped up nicely. With the machine running, slowly drizzle in the olive oil, followed by the water and lemon juice. Taste and season with salt and pepper. Set this aside, too.
3. **Whipped ricotta:** Grab a large bowl and whisk the ricotta and honey together vigorously until it's light and smooth. Set aside.
4. **Marinated pears:** In a large bowl, whisk together the vinegar, oil, salt, and pepper. Add the pear and onion slices, and gently toss until they're coated. Let marinate for at least 10 minutes.
5. **Pear and onion sauté:** Heat a non-stick pan over medium heat. Add the marinated pear and onion, sautéing until they're nice and golden brown. Once done, transfer to a medium bowl and set aside, but don't clean the pan just yet!
6. **Balsamic glaze:** To the same pan, immediately pour in the balsamic vinegar and honey. Bring it to a quick boil, then remove from heat. Let it cool to room temperature in a small bowl.
7. **Toast the bread:** Preheat your broiler. Brush both sides of your bread slices with olive oil, then pop them under the broiler until golden and crispy on both sides.
8. **Assemble the tartine:** Spread a little balsamic mayonnaise on top of each slice of toasted bread. Top with a generous scoop of pistachio pesto and whipped ricotta.
9. **For the salad:** In a small bowl, toss the marinated pear and onion with some fresh arugula. Season with salt and pepper to taste. Spoon the salad on top of toasts or add some prosciutto and drizzle with the balsamic glaze.

**TABLE TALK TIPS:** The key here is really good balsamic vinegar, so don't just grab any bottle off the shelf. I like to search out one with a PGI label, which stands for Protected Geographical Indication (fancy, right?). Basically, it means the vinegar comes from a specific place known for making it the right way and the taste is guaranteed to be top-notch. So, when you see that little PGI logo, you know you're getting the real deal—something with quality and authenticity that you can feel good about using. Plus, it adds an extra level of deliciousness to this already tasty tartine.

 **NOTES FOR NEXT TIME:**

**TABLE TALK TIPS:** If your eggplant weighs more than 12 ounces, you may need to bump up the salt and lemon juice in step 5 to balance the flavors. The dip should be bold and flavorful but never overpowering.

Baba ghanoush is wonderfully customizable: Mix in a pinch of smoked paprika or cumin. Swirl in a dollop of Greek yogurt for an extra creamy, tangy twist. Try folding in finely chopped parsley, mint, or cilantro. A drizzle of chili oil or a sprinkle of Aleppo pepper also does the trick. You can even give it a nutty crunch by topping it with toasted pine nuts or sesame seeds.

# Baba Ghanoush
## (Smoky Egg Plant Dip)

I first made baba ghanoush over 20 years ago when eggplants from my CSA started piling up and it quickly became a staple in my kitchen. This Lebanese classic is all about smoky, fire-roasted eggplant blended with tahini, lemon, and garlic for a creamy, tangy spread. I char the eggplant until the skin blisters, then mellow the garlic in lemon juice before mixing everything together. With a few simple tweaks—herbs, spices, or a drizzle of chili oil—it's a timeless dip that always feels fresh.

**What you need:**

1 eggplant (12 oz / 340 g)

2 teaspoons lemon juice plus extra for seasoning

1–2 garlic cloves (minced to a paste)

½ teaspoon table salt

2 tablespoons tahini

2 tablespoons extra-virgin olive oil or garlic confit oil , divided

2 teaspoons fresh parsley, chopped

1. **Set Up for Roasting:** Use a paring knife to poke about six holes in the eggplant. This helps release steam and prevents unexpected eggplant explosions.
   - **Oven Method:** Move an oven rack 8 inches from broiler and preheat the broiler. Line a rimmed baking sheet with aluminum foil for easy cleanup.
   - **Charcoal Grill:** Open bottom vent, light a full chimney of charcoal (about 6 quarts), and pour the hot coals evenly over the grill. Place the cooking grate, cover and open the lid vent. Let grill heat up for about 5 minutes.
   - **Gas Grill:** Turn all burners to high, cover, and preheat grill for about 15 minutes. Then reduce the burners to medium-high.

2. **Roast the eggplants:** Place eggplant on your prepared baking sheet or directly on grill grates. Cook for 20 minutes, then flip them and continue cooking for another 10 minutes. The skin should be deeply charred, with a smoky aroma like burning leaves. Once done, transfer eggplant to a plate and let cool completely, about 30 minutes.

3. **Prep the garlic mixture:** While the eggplant cools, mix lemon juice, garlic, and salt in a medium bowl. Let this sit to mellow the garlic's sharpness.

4. **Scoop and chop:** Once the eggplant is cool, split lengthwise through the skin. Peel the skin back and discard it, then scoop out the soft flesh. Chop the flesh finely with a chef's knife and add it to the bowl with the lemon juice mixture.

5. **Mix and season:** Add tahini and 1 tablespoon olive oil, stirring until smooth and creamy. If you like an extra smooth baba ghanoush, use your blender or hand blender, blending to reach desired consistency. I often add some olive oil, about 1 tablespoon at a time, to achieve smooth texture. Let the baba ghanoush sit for about 20 minutes to let flavors meld, giving it a stir now and then. Taste and adjust with more lemon juice and salt as desired.

6. **Garnish:** Spread baba ghanoush in a shallow serving bowl. Drizzle with the remaining 1 tablespoon olive oil, sprinkle with parsley, and serve with your favorite dippers like pita bread, cut vegetables, crackers — so many options!

# Rosemary Ricotta Toast with Figs

Have you noticed those little clamshell packages of fresh figs popping up at the grocery store? If not, start scanning the produce aisle, especially near the berries, from May through fall. If the only fig you've ever had is inside a Fig Newton, get ready for a revelation. Fresh figs are creamy, sweet, and juicy—like nature's candy with a subtle elegance. They're high in natural sugars but low in acid, making them perfect for eating whole, baking into tarts, whipping up into compotes or even blending into smoothies.

**What you need:**

2 tablespoons garlic confit oil or olive oil

½ cup (115 g) whole milk ricotta

1½ teaspoons rosemary, minced, from about 1 sprig

Tuscan sea salt (pg.225) or Kosher salt, to taste

Ground black pepper, to taste

2 slices brown bread or rye bread

2 oz (55 g) prosciutto or salami, thinly sliced

3 oz (85 g) figs, quartered or halved, depending on size

2 cups (50 g) baby arugula

½ lemon, quartered

 NOTES FOR NEXT TIME:

1. **Whip the ricotta:** Toss ricotta and a pinch of fresh rosemary into a small food processor or use a hand blender. Blend until smooth, creamy, and just a little fluffy, about a minute. Season with salt and pepper. Taste it! It should make you smile.

2. **Grill the bread:** Adjust your oven rack to 6 inches below the top heating element (broiler). Preheat broiler to 450°F (232°C). Brush both sides of your bread with that garlic confit oil (pg.229) or plain olive oil. Place on a baking sheet and toast the bread until golden and toasty on both sides. Think crunchy perfection.

3. **Assemble:** Spread each toast with a generous layer of whipped ricotta. Lay on a few slices of prosciutto (or skip it if you're keeping things vegetarian). Add fresh fig slices (or jam, berries, peaches—whatever you've got). Drizzle with extra chili oil if you're in the mood for more heat, and sprinkle with a pinch of salt

4. **Toss your greens:** In a bowl, mix arugula with a drizzle of olive oil, a squeeze of lemon juice, and a little salt and pepper. Serve the salad alongside your toasts—or pile it right on top if you're feeling wild.

**TABLE TALK TIPS:** Fresh figs hard to find? Fig jam, berries, or peaches make excellent stand-ins. Going vegetarian? Try salted nut butter or grilled eggplant instead of prosciutto. If your ricotta's a bit too wet, pop it in a mesh strainer over a bowl while you prep—it'll be just right when you're ready.

# Bourbon-Glazed Salmon Bites

One night, some friends and I got together for a cozy, low-key dinner, bringing along ingredients that felt a bit like treasures. A few of the guests had even hunted or fished for their contributions, which inspired me to come up with something just as special for the meal. That's how these bourbon-glazed salmon bites were born!

**Salmon**

6 oz (170 g) salmon fillets (1 inch / 2.5 cm thick, skin-on, cut into 1–2 inch / 2.5–5 cm cubes)

¼ teaspoon kosher salt

¼ teaspoon black pepper

2 teaspoons olive oil

**Bourbon Glaze**

1 teaspoon olive oil

1 garlic clove, minced

¼ cup shallots, diced

½ cup (100 g) brown sugar

⅛ teaspoon beef Better Than Bouillon® concentrate

2 tablespoons soy sauce

2 tablespoons red wine vinegar

1 tablespoon bourbon

¾ teaspoon cornstarch

**Finishing Touches**

1 teaspoon prepared wasabi

1 green onion (sliced)

1. **Preheat oven:** Adjust oven rack to middle position and heat oven to 300°F (150°C).

2. **Prepare the salmon:** Cut salmon into 6 cubes and pat dry with paper towels. Season lightly with salt and pepper.

3. **Make the glaze:** Heat oil in a small saucepan. Add garlic and shallots and saute, until soft, about 2-3 minutes. Whisk together brown sugar, bourbon, beef bouillon, soy, vinegar, and cornstarch in the saucepan, continuing to stir until no lumps remain. Bring to a boil over medium-high heat, stirring to combine ingredients and dissolve sugar. Reduce heat to a simmer and cook for 5-7 minutes, or until sauce has reduced and is thick enough to coat the back of a spoon. Remove from heat. Transfer 1 tablespoon glaze to a small bowl and set aside. While the glaze may seem thin, it will thicken as it cools.

4. **Sear the salmon:** Heat a cast-iron or oven safe skillet over medium-high heat. Add 1 tablespoon oil and swirl to coat the pan. Once oil is shimmering, add salmon cubes, flesh side down, leaving space between each piece. Sear for 1-2 minutes until the flesh side is golden brown but not fully cooked through. Remove from the heat. Flip the cubes and brush tops of cubes with 1 tablespoon glaze. Transfer skillet to oven and cook until centers are still translucent when checked with tip of paring knife and register 125°F (52°C), 3-4 minutes. Wash and dry brush to avoid cross contamination..

5. **Serve:** Using a fish spatula, remove skin from the salmon and transfer glazed salmon bites to a serving plate. Place a small dot of wasabi on top of each piece, but don't go too heavy or your eyes will begin to water and your mouth will be on fire! Spoon more glaze over each salmon bite and sprinkle with green onions. Add a decorative toothpick and serve.

**NOTES FOR NEXT TIME:**

**TABLE TALK TIPS:** I love using sustainably raised or wild-caught salmon in recipes like this, not just because it tastes amazing, but because it's better for our oceans and future fish supplies. If you can, try picking up some local salmon at a farmers" market or food co-op; it really makes a difference! This recipe is simple and comes together quickly in a cast-iron skillet, giving you beautifully caramelized, flavorful bites of salmon.

**Minnesota Bootlegger**
Pg. 39

**Dr. Werley Whiskey Sours**
Pg. 43

**Blackberry Mocktail**
Pg. 41

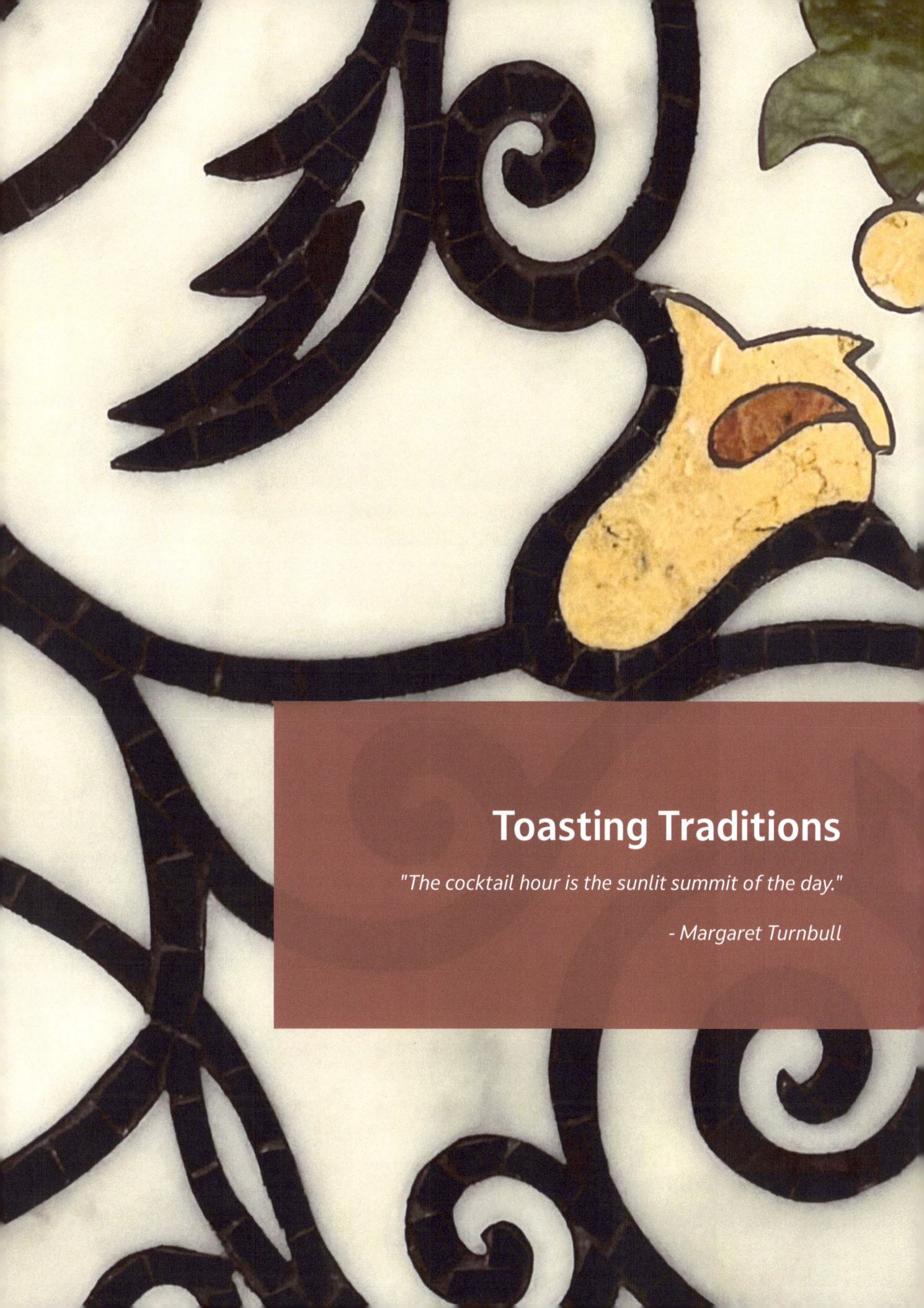

# Toasting Traditions

*"The cocktail hour is the sunlit summit of the day."*

*- Margaret Turnbull*

# Minnesota Bootlegger

Boating isn't the only tradition that kicks off on Memorial Day in the Land of 10,000 Lakes—it's also the start of Bootleg season. This refreshing, citrusy cocktail is Minnesota's signature sip, with a history as spirited as its ingredients.

Ask around and you'll hear plenty of stories about its origins. The Minikahda Club in Minneapolis and Woodhill Country Club in Wayzata both claim to have poured the first Bootleg and their members defend that claim with gusto. Today, this hometown favorite isn't just for clubhouses—it's a staple at weddings, summer gatherings, and lakeside toasts.

**Bootlegger Mix (10 servings):**

*2 to 3 large bunches young mint*

*1 can (12 ounces / 355 g) frozen lemonade concentrate, slightly thawed*

*1 can (12 ounces / 355 g) frozen limeade concentrate, slightly thawed*

*Juice of 1 lime*

**Bootlegger Cocktail (Serves 1):**

*Ice*

*2 ounces (60 ml) vodka, rum, or gin (your choice)*

*1 to 2 tablespoons bootlegger mix*

*Club soda*

*Lime slices, for garnish*

1. **Make the bootleg mix:** Remove mint leaves from stems, setting aside a few for garnish. In a blender or food processor, combine mint leaves, lemonade concentrate, limeade concentrate, and lime juice. Blend until smooth. Place in freezer until ready to use.
2. **Assemble the cocktail:** Fill a glass with ice. Add 2 ounces of your preferred liquor. Pour in club soda until the glass is nearly full. Stir in 1 to 2 tablespoons of Bootleg mix, adjusting to taste.
3. **Finishing touches:** Garnish with a lime slice and a fresh mint leaf. Sip and savor Minnesota's signature summer cocktail. Cheers!

**TABLE TALK TIPS:** You can make a batch of this mix ahead of time and freeze for your next happy hour. After blending the mix, place in a resealable freezer bag and pop in the freezer. It will stay fresh for up to two weeks.

**NOTES FOR NEXT TIME:**

Limoncello Sorbet Spritz | 41     Blackberry Mojito

Watermelon     42 | Twist on a Dirty Martini

# Limoncello Sorbet Spritz

With summer's arrival, the craving for refreshing, sun-kissed cocktails comes! Nothing captures the essence of warmer weather quite like this Limoncello Sorbet Spritz. It starts with limoncello, the quintessential Italian lemon liqueur known for its bright, citrusy sweetness. Add crisp, bubbly prosecco and a scoop of luscious lemon sorbet, and you have a drink that's both elegant and irresistibly smooth. The sorbet infuses the cocktail with an extra layer of lemon flavor, making each sip pure heaven. Finished with zesty lemon sparkling water and a fragrant sprig of fresh mint, this effervescent cocktail is truly summer in a glass.

**What you need (Serves 1):**

*2 ounces (60 ml) Limoncello*

*1 small scoop lemon sorbet*

*2 to 3 ounces (60–90 ml) prosecco*

*Lemon sparkling water, to top*

*Ice*

*Fresh mint and lemon wedge, for garnish*

1. **Make the spritz:** Fill a footed glass like a wine glass or martini glass with ice and add a scoop of lemon sorbet. Pour the limoncello over the ice and sorbet. Add the chilled prosecco. Top with lemon sparkling water for an extra refreshing fizz. Garnish with a sprig of fresh mint and lemon wedge.

**TABLE TALK TIPS:** For a non-alcoholic version, omit the limoncello and prosecco. Instead, use lemonade and additional lemon sparkling water for a refreshing mocktail. Keep limoncello chilled in the freezer—its high alcohol content prevents it from freezing solid, making it perfectly icy and smooth. Use a high-quality, well-chilled prosecco or a dry sparkling wine for best results.

# Blackberry Mojito
## (Mocktail or Cocktail)

In the dead of winter, I love sipping a glass of prosecco— this drink adds a fun twist to my usual, with the option to make it a mocktail. The magic is in the muddling: gently pressing fresh mint leaves and juicy blackberries with the back of a wooden spoon (or a muddler) to release their bright, fragrant oils and sweet berry juices. The result? A refreshing, vibrant sip that feels like a little taste of summer in the middle of January.

**What you need (Serves 2):**

*6 ounces (170 g) fresh blackberries*

*12 fresh mint leaves*

*Juice of 1 lime*

*2 tablespoons simple syrup\* (see note for homemade recipe)*

*Club soda, soda water or sparkling water (or prosecco for a cocktail twist!)*

*Extra blackberries, mint, and lime slices, for garnish*

1. **Getting started:** In each of 2 glasses, place 6 blackberries, 6 mint leaves, 2 tablespoons lime juice, and 4 tablespoons simple syrup.

2. **Muddle ingredients:** Muddle blackberries and mint to extract flavors: using a muddler or the back of a wooden spoon. Gently press down and twist to release blackberry juices and mint essential oils.

3. **Top it off:** Fill the glasses with ice, add 2/3 cup sparkling water (or prosecco for a cocktail), and stir gently.

4. **Serve:** Garnish with extra blackberries, mint leaves, and lime slices. Enjoy!

**TABLE TALK TIPS:** Create your own homemade simple syrup by bringing 1 cup water and 1 cup sugar (white or raw) to a boil. Stir until sugar dissolves, remove from heat and let cool completely.

# Watermelon Lime Mocktail

Got a watermelon and only two of you to enjoy it? We've got the perfect solution to use up that leftover watermelon; a refreshingly zesty Watermelon Lime and Mint Mocktail (non-alcoholic)! It's the perfect thirst-quencher for those hot summer days and oh-so-simple to whip up.

*6 cups (900 g) seedless watermelon chunks (from ½ small watermelon), plus small wedges for garnish*

*6 tablespoons sugar or honey (see note on honey measurements)*

*Juice of 2 to 3 limes (about ⅓ cup / 80 ml)*

*⅓ cup (80 ml) water*

*Club soda or sparkling water*

*Fresh mint sprigs, for garnish*

1. **Mix together ingredients:** Combine watermelon, sugar, and lime juice in a blender. Puree until smooth, about 30 seconds. Taste and adjust sweetness if needed.

2. **To serve:** Fill glasses with ice cubes. Pour the watermelon mixture over the ice, filling each glass about two-thirds full. Top off with water or soda and give it a gentle stir. Serve immediately, garnished with mint sprigs and watermelon wedges,

**TABLE TALK TIPS:** If using honey instead of sugar, start with half the amount of sweetener. Taste. Add more honey to reach desired sweetness.

**Want to turn this mocktail into a cocktail?** Simply add 1-2 ounces of white rum or vodka per serving after blending the watermelon mixture. Stir well before topping with club soda.

# Twist on a Dirty Martini

A classic dirty martini gets its signature briny kick from olive juice, but why stop there? If you love a salty, tangy twist in your cocktail, consider using other brines you might already have in the fridge. My two favorites? The bright, slightly sweet brine from banana peppers and the bold, spicy kick of jalapeño brine. Each one brings a unique depth of flavor to the martini, transforming it into something unexpected and exciting. Whether you prefer a touch of heat or a vinegary zing, this twist on a dirty martini is sure to shake up your usual cocktail routine.

**What you need (Serves 2):**

*6 ounces (180 ml) vodka*

*1 ounce (30 ml) dry vermouth*

*1 ounce (30 ml) brine of choice (jarred banana pepper or jalapeño brine recommended)*

*Garnish of choice: sliced lemon, stuffed olives, cocktail onions or a pepper slice*

1. **Make the mix:** In a mixing glass, combine vodka, dry vermouth, and your chosen brine. Stir well to blend the flavors.

2. **Stir or shake:** Fill a separate glass or cocktail shaker with ice and pour in the martini mixture. Stir gently if serving on the rocks, or shake if you prefer a more diluted, chilled martini.

3. **Serve:** Strain into chilled martini glasses or pour over fresh ice in a rocks glass. Garnish with your choice of a lemon slice, stuffed olive, cocktail onion or even a slice of banana pepper or jalapeño for an extra flavor boost.

**TABLE TALK TIPS:** This martini is a bold twist on a classic, offering a briny, savory sip that pairs beautifully with salty appetizers or a simple cheese plate. Cheers to discovering new ways to enjoy an old favorite!

# DWWS (Dr. Werley Whiskey Sour)

Since the 1960's, the Dr. John Werley family (my husband's father) has spent a couple of weeks out of every year at the beach on Hatteras Island, North Carolina where there was always a cocktail hour on the deck before dinner. This Whiskey Sour Recipe was Dr. Werley's creation and friends quicky dubbed it the DWWS (Dr. Werley Whiskey Sour).

### What you need (1 pitcher):

- 1 can (12 ounces / 355 ml) frozen pink lemonade concentrate
- 12 ounces (355 ml) Windsor Canadian Whiskey®
- 12 ounces (355 ml) water
- Ice
- 1 jar (6 ounces / 175 g) maraschino cherries with juice

NOTES FOR NEXT TIME:

1. **Before you begin:** This recipe uses a 1:1:1 ratio of ingredients. First, empty the frozen pink lemonade from the can directly into a large pitcher. Using the now empty frozen pink lemonade can, fill with Windsor Canadian whiskey. Add the whiskey to the pitcher to combine with the frozen pink lemonade.

2. **Mix it up:** Fill the empty frozen lemonade can with water and add to the pitcher, stirring to combine lemonade, whiskey, and water. Add another ½ can of water if you want less alcohol per drink.

3. **To serve:** Pour into an ice-filled glass. Top with a splash of maraschino cherry juice and garnish with a cherry or two.

4. **Taste and adjust:** If you prefer a sweeter whiskey sour, add cherry juice right to the glass. If it's too strong, let the ice begin to melt. As the ice melts, it will dilute the drink. If it's still stiffer than you'd like, top off your glass with more water.

**TABLE TALK TIPS:** The Werley Family recommends using Windsor Canadian Whiskey. Do NOT follow the lemonade directions on the lemonade package! Just pour frozen lemonade from the can directly into the pitcher.

# Blood Red Orange Margarita

Few things feel as festive as a beautifully balanced margarita and this Blood Orange Margarita brings a stunning twist to the classic. The deep crimson hued blood oranges add a burst of color and a citrusy sweetness. A visual treat and vibrant, refreshing cocktail!

**What you need (Serves 1):**

½ lime, cut into 3 wedges

½ blood orange, cut into 3 slices

2 ounces (60 ml) reposado tequila*

1 ounce (30 ml) Cointreau® or another orange liqueur

Splash of fresh lime juice

Float of Grand Marnier®

Salt, for rim of glass

*Reposado tequila is tequila that has been aged in barrels for a minimum of two months and up to a year. The word reposado is Spanish for "rested."

NOTES FOR NEXT TIME:

1. **How to salt the rim of a glass:** A salted rim enhances the flavors of a margarita by balancing the citrus and sweetness. Here's how to do it properly: Moisten the rim by cutting a small slit in a lime wedge and running it along the rim of the glass. For a more uniform application, dip the rim into a small saucer of citrus juice or water. Keep the glass upside down to prevent liquid from dripping down the sides.

2. **Apply the salt:** Pour salt onto a second saucer. If you want to keep the salt on the outer edge only, hold the glass at 45-degree angle and roll it gently through the salt. This prevents salt from getting inside the glass. See Table Talk Tips below.

3. **Let it set:** Allow the glass to sit for a minute or two before pouring in your cocktail. This helps the salt adhere properly.

4. **Mix the drink:** In a tall glass, add ice, lime wedges and blood orange slices. Using a muddler or the back of a wooden spoon, gently press down and twist to release the juices. Transfer the ice, muddled fruit and any juices to a cocktail shaker. Add tequila, Cointreau, and an extra splash of lime juice, then shake well until chilled.

5. **Finishing touches:** Strain the mixture into a prepared glass filled with fresh ice. To float the Grand Marnier®, hold a small inverted teaspoon over the drink and slowly pour the Grand Marnier® over the back of the spoon. This technique allows it to sit briefly on top before sinking in for a layered effect. Alternatively, you can simply pour it directly on top.

**TABLE TALK TIPS:**
- Salt half the rim for guests who prefer to sip from an unsalted section.
- Experiment with different rim flavors. Try grapefruit juice, pineapple juice, or even cranberry juice instead of lime.
- Enhance the salt blend. Mix in chili powder for a spicy twist, or swap the salt for sugar if you prefer a sweeter rim.

If you prefer a slightly sweeter margarita, stir in a little simple syrup to taste. Make your own homemade simple syrup by bringing 1 cup water and 1 cup sugar (white or raw) to a boil. Stir until the sugar dissolves, remove from heat, and let cool completely.

# Slope-side Hot Chocolate

There's nothing quite like a day on the slopes to work up an appetite for a good hot chocolate. In our family, skiing isn't just a winter activity, it's a full-on tradition. From family trips to the North Shore in Minnesota, carving turns at Lutsen Mountain, to spring break road trips for Big Sky powder, skiing has been our winter playground. Then there's Zach, our racer, taking us from Colorado training camps to every local Midwest hill for USSA and FIS races. And through it all, we've had one universal measure for a resort's greatness: the hot chocolate.

Now, I'm not talking about the kind where you rip open a packet of instant mix and stir it into hot water (though we've all been there). No, I mean the velvety, rich, almost-like-drinking-a-melted-chocolate-bar kind of hot chocolate—the kind that makes you want to savor every sip while your toes thaw out.

But then 2020 happened. The ski chalet restaurants were closed, and with it went our beloved slope-side hot chocolate tradition. Determined to keep the magic alive, I set out to recreate our ultimate favorite. Hence, this recipe was born.

**What you need (Serves 1 to 2):**

*1 cup water*

*2 tablespoons unsweetened cocoa powder, preferably Dutch-processed*

*1 ½ cups (360 ml) whole milk*

*2 ½ ounces (70 g) bittersweet chocolate, chopped or chips*

*1 to 2 tablespoons granulated sugar or brown sugar*

*Tiny pinch fine sea salt*

*½ teaspoon vanilla extract*

*Whipped cream or marshmallows, for serving*

1. **Make the base:** Pour about a cup of water into a small pot and bring it to a boil. Whisk in the cocoa powder—don't stress if it's a little clumpy; it'll smooth out soon enough.

2. **Add milk:** Turn heat down to medium and slowly whisk in milk, making sure to get all the cocoa off the sides of the pot. This is where the magic starts happening

3. **Melt chocolate:** Once the milk is hot and just starting to simmer, whisk in the chocolate, a tablespoon of sugar, and the tiniest pinch of salt. Drop the heat to low and whisk until the chocolate melts into pure silky goodness. Give it a taste—if sweet-tooth is unsatisfied, add a bit more sugar. Then turn off the heat and stir in vanilla.

4. **Serve:** Pour into your favorite mugs and pile on the whipped cream or marshmallows—or both! Sip, smile, and repeat.

 **NOTES FOR NEXT TIME:**

**Leftover Roasted Chicken Noodle Soup**  Pg.65

**Mason Jar Gazpacho**  Pg.71

**Baked Onion Soup**  Pg.57

# Soups to Savor

"Soup is a lot like a family. Each ingredient enhances the others"

- Marge Kennedy

# Tomato and Fennel Soup

A homemade tomato and fennel soup supper that's fast, velvety without cream, and just enough for two. Making tomato soup always reminds me of cozy Sunday lunches after church. My mom, who was a Family and Youth Director before becoming a Methodist pastor, worked most Sundays, leaving Dad in charge of lunch for my brother and me.

Dad loved anything tomato-related, especially a good tomato soup, which he would make with the tomatoes and milk he grew up with on his family's dairy farm in Clatonia, Nebraska. With six siblings and rows of tomato plants in the garden, he learned to whip up a simple, creamy tomato soup from scratch—a tradition he brought to our own Sunday lunches. This version has the same soul-warming flavor (without the cream) and is almost as easy as opening a can!

**What you need:**

*1 large fennel bulb, coarsely chopped*

*¼ cup (55 g) unsalted butter*

*½ large yellow onion or 1 small yellow onion, coarsely chopped*

*3 cloves garlic, minced*

*1 can (28 ounces / 794 g) whole tomatoes*

*1 cup (240 ml) vegetable broth or chicken broth, or use Better than Bouillon® concentrate (1 cup /240 ml water mixed with 1 teaspoon concentrate)*

*2 tablespoons packed light brown sugar*

*¼ cup (60 ml) Pernod® (anise-flavored liqueur)*

*Salt and freshly ground black pepper, to taste*

*1 tablespoon unsalted butter (optional)*

*1 sprig fresh fennel, for garnish*

 NOTES FOR NEXT TIME:

1. **Build the base:** Cut tops from the fennel bulbs. Coarsely chop bulbs. In a large saucepan, melt butter. Saute fennel, onion and garlic over low heat until softened, 15 minutes, stirring occasionally.

2. **Make it a tomato soup:** Add tomatoes and their juice, broth, and sugar, breaking up tomatoes with wooden spoon. Bring to a boil. Reduce heat, cover and simmer for 30 minutes. Remove from heat.
   **For the blender:** Transfer soup to a blender jar and process until smooth and creamy, about 2 minutes. Return soup to saucepan reheat and add Pernod.
   **For the immersion blender:** Place blender directly in saucepan so blades are submerged (you may need to tilt saucepan slightly) and blend until smooth and creamy, about 3 minutes, scraping down sides of saucepan as needed. Add Pernod and reheat.

3. **Taste and adjust seasoning:** Taste and season with salt and pepper. Canned tomatoes vary in flavor, which means you will need to adjust the seasoning of the soup a bit at the end. Taste and, if necessary, add a little more sugar to balance out tomatoes acidity, and butter for richness. Add more broth if too thick. I usually add another ½ teaspoon of salt. Blend again if needed.

4. **Finishing touches:** Bring soup to simmer over medium heat. Ladle into bowls, garnish with fennel sprig, and serve with sandwiches.

**TABLE TALK TIPS:** Make ahead and freeze! I love to make a big pot of Tomato and Fennel Soup (double the recipe) to freeze for a simple supper later in the week. Make ahead as the flavor gets better a day or two after sitting in the refrigerator. This any-season soup uses canned tomatoes – you don't have to wait for tomato season to enjoy.

# Roasted Carrot Soup

This roasted carrot soup was born out of abundance—those generous, earthy gifts that came straight from the soil at Spring Hill Farm. As CSA members, we'd arrive early in the morning to help harvest and assemble vegetable shares, packing just-picked produce into cloth tote bags to be delivered that same day. Some weeks, the carrots would come in heavy—five pounds or more of vibrant orange roots, still cool from the earth.

Harvest days always ended with a potluck lunch under the big tree, the branches stretching wide to shade our picnic table. Looking out over the rows of vegetables we had just picked, we'd pass around homemade dishes and stories. My roasted carrot soup quickly became a favorite at those gatherings—simple, comforting, and rich with the natural sweetness of freshly pulled carrots. It was requested often enough that I began making it every time I signed up for harvest and, eventually, it became my very first published recipe in the Spring Hill CSA cookbook.

### What you need:

- 1 pound (450 g) carrots, cut into 1-inch chunks
- 2 small Yukon Gold potatoes, cut into 1-inch chunks
- 1 large yellow onion, cut into 1-inch chunks
- 3 to 5 garlic cloves, peeled
- 2 to 4 tablespoons olive oil
- Sea salt and freshly ground black pepper, to taste
- 2 thyme sprigs
- 1 bay leaf
- 1 quart (4 cups / 950 ml) vegetable or chicken stock, or water
- ½ cup (120 ml) light cream or coconut milk
- 1 to 2 tablespoons maple syrup
- 2 to 3 tablespoons crème fraîche or sour cream, stirred with a fork until loosened
- 2 teaspoons minced parsley for garnish

1. **Roast vegetables:** Preheat the oven to 425°F (220°C). Toss vegetables with olive oil and season with ½ teaspoon salt and some pepper. Put them on a baking sheet with thyme and bay leaf then roast until tender and glazed, turning them with a spatula 2 or 3 times, checking for doneness at 45 minutes.

2. **Blend:** Transfer vegetables to a soup pot, add the stock and bring to a boil. Simmer until the carrots are soft, about 20 minutes. Cool slightly. Using a hand blender or food processor, puree until smooth. Return puree to the pot. Taste and adjust seasoning, adding ¼ teaspoon of salt at a time. Season with ¼ teaspoon pepper. Stir, taste and adjust seasoning. Stir in maple syrup, adding 1 tablespoon at a time to desired sweetness. Stir in enough cream (up to ½ cup) to achieve desired consistency. Reminder: If freezing, hold back cream until you thaw and reheat.

3. **Finishing touches:** Ladle soup into bowls, swirl a spoonful of crème fraiche into each, add a little minced parsley and serve.

**TABLE TALK TIPS:** If you decide to freeze the soup, do not add the cream or milk until right before serving.

# Fall Farmer's Market Soup

Who needs a thin, brothy veggie concoction when winter rolls in like a grump? This is the kind of soup that pulls up a chair, hands you a thick pair of socks, and says, "We're in this together." I dreamed it up after a chilly October morning stroll through the Mill City Farmers Market, where I stuffed my tote with earthy mushrooms, root veggies, and a few too many "just because" finds. Canned cannellini beans make it hearty without extra fuss, while a slice of toasted bread blended in creates that creamy texture—no cream required. A splash of balsamic at the finish ties everything together with a bright little kick.

**What you need:**

- 2 tablespoons vegetable oil
- 2 medium carrots, peeled and cut into ¾-inch (2 cm) pieces
- 1 large parsnip, peeled and cut into ¾-inch (2 cm) pieces
- 1 small onion, peeled and cut into ½-inch (1.25 cm) pieces
- 3 cloves garlic, minced
- 4 cups (960 ml) low-sodium chicken broth or vegetable broth
- 1 medium russet potato, peeled and cut into 1-inch (2.5 cm) pieces, or substitute sweet potato
- 1 teaspoon minced fresh thyme leaves
- 1 sprig fresh rosemary
- 1 bay leaf
- 1 slice hearty white sandwich bread, lightly toasted (omit to keep gluten-free)
- 1 cup (30 g) baby spinach, stemmed and chopped
- ½ can (7 ounces / 200 g) cannellini beans, drained and rinsed
- ½ cup (45 g) chestnut or cremini mushrooms, trimmed and cleaned
- 5 ounces (140 g) frozen peas
- Balsamic vinegar, to taste
- Salt and freshly ground black pepper, to taste

1. **Build the base:** Heat oil in large heavy-bottomed pot or Dutch oven over medium-high heat until oil begins to shimmer. Add carrots, parsnip, and onion, cooking until lightly browned and softened, about 5 to 7 minutes.

2. **Add layers of flavor:** Stir in garlic and cook until fragrant, about 30 seconds. Add broth, potatoes, thyme, rosemary, and bay leaf. Give it a stir and bring to boil. Reduce heat to low, cover, and simmer until vegetables are fork tender, about 15 minutes.

3. **Blend:** Remove and discard rosemary and bay leaf. Transfer 1 ½ cups solids, ½ cup broth, and bread to a blender or the beaker of a hand immersion blender. Puree until smooth. Stir puree back into pot, add spinach, cannellini beans, mushrooms, and peas; cook over medium heat until spinach is tender and mushrooms and beans are heated through, about 8 minutes.

4. **Finishing touches:** Stir in 1 tablespoon vinegar and season with salt and pepper. Taste and adjust seasoning by adding more salt and vinegar. Garnish with Parmesan and toasted croutons, if desired. Pass extra vinegar at the table.

**NOTES FOR NEXT TIME:**

**TABLE TALK TIPS:** When you're cooking just for two, opening a whole carton of broth can feel wasteful. That's where soup concentrates like Better than Bouillon really shine. A teaspoon mixed with a cup of water makes a quick, flavorful base, and the jar keeps in the fridge for ages. They make both a roasted chicken and a vegetable version, so you can match the broth to whatever soup you're stirring up.

# Baked Onion Soup

In 1954, the Food News Department of The New York Times released a pamphlet called "Soups," featuring 20 recipes for soups "thick and thin, hot and cold." Among them was a classic French onion soup, which I've lovingly updated with sherry and wine for extra depth. While caramelizing the onions takes some patience, it's a process that rewards you with unparalleled richness. The other day, I filled my slow cooker with yellow onions, added a generous chunk of butter, and let it do its magic. When it's time to make the soup, I use buttery, skillet-toasted croutons in place of traditional bread slices. This tweak makes the soup easier to eat and adds a satisfying crunch.

**Caramelized Onions**

⅓ cup (75 g / 5 tablespoons) unsalted butter, melted

3 to 4 pounds (1.36–1.81 kg) yellow onions, peeled and thinly sliced

**For the Soup**

1 quart (4 cups / 950 ml) beef stock — use a high-quality bone broth like Bonafide® or use a roasted beef base like Better Than Bouillon®

1 cup (240 ml) dry white wine

1 tablespoon dry sherry

1 tablespoon all-purpose flour

½ teaspoon black pepper, plus more to taste

4 to 6 slices French bread (½-inch / 1.25 cm thick), cut into crouton-sized pieces

1 tablespoon olive oil

1 tablespoon unsalted butter

¼ teaspoon salt, plus more to taste

¾ cup grated Gruyère cheese

1. **Caramelize the onions:** Place the sliced onions in a slow cooker. Pour melted butter over onions and stir to coat. Cover and cook on HIGH for 5 to 7 hours, stirring occasionally to keep from burning. The onions should be deeply golden and caramelized. I like to do this overnight. If not using immediately, let the onions cool, then store. See "Table Talk Tip" below.

2. **Make the soup:** Heat the beef stock in a saucepan or microwave until warm. Set aside. In a large, heavy-bottomed pot (like a 3-quart Dutch oven), combine the caramelized onions, wine, and sherry. Bring the mixture to a boil.

3. **Thicken and simmer:** Stir flour into onion mixture and cook for 1 to 2 minutes to remove the raw flour taste. Slowly add the warm broth, salt, and black pepper. Bring to a boil, then reduce heat and simmer uncovered for 10 minutes. Adjust seasoning with more salt and pepper if needed.

4. **Prepare the croutons:** Heat the olive oil and butter in a large skillet over low to medium heat. Add the bread pieces and ⅛ teaspoon salt. Toss frequently for about 10 minutes, until croutons are golden and crisp. Add more oil if needed.

5. **Assemble and serve:** Preheat the broiler and arrange ovenproof bowls or ramekins on a baking sheet. Divide the soup between the bowls. Top with croutons, and generously sprinkle each bowl with Gruyère cheese. Place under the broiler for 1 to 2 minutes, watching carefully, until the cheese is melted and bubbly. Serve immediately.

**TABLE TALK TIPS:** Make a large batch of caramelized onions—they freeze beautifully and are a game-changer for quick meals. To store: If not using immediately, let the onions cool. Store in an airtight container in the refrigerator for up to 1 week, or freeze in ice cube trays (tablespoon portions), to easily add to soups and pasta. Transfer to a freezer bag for up to 2 months. The soup can be made up to "prepare the croutons" or step 4 and stored in the freezer up to 2 months. Thaw and reheat before topping with freshly made croutons and cheese.

# Soupe Au Pistou
## (Vegetable Soup with Pesto)

Thinking of Soupe au Pistou transports me to Provence and the quiet week Mark and I spent wandering its sun-drenched villages. We discovered a tiny bistro called Le Paradou, where every evening, a steaming bowl of this Provençal vegetable soup would appear before our meal. Perfect when the mistral winds are blowing! The soup was served family-style — a large bowl with a ladle so each guest could scoop their own, adding a generous spoonful of pistou for a final, fragrant touch.

**Pistou**

½ cup (15 g) fresh basil leaves

1 ounce (28 g / 1/2 cup) Parmesan cheese, grated

⅓ cup (80 ml) extra-virgin olive oil

1–2 garlic cloves, minced

**Soup**

1 tablespoon extra-virgin olive oil

1 garlic clove, sliced

1 bay leaf

1 fresh thyme sprig

1 leek, white and light green parts only, halved lengthwise, sliced ½-inch (1.25 cm) thick, and washed thoroughly

1 celery rib, cut into ½-inch (1.25 cm) pieces

1 carrot, peeled and sliced ¼-inch (0.6 cm) thick

Salt and freshly ground black pepper, to taste

3 cups (720 ml) vegetable or chicken broth

1 cup (240 ml) water

2 small gold potatoes, scrubbed and cut into 1/4-inch (0.6 cm) dice

1 small eggplant or slender courgette/zucchini, quartered lengthwise and cut into ¼-inch (0.6 cm) dice

½ cup (40 g) orecchiette or other short pasta

4 ounces (115 g) haricots verts or green beans, trimmed and cut into ½-inch (1.25 cm) lengths

1 cup (170 g) white beans, such as cannellini or navy beans

**Good to know before you start:**

*Courgette:* British term for zucchini; also the French term.

*White beans:* While you could use fresh beans or dried beans, I opt for canned cannellini beans.

1. **First make the pistou:** Using a pestle and mortar, pound the garlic to a paste with a pinch of salt. Add the basil and a splash of extra virgin olive oil and continue pounding to make a green paste. Now stir in the remaining oil and Parmesan. Set aside.

2. **To make the soup:** Heat a large splash of olive oil in a large saucepan or Dutch oven over a low-medium heat. When it is hot, add the garlic, bay leaves, thyme sprigs, leek, celery, carrot, and ½ teaspoon salt and cook for 8 to 10 minutes until vegetables are softened but without color. Stir them frequently to keep them from browning.

3. **Add the veggies:** Add the potatoes, eggplant/courgettes, broth, and water, bringing to a boil, scraping up any bits stuck to the bottom of the pan. Simmer until the potatoes are tender, 10 minutes. Add the green beans and continue to simmer for another 5 minutes.

4. **Stir in the pasta:** You might need to add another cup of water and simmer until slightly softened, 5 minutes— the soup will become quite thick with the starch from the pasta. Stir in the cannellini beans and their liquid, simmer until pasta and vegetables are tender, about 3 to 5 minutes. Remove the bay leaves and the thyme. Season with salt and pepper to taste.

5. **Serve:** Divide the soup among serving bowls with the pistou served on the side, to be stirred into the soup just before eating.

**TABLE TALK TIPS:** If you don't have a mortar and pestle, you can use a food processor, a spice grinder, a rolling pin, a meat hammer, a heavy pan, a sturdy ziplock bag with a heavy object to crush against or even an empty wine bottle!

**NOTES FOR NEXT TIME:**

# Roasted Red Pepper Soup
## with Smoked Gouda and Coconut-Lime Cream

One of my favorite après-ski memories comes from a day at A-Basin in Summit County, Colorado. After a long morning on the slopes, Mark and I ducked into the Black Mountain Lodge for lunch, where a roasted red pepper and gouda soup caught my eye. Rich, velvety, and topped with sour cream and chives, it was the kind of cozy bowl you don't forget. I couldn't wait until we got home to Minnesota to make it, so I recreated it right in our vacation rental kitchen! The magic is in roasting the peppers yourself for that smoky-sweet flavor, though jarred peppers work in a pinch—just watch the salt. This small-batch version serves two perfectly (with just enough to freeze for later) and gets its luxurious creaminess from smoked gouda. A drizzle of cilantro-lime cream ties it all together with a bright, fresh finish.

**Coconut-Lime Cream**

⅓ cup (80 ml) coconut cream or sour cream (see notes)

1 tablespoon fresh-squeezed lime juice

½ teaspoon garlic powder

¼ teaspoon salt

Cilantro, for garnish (optional)

**Red Pepper and Gouda Soup**

4 red bell peppers, trimmed, cored, and halved

1 ½ teaspoons olive oil

1 garlic clove, minced, about 1 teaspoon

½ medium red onion, chopped

¼ teaspoon ground cumin

¼ teaspoon smoked paprika

1 tablespoon tomato paste

1 ½ teaspoons rose harissa

1 ½ teaspoons cornstarch or all-purpose flour

2 cups (480 ml) low-sodium chicken or vegetable broth, plus extra as needed

1 bay leaf

¼ cup (60 ml) half-and-half

1 tablespoon dry sherry

½ cup (50 g) smoked Gouda, shredded

1 tablespoon fresh cilantro leaves, minced, for garnish

Salt and freshly ground black pepper, to taste

1. **Make the coconut-lime cream:** Whisk all the ingredients together in a small bowl and season with salt and pepper to taste. Cover and refrigerate until needed.

2. **Roast the peppers:** Preheat the broiler with the rack 6 inches from heat source. Line a baking sheet with foil for easy cleanup. Toss the halved peppers with 1 ½ teaspoons olive oil, ¼ teaspoon salt, and a pinch of black pepper. Place them cut side down on the prepared sheet. Broil until the skins are charred and puffed but flesh is still firm, about 4–7 minutes, rotating the pan halfway through.

3. **Peel peppers:** Transfer the broiled peppers to a bowl, cover with foil, and let steam for 10 to 15 minutes. Peel away any loose skins (don't worry if some stay on) and chop the peppers. Make ahead tip: Store in an airtight container in the fridge for up to 3 days.

4. **Cook the soup:** In a Dutch oven over low heat, cook the garlic in 1 teaspoon olive oil, stirring constantly, until foamy and lightly golden, about 8 to 10 minutes. Add the onion, increase heat to medium, and cook until softened, about 5 to 7 minutes. Stir in the cumin and smoked paprika; cook until fragrant, about 30 seconds. Add the tomato paste, harissa, and cornstarch, stirring for 1 minute to deepen the flavors. Slowly whisk in the broth, smoothing out any lumps. Stir in the bay leaf and chopped roasted peppers. Bring to a gentle simmer and cook until the peppers are very tender, about 5 to 7 minutes.

5. **Blend:** Remove the bay leaf. Using an immersion blender (or blending in batches), puree the soup until completely smooth. For extra silkiness, strain through a fine-mesh sieve into a clean pot, pressing with a spoon to extract all the liquid.

6. **Finishing touches:** Stir in half-and-half, sherry, and extra broth as needed to adjust consistency. Gently heat over low (do not boil). Stir in smoked gouda, blending once more for a velvety texture. Stir in the cilantro and season with salt and pepper to taste. Ladle into bowls and drizzle with the cilantro lime cream.

**TABLE TALK TIPS:** For the coconut-lime cream I use canned coconut cream. It's thicker and richer than canned coconut milk because it has less water and more coconut meat. If you cannot find coconut cream you can substitute sour cream.

**NOTES FOR NEXT TIME:**

**Freezing Tip:** Let the soup cool completely before storing in airtight glass jars (leave 1-inch space at the top). Label and freeze for up to 3 months.

**About rose harissa:** Rose harissa is one of my secret kitchen weapons! This North African chili paste gets a floral twist from rose petals, adding a sweet balance to its heat. I use Belazu® brand (buy online) for its punchy, well-rounded flavor, but if you're using a milder supermarket version, just add about 50% more.

# Asparagus, Leek & Edamame Soup

The arrival of spring means one thing in my kitchen: asparagus season. There's nothing quite like the taste of fresh picked, locally grown asparagus—sweet, grassy, and just a little nutty. It's one of those fleeting ingredients that reminds me to savor the season while it lasts. This velvety soup is my way of celebrating spring's best, blending tender asparagus with leeks and edamame for a bright, fresh flavor. The secret to its silky-smooth texture? Running the puréed soup through a fine mesh sieve—a small extra step that makes all the difference.

**Soup**

1 teaspoon unsalted butter

1 tablespoon + 1 teaspoon olive oil, divided

1 cup (100 g) thinly sliced leeks (white and light green parts only)

1 shallot, minced

1 garlic clove, minced

3 cups (720 ml) vegetable or chicken broth, or 3 teaspoons (15 ml) Better Than Bouillon® mixed with water

½ cup (100 g) rice

1 ¼ cups (225g) shelled edamame, fresh or frozen

1 teaspoon grated lemon zest

½ pound (225 g) asparagus, stems cut into 1-inch (2.5 cm) pieces (tips reserved for garnish)

½ teaspoon kosher salt

⅛ teaspoon freshly ground black pepper

¼ cup (60 ml) heavy cream (optional)

Chopped chives, for garnish

**Ricotta Crostini**

4 slices (1/2-inch / 1.25 cm thick) baguette, cut on the bias

½ cup (125 g) fresh ricotta

2 teaspoons minced fresh tarragon or chives

1 garlic clove, peeled and halved

1. **Sauté the aromatics:** In a medium saucepan, heat 1 tablespoon olive oil and melt the butter over medium-low heat. Stir in the leeks and shallot, cooking until soft, about 5 minutes. Add the garlic and cook for 30 seconds until fragrant.
2. **Simmer the soup:** Pour in the broth, then add the rice, edamame, and lemon zest. Increase the heat and bring the soup to a boil. Reduce to a simmer and cook until rice is just tender, about 15 minutes.
3. **Cook the asparagus:** Add asparagus stems, salt, and pepper. Return to a boil, then reduce heat to a simmer, cover, and cook until vegetables are tender, about 10–12 minutes.
4. **Blend & strain:** Purée the soup using an immersion blender or a food processor until smooth. Strain through a fine mesh sieve, discarding any solids. Return the soup to the pot, taste and decide if you want to add cream. If you add, stir it in now and heat through. Otherwise, skip the cream and heat the soup. If soup seems too thick, add more broth.
5. **Sauté the asparagus tips:** In a small nonstick skillet, heat remaining 1 teaspoon olive oil over medium heat. Add reserved asparagus tips and sauté until tender, about 5 minutes.
6. **Make crostini.** Heat oven to 350°F (175°C). Place bread slices on a baking sheet and toast, turning halfway through, until bread is golden and dry to the touch, about 10 minutes. While bread toasts, season ricotta with tarragon, salt and pepper. Rub hot crostini with cut side of halved garlic cloves and slather with ricotta. Ladle soup into warm bowls and garnish with asparagus tips and cut chives. Serve with crostini.

**TABLE TALK TIPS:** Sourcing asparagus from a local food cooperative or farmers' market is what makes this soup truly special. It's heirloom cooking at its best, using ingredients that connect us to the land and the season. So grab a bunch of the freshest asparagus you can find and let's make something delicious!

 **NOTES FOR NEXT TIME:**

# Leftover Roasted Chicken Noodle Soup

There's nothing quite like homemade chicken noodle soup, especially when it's served up fresh in my aunt's farm kitchen. Growing up, our family would pile in for a weekend at the farm and, sure enough, she'd have a spread waiting: pots of chili, her classic chicken noodle soup, and trays of runzas, all set to feed our crowd of 24. This version of her soup is the ultimate comfort food but with a twist: a bright, herby mint mojo sauce that takes it up a notch. It's also a great way to use up any leftover roasted chicken. Once you've made this, you'll never go back to the canned stuff. Simple, flavorful, and totally worth it.

**What you need:**

- 1 tablespoon unsalted butter
- 1 small onion, diced
- 1 carrot, diced
- 1 stalk celery, diced
- 1 small parsnip, diced
- 1 small leek, thinly sliced, white and light green parts only
- 6 cups (1.4 L) water
- 2 tablespoons Better Than Bouillon® concentrate, roasted chicken flavor
- ⅛ pound (2 oz / 55 g) egg noodles, or fettuccine noodles broken into pieces
- 1 cup (125 g) leftover rotisserie chicken or roasted chicken, shredded
- Mint mojo sauce, for garnish, (optional, see pg.222)

1. **Sauté the aromatics:** Get out a heavy-bottomed pot or Dutch oven and melt the butter over medium heat. Now, toss in the chopped onion, carrot, celery, parsnips, and leeks, cook until just tender, about 5 minutes. Pour in the water and stir in 2 tablespoons Better Than Bouillon® to really bring out those flavors. Set over medium heat, bring everything up to a boil, adjust the heat to let it simmer until the veggies are tender and perfect.

2. **Cook the noodles:** While that's cooking, start a second pot with well-salted water (we're going for "sea-level salty") to cook the noodles. Once it's boiling, in go the noodles to cook them until they're just right — al dente (firm to the bite but tender throughout.

3. **Finishing touches:** Add cooked chicken to the pot with the broth and veggies, giving it all a taste. Add a little more bouillon or salt if needed. To serve, place a scoop of cooked noodles into each soup bowl, then ladle that comforting vegetable and chicken soup over the top.

**TABLE TALK TIPS:** For a bright, fresh finish, drizzle a little mint mojo sauce (pg.222) No left over roasted chicken? Make your own homemade stock (pg. 222) and use the pouched chicken meat from the stock.

**NOTES FOR NEXT TIME:**

# Kim's Award Winning White Chicken Chili

Kim is a dear friend. We met years ago through our small group at church and she's been instrumental in helping me test nearly every recipe in this cookbook. When she offered to share her award-winning white bean chicken chili—yes, she's taken home more than a few trophies for this one—we were thrilled! It's a little pot of comfort with big flavor. Now, the only debate left is how you like yours: thick and hearty, or with a little more broth like Mark and I prefer. Either way, I can't wait to hear what you think when you try it.

**What you need:**

½ pound (225 g) dried white beans (Great Northern, cannellini, or Italian kidney beans)

1 tablespoon chicken stock base (like Better Than Bouillon®), divided

½ large onion, chopped

Peanut oil or vegetable oil (enough for sautéing)

3–4 large garlic cloves, thinly sliced

4 ounces (115 g) canned chopped green chilies, drained

1 teaspoon dried oregano

1½ teaspoons ground cumin

½ teaspoon cayenne pepper (or more if you like it spicier)

1½ teaspoons chipotle pepper in adobo sauce, puréed (tip: purée the whole can, freeze in small portions, and defrost as needed)

1 large Anaheim chili, roasted and diced

1 small sweet red bell pepper, roasted and diced

3 cups (375 g) cooked, diced chicken (rotisserie chicken works great)

½ cup (120 g) sour cream

1½ cups (150 g) shredded Monterey Jack cheese

**Toppings** (optional, but amazing)

Chopped green onions

Fresh cilantro

Diced tomatoes

Chopped jalapeños

Store-bought tortilla strips or Fritos®

Shredded Monterey Jack or crumbled blue cheese

1. **Get those beans ready (optional - see note):** To soak, place beans in a bowl and cover with about 4 inches of water. Let them hang out for at least 4 hours or overnight. Drain and rinse under cold running water.

2. **Cook the beans:** Place the soaked (or unsoaked), rinsed, and drained beans in a deep pot with 4 cups of cold water. Bring to a boil, then lower the heat and simmer gently, covered, for 1 to 1½ hours. Stir in about 2 teaspoons of stock base to flavor the beans. Give the beans an occasional stir and skim off any foam and skins. Cook until very tender but still with a little bite. Keep an eye on the water level—you want a very gentle simmer and enough liquid to prevent scorching. Yes, I'm speaking from experience.

3. **Roast those peppers:** Move your oven rack about 6 inches below the broiler and preheat. Line a baking sheet with foil. Halve the Anaheim and red bell peppers lengthwise, leaving stems intact. Remove seeds, drizzle with a little oil, sprinkle with salt and pepper, and place cut-side down on the sheet. Broil for 4–7 minutes until charred. Let cool, then cut off the stems and peel off any loose skin. Discard any remaining skin that slips off easily and discard.

4. **Sauté the flavor base:** Heat a swirl of oil in a sauté pan. Add the onion and garlic and cook until soft and fragrant, about 3–4 minutes. Stir in green chilies, puréed chipotle, roasted peppers, cumin, oregano, and cayenne. Take a moment to breathe in the aroma—it's chili magic in the making.

5. **Make it a chili:** Add 1 teaspoon stock base, the sautéed mixture, and the chicken to your pot of beans. Add more water and stock base, if needed. Simmer gently for another 30 minutes, letting all the flavors come together. Taste and adjust seasoning

At this point, you can pause and refrigerate overnight for even better flavor, or freeze for later. When reheating, you may want to add a splash of water to loosen things up.

Just before serving, stir in the sour cream and shredded cheese. If chili is too thick, add a little more broth. Heat until the cheese is fully melted and the chili is creamy and hot.

6. **Finishing touches:** Ladle into bowls and let everyone go wild with toppings.

**TABLE TALK TIPS:** Soaking speeds up cooking and can make the beans easier to digest—but it's totally optional (see step 1). No soak? No problem. They'll just need a bit longer to cook (see step 2).

**NOTES FOR NEXT TIME:**

67

## Icelandic Fish Stew (Plokkfiskur)

This hearty fish stew is my tribute to Iceland—a land of dramatic coastlines and a cuisine that makes the most of every catch. On a visit there, I discovered plokkfiskur, a humble mash of leftover fish, potatoes, onions and milk, seasoned simply with black pepper. Every cook adds their own twist and I couldn't shake the memory of how comforting it was. Back home, I reimagined it for two; halibut simmered in clam juice and white wine, thickened with potatoes and tomato paste and finished with cream, Gouda, and a squeeze of lemon. Rustic yet refined, it's an ode to Iceland's shores, made for sharing.

**For fish:**

- ½ teaspoon kosher salt
- ½ teaspoon sugar
- ¼ teaspoon freshly ground black pepper
- ½ lb (225 g) halibut, or other white fish such as cod or striped bass, cut into 2 × 1-inch (5 × 2.5 cm) pieces

**Fish Stew**

1 leek, white and pale green parts only, tough outer layer removed, sliced into ¼-inch (6 mm) rounds

1 tablespoon unsalted butter

1 tablespoon olive oil

1 celery stalk, thinly sliced

½ cup (70 g) shallots, diced

½ teaspoon salt

¼ teaspoon curry powder

1 tablespoon tomato paste

½ cup (120 ml) white wine

½ lb (225 g) baby creamer Yukon gold potatoes, halved (quartered if larger than 1½ in / 4 cm in diameter)

1 cup (240 ml) bottled clam juice

1 bay leaf

½ cup (120 ml) heavy cream

2 ounces (55 g) Gouda cheese, shredded

2 teaspoons fresh lemon juice

**Garnish**

¼ cup (60 ml) heavy cream, whipped (optional)

chives (optional)

celery leaves (optional)

1. **Season the fish:** If fish is frozen, move it to the refrigerator the night before making the stew. In a small bowl, mix together ½ teaspoon salt, sugar, and pepper. Sprinkle fish evenly on all sides with salt mixture and place on wire rack set in rimmed baking sheet. Refrigerate at least 30 and up to 45 minutes.

2. **Make the stock:** Cut leeks into ¼" rounds. Rinse, tossing with hands so that leeks separate into individual rings, and drain thoroughly. In a medium sized stock pot over medium heat, melt butter and oil together. Add leeks, celery, and shallots, making sure the vegetables are tossed enough to coat. Cover pot and cook until leeks begin to soften, 5-6 minutes.

3. **Build flavor:** Add salt, curry powder, and tomato paste. Stir well and cook just until fragrant, about 30 seconds. Pour in the wine and simmer for about 1 minute. Add potatoes, clam juice, bay leaf, and ½-cup water; bring to a boil until potatoes are fork tender, about 10 – 12 minutes. Cut fish into 2 × 1-inch (5 × 2.5 cm) pieces and add fish to the pot along with ½ cup cream, gently stirring to combine. Cook until fish is opaque, about 3 – 4 minutes.

4. **Finishing touches:** In a small bowl add ¼ cup of heavy whipping cream. Using a whisk, beat until soft peaks form, set aside. Grate the gouda cheese into another bowl. Remove bay leaves from stew and stir in gouda and lemon juice, letting sit for 3 – 5 minutes.

5. **Taste and adjust seasoning:** Add more wine to achieve desired consistency. Too bland? Add ¼ teaspoon of salt at a time. For brighter citrus flavor? Add ½ teaspoon of lemon juice at a time. Serve the soup with a spoonful of whipped cream, chives, and celery leaves.

**NOTES FOR NEXT TIME:**

Heirloom Tomato Gazpacho | 72

72 | Cantaloupe and Sweet Corn Gazpacho

Peach and Cucumber Gazpacho | 73

75 | Strawberry Gazpacho

# Sips of Summer: Mason Jar Gazpacho

There's something about wandering a farmer's market or pulling over at a roadside produce stand that makes summer feel just right. The heirloom tomatoes are warm from the sun, their skins slightly split from ripeness. The melons are so fragrant and sweet, you can smell them before you see them. And the peaches? Soft, juicy, and just begging to be eaten over the sink.

These are the flavors of summer, and gazpacho is the perfect way to capture them in their purest form. Whether it's the classic, sun-kissed heirloom tomato gazpacho, the refreshing balance of peach and cucumber, or the unexpected sweetness of melon and strawberries, each sip is a taste of the season. I love serving these in individual mason jars—perfectly chilled, easy to serve, and just the right portion for one. No cooking required, just a little blending and a few fresh ingredients to celebrate the best of what's in season.

**TABLE TALK TIPS:**

- **Avoid the mistake of not seasoning the soup.** Cold soups require a surprising amount of seasoning, even more than hot soups. That means more salt, yes, but also more acid (think lime juice) and heat (like chilies). Taste, season, chill, and then—this is key—taste and re-season after it's chilled. You'll be floored by how much the flavors become muted after a rest in the fridge.

- **Serve cold.** Chill gazpacho at least 3 hours before serving – this is when the vegetable and fruit flavors really mesh.

- **Don't forget the toppings.** They will not only make the soup look appetizing, but will add some needed texture. Make sure to add right before serving so they don't lose their crispy crunchiness.

- **Store gazpacho in an airtight container** in the refrigerator for up to 4-5 days.

**NOTES FOR NEXT TIME:**

# Heirloom Tomato Gazpacho

**What you need:**

½ cup (75 g) red onion, roughly chopped (reserve ¼ cup / 40g, diced into 1 cm pieces for garnish)

1 ½ lbs. (680 g) heirloom tomatoes, cored and chopped (reserve ½ cup / 85 g, diced into 1 cm pieces for garnish)

1 cup (130 g) cucumber, peeled, seeded, and chopped, reserve ⅜ cup / 50g, diced into 1 cm pieces for garnish

1 cup (150 g) red bell pepper, seeded and chopped, reserve 2 tablespoons, diced into 1 cm pieces for garnish

½ teaspoon kosher salt, divided, plus more to taste

2 ½ teaspoons fresh lemon juice, divided

2 tablespoons olive oil, divided

1 teaspoon minced fresh flat-leaf parsley

Freshly ground black pepper, to taste

1 garlic clove, minced

¼ teaspoon minced fresh thyme

1 tablespoon balsamic vinegar, rice vinegar, or sherry vinegar

1 cup (50 g) cubed French bread, crusts removed

½ tablespoon sugar

Crème fraîche and balsamic reduction, for garnish

1. **Prepare the garnish:** In small bowl, combine ¼ cup diced onion, ½ cup tomatoes, ⅜ cup cucumber, and 2 tablespoons bell pepper with ¼ teaspoon salt, ½ teaspoon lemon juice, 1 tablespoon olive oil, parsley, and a pinch of black pepper. Cover and refrigerate until ready to serve.

2. **Make the soup base:** In a food processor, combine remaining ¼ cup onion, 2 teaspoons lemon juice, ¼ teaspoon salt, sugar, garlic, thyme, vinegar, and bread. Puree until smooth, about 2 minutes, scraping down the sides as needed.

3. **Blend the gazpacho:** Add the remaining tomatoes, cucumber, and bell pepper to the processor and puree until completely smooth (2 to 4 minutes). Season with black pepper. Transfer to a bowl, cover, and refrigerate for at least 1 hour or up to 1 day.

4. **Final blending:** Just before serving, return soup to the food processor. With motor running, slowly drizzle in remaining 1 tablespoon olive oil and blend for 1 minute. Taste and adjust seasoning with vinegar, salt and pepper. Ladle gazpacho into two 10-ounce mason jars. Cover and chill until ready to serve. Garnish each jar with crème fraîche and a spoonful of reserved diced vegetables.

# Cantaloupe and Sweet Corn Gazpacho

**What you need:**

2 corn ears, husks removed, kernels cut from cob

1 shallot clove, peeled and roughly chopped

½ tablespoon (7 ml) avocado oil

Kosher salt and freshly ground black pepper, to taste

¼ yellow bell pepper, ribs and seeds removed, roughly chopped (plus 1 tablespoon / 10 g finely diced, reserved for garnish)

½ cantaloupe, skin and seeds removed, roughly chopped (plus 1 tablespoon / 10 g finely diced, reserved for garnish)

2 red or yellow tomatoes, cored and seeds removed, roughly chopped (plus 1 tablespoon / 10 g finely diced, reserved for garnish, or use thinly sliced cherry tomatoes)

5 tablespoons (30 ml) extra-virgin olive oil, divided

¼ Fresno or red jalapeño pepper, cored and seeds removed, small dice (optional)

¾ teaspoon chopped fresh cilantro or mint (optional)

Fresh lime juice, to taste

# Cantaloupe and Sweet Corn Gazpacho *(continued)*

1. **Sauté the corn:** In a small Dutch oven or skillet, cook shallots and corn kernels in avocado oil over medium heat. Add ¼ teaspoon salt and ⅛ teaspoon fresh ground pepper and stir frequently until corn has softened and shallots are translucent. If the corn begins popping – remove from heat. Once done, remove from the pot and chill down for about 5 minutes or chill completely in the refrigerator.

2. **Prepare vegetables:** In a large bowl, combine roughly chopped vegetables and fruit. *Reminder: reserve 1 tablespoon each of the melon, tomato, and peppers for garnish.* Add cooked corn and shallot mixture, along with the jalapeno, if desired, to the large bowl and toss with 1 tablespoon olive oil. Season with salt. You can prepare the vegetable and fruit mixture up to 2 days in advance.

3. **Process the soup:** Combine mixed vegetables and fruit in a blender. Please do not fill the blender more than half full; we want to "pulverize" the fruits and vegetables. You will need to divide the process into a couple of batches.

   Starting with the setting on low, turn on blender and increase speed to high. All ingredients should blend easily. If they don't, add 1 tablespoon olive oil and 1 tablespoon water at a time until everything turns in the machine. Continue blending on high until the gazpacho is smooth (this may take 2-3 minutes). Just before turning the machine off, add 1 tablespoon of olive oil and blend briefly until combined.

   Turn off the machine and strain gazpacho through a fine mesh strainer. Use a ladle or spatula to push the liquid through, leaving pulp and tomato skins in the strainer. This will result in a silky and creamy texture. Note: If you are short on time or enjoy a chunkier version of this gazpacho, you can skip this step.

   Repeat steps 5 thru 8 until all the vegetable and fruit mixture has been processed. Adjust the consistency with more olive oil or water, and season gazpacho with salt and lime juice to your liking. Chill the soup in an airtight container in the refrigerator for at least 3 hours. Keep the cilantro or mint, and reserved finely diced vegetables for garnish.

# Peach and Cucumber Gazpacho

### What you need:

*2 ripe peaches (225 g / ½ lb), halved and pitted; cut one peach into 2-inch [5 cm] pieces, the other peach into ¾-inch [2 cm] pieces)*

*2–3 cucumbers (340 g / ¾ lb), peeled and seeded; cut into 2-inch [5 cm] pieces, the remaining into ¾-inch [2 cm] pieces)*

*1 cup (240 ml) ice water, divided*

*1 scallion, chopped*

*1 jalapeño chile, stemmed, halved, and seeded (half chopped coarse; ½ tsp finely chopped reserved for garnish, if desired)*

*¾ teaspoon table salt*

*½ teaspoon sugar*

*½ cup (120 g) plain whole-milk yogurt*

*1 ½ tablespoon seasoned rice vinegar, divided*

*¼ tsp black pepper*

*2 tablespoon minced fresh mint, plus extra shredded mint for garnish*

*Extra virgin olive oil, for drizzling*

## Peach and Cucumber Gazpacho *(continued)*

1. **Blend ingredients:** In a blender, combine the 2-inch pieces of peach and cucumber, ½ cup ice water, scallion, coarsely chopped jalapeño, salt, sugar, and mint. Blend until completely smooth, about 2 minutes.

2. **Strain the soup:** Pour soup into a fine-mesh strainer, set over a large bowl. Using the back of a ladle or a rubber spatula press the soup through.

3. **Season:** Whisk in the yogurt, 1 tablespoon of vinegar, pepper, and the remaining ½ cup ice water. Cover and refrigerate to meld flavors for at least 20 minutes or up to 12 hours.

4. **Prepare the toppings:** Meanwhile, in a bowl, combine ¾-inch pieces of peach and cucumber, finely chopped jalapeño and remaining ½ tablespoon of vinegar.

5. **Serve and enjoy:** Stir mint into the soup and season with salt and pepper to taste. Serve the gazpacho cold, topping individual portions with the peach-cucumber salad and shredded mint, and drizzling with olive oil.

## Strawberry Gazpacho

**What you need:**

¼ (50 g) English cucumber, peeled

2 ¼ cups (340 g) ripe heirloom tomatoes, halved, about 1 lb

¾ cup (100 g) ripe strawberries, hulled, about 5 oz

½ jalapeño or milder chili (such as Fresno), deseeded if preferred

1 medium shallot clove, peeled

1 garlic clove, peeled

1 to 2 teaspoons sumac (Note: substitute with paprika plus grated lemon zest, if preferred)

1 to 2 tablespoons agave syrup or honey

1 tablespoon vinegar (white balsamic, white wine, champagne, or sherry)

¼ cup (60 ml) extra-virgin olive oil (lemon-infused olive oil makes a great twist)

Juice and zest of 1 lime or small lemon

1 to 2 teaspoons sea salt, to taste

½ to 1 teaspoon freshly ground black pepper

**Garnishes** *(optional)*

Halved cherry tomatoes

Sliced strawberries

Fresh herbs

Extra drizzle of olive oil

1. **Load the blender:** Toss the cucumber, tomatoes, strawberries, jalapeño, shallot, garlic, vinegar, lime or lemon juice and zest, olive oil, salt, sumac, agave or honey, and pepper into a high-powered blender or food processor.

2. **Blitz away:** Blend until everything is silky smooth. Taste as you go — this is your moment to play. Need more brightness? Splash in a bit more vinegar. Want it sweeter? Add another drizzle of agave or honey. Or maybe it just needs a pinch more salt to make the flavors pop.

3. **Chill out:** Pour the gazpacho into an airtight container (or straight into mason jars if you're feeling ahead of the game) and refrigerate for at least 3 hours.

4. **Serve:** Pour into chilled mason jars or bowls. Top with cherry tomatoes, strawberries, a few sprigs of fresh herbs, and a final drizzle of olive oil.

**Aunt Sherril's Runzas**
Pg.80

**Short Rib Burger**
Pg.82

**Crispy Lamb Pitas**
Pg.83

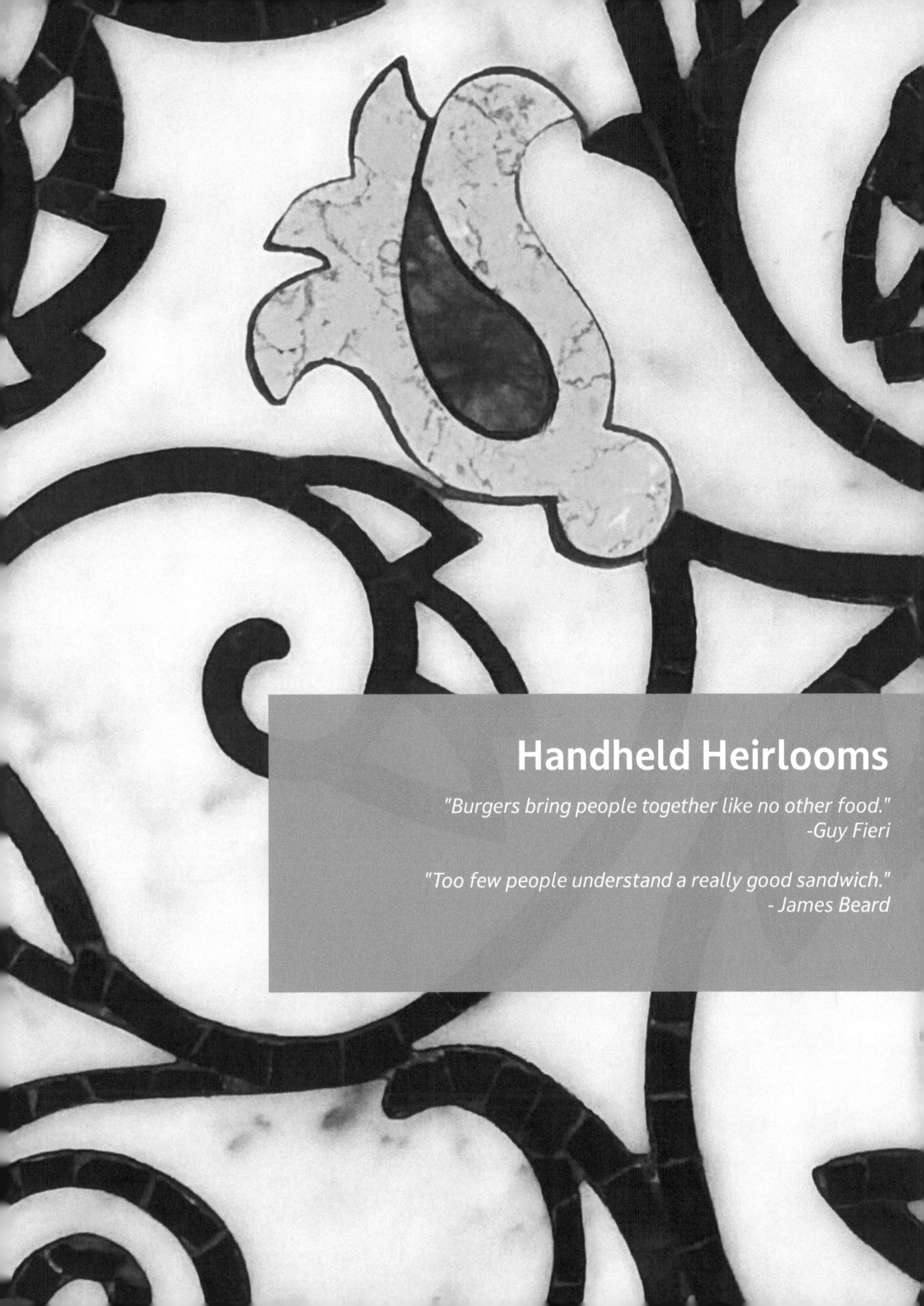

# Handheld Heirlooms

"Burgers bring people together like no other food."
-Guy Fieri

"Too few people understand a really good sandwich."
- James Beard

Philly Cheesesteaks for Two | 79

80 | Aunt Sheree's Rum Recipe

Short Rib Burgers | 82

83 | Crispy Lamb Pita

# Philly Cheesesteaks

Let me take you back to an unforgettable holiday weekend one fall - a long weekend when there was no school, where Mark, the boys, and I hit the history trifecta: Boston, Philly, and Washington, D.C. Amid the Liberty Bell and all the historic stops, Mark introduced us to the magic of Pat's cheesesteaks of Philadelphia. Those melty, meaty, cheesy bites? They were life-changing. Back home, we had to recreate the magic—minus the "Wiz." Provolone, pepper jack or American cheese? Your call. These weeknight wonders are also perfect for using up that surplus of peppers from your garden.

**What you need:**

¾ to 1 lb (340–450 g) flank steak

2 Italian sub rolls, 8-inch (20 cm), split lengthwise

1 tablespoon vegetable oil

1 tablespoon unsalted butter or ghee

¼ teaspoon salt

¼ teaspoon black pepper

2 tablespoons grated Parmesan cheese

4 slices (4 oz / 115 g) provolone, American cheese, or pepper jack

½ yellow onion, thinly sliced into half-moons

½ red bell pepper, thinly sliced

½ yellow bell pepper, thinly sliced

Hot sauce (optional)

 **NOTES FOR NEXT TIME:**

1. **Freeze the steak:** Place your flank steak on a baking sheet and pop it in the freezer for about an hour, just until it's firm. This makes slicing easier.

2. **Toast the rolls:** Adjust your oven rack to the middle position and preheat to 400°F (200°C). To make room for the steak filling, the bun can be hollowed out before adding the sandwich ingredients. Now, spread those split rolls on a baking sheet and toast them until lightly browned. This gives them a nice crunch to stand up to all that cheesy goodness.

3. **Slice the steak:** Using your sharpest knife, slice the steak as thinly as you can against the grain. Mound the slices on a cutting board and give them a rough chop—about 10-20 times.

4. **Cook the meat:** Heat 1 tablespoon vegetable oil and melt the butter in a (10-inch) cast iron skillet over high heat. When it's just starting to smoke and the butter starts turning brown, add the steak in an even layer. Let it sear without stirring until one side is deeply browned, about 2 - 3 minutes.

5. **Add the veggies:** Toss in the onions and peppers. Stir everything together and cook until the steak is no longer pink and the veggies are soft, about 4-5 minutes, stirring occasionally.

6. **Season and cheese it up:** Sprinkle the mixture with salt and pepper. Reduce the heat to medium and sprinkle Parmesan cheese over meat and veggies. And if looking for a bit more heat, add some hot sauce. Lay the cheese slices on top and let it melt for about 2 minutes. Then use a heatproof spatula to fold the gooey cheese into the meat mixture. Divide the cheesy steak mixture evenly among the toasted rolls. Serve immediately. History lessons are optional, but these cheesesteaks? Mandatory. Enjoy!

# Aunt Sherril's Runza Recipe

Trying to imagine a runza? This homemade Nebraska runza sandwich recipe inspired by my aunt's farm kitchen is simply ground beef and cabbage, all wrapped-up in a fresh baked bread bun. This recipe makes 8 sandwiches. Two for now, freeze the rest for later.

**For the dough** *(or use 1 lb frozen bread dough)*

¾ cup (180 ml) warm water, 110°F (43°C)

½ cup (120 ml) sweetened condensed milk

¼ cup (60 ml) vegetable oil

2 tablespoons sugar

1 large egg

3 ½ cups (440 g) all-purpose flour, plus extra for rolling

2 (¼-oz / 7 g each) packets instant or rapid-rise yeast

1 teaspoon salt

**For the filling**

4 tablespoons (55 g) unsalted butter, divided

1 ½ pounds (680 g) 90% lean ground beef

1 ½ tablespoons Worcestershire sauce

½ teaspoon garlic powder

½ teaspoon onion salt

1 teaspoon dried oregano

1 teaspoon dried basil

Pinch of red pepper flakes

Dash of hot sauce (optional)

Salt and black pepper, to taste

1 large white onion, finely chopped, about 1 cup / 150 g

½ red or green bell pepper, finely chopped, about ½ cup / 75 g (optional)

½ small head cabbage, chopped, about 3 cups / 200 g

8 slices deli American cheese or pepper jack, about 8 oz / 225 g

1. **Make the dough:** Let's start by lightly greasing a large bowl with cooking spray. Warm some water, targeting the temperature to be around 110°F (43°C). If you don't have a thermometer, test water to make sure it's almost, but not, too hot to touch.

   **Using a stand mixer:** Mix water, sweetened condensed milk, oil, sugar, and egg in large glass measuring cup that holds 2 - 4 cups liquid. In the bowl of a standing mixer fitted with a dough hook, mix flour, yeast, and salt together. With mixer on low, slowly add the water mixture. After dough comes together (we are looking to see that the flour is well mixed in). Increase speed to medium and mix until shiny and smooth, 4 to 6 minutes. With floured hands, turn dough out onto heavily floured work surface. Shape dough into a ball, and place in the greased bowl.

   **To make dough by hand:** Combine dry ingredients in large bowl, making a well in center of dry ingredients. Pour the wet ingredients into the well, incorporating all the flour using a fork or wooden spoon. Mix for about 1-2 minutes using the wooden spoon – it will be hard to mix. Don't worry about tidy dough here, just get the flour all mixed in and turn dough out onto heavily floured work surface. With floured hands, knead until shiny and smooth, about 10 minutes.

   **If using frozen dough:** Thaw and let rise according to package directions.

2. **Let it rise:** Cover bowl with plastic wrap or a wet kitchen towel and let rest in a warm place until doubled in size, about 1 hour.

3. **Cook the Filling:** Melt 1 tablespoon butter in large skillet over medium-high heat. Add beef and cook until just beginning to brown, about 6 minutes, breaking up any large clumps. Stir in Worcestershire sauce, garlic powder, onion salt, oregano, basil, and red pepper flakes. Simmer for about 30 seconds. Using a slotted spoon, transfer beef to paper towel-lined plate.

Melt 1 tablespoon butter in the now-empty pan. Add onion and peppers (if using) and cook until softened, about 3 minutes. Now we will add the cabbage and toss until just beginning to wilt, 2 to 4 minutes (I prefer to have it a bit crunchy). Return beef to pan and season with salt and pepper and hot sauce for an extra kick.

4. **Assemble Runzas:** Adjust oven racks to the upper-middle and lower-middle positions and heat oven to 350°F (175°C). Coat 2 baking sheets with cooking spray. Pro tip: Spray baking sheets over open dishwasher door to contain the oil! Divide dough into 8 equal pieces, gently forming 8 small balls. Working on lightly floured work surface, roll each piece of dough into 7-inch (18 cm) circle– it does not have to be a perfect circle. Place one dough round in a deep cereal bowl and top with one slice of cheese. Spoon ¾ cup filling over cheese and pinch edges of dough together to form bun. Transfer bun, seam side down, to prepared baking sheet. Repeat with remaining dough, cheese, and filling, placing 4 buns on each baking sheet. Cover buns with plastic wrap or wet kitchen towel and let rise until puffed, about 20 minutes.

5. **Bake:** Until golden brown, about 20 minutes, switching and rotating position of baking sheets halfway through baking time. Brush buns with melted butter and serve with ketchup! Or just rub buns with a stick of butter while they are still warm.

**TABLE TALK TIPS:** Making runza's for two? Make and freeze. Baked runzas freeze well. Wrap each runza in plastic wrap and store in air-tight container. Thaw in refrigerator and reheat in a 350°F (175°C) oven for about 10 minutes.

**NOTES FOR NEXT TIME:**

# Short Rib Burgers
## with Scallion-Miso Mayo

Some burgers are just burgers, but this short rib burger will rival your favorite pub-style burger. Grinding your own beef might seem like an extra step, but trust me, the result is worth it. With a perfectly seared crust and juicy, rosy interior, this burger is elevated by the tangy umami punch of scallion-miso mayo. Whether you're celebrating a special occasion or simply treating yourself, this is the ultimate burger for two.

**Burgers**

*1 pound (450 g) boneless beef short ribs, trimmed and cut into ½-inch (1.25 cm) cubes or sirloin steak tips or chuck-eye roast (12 ounces / 340 g), trimmed*

*½ teaspoon table salt*

*½ teaspoon black pepper*

*1 teaspoon vegetable oil*

*2 hamburger buns, toasted and buttered*

**Scallion-Miso Mayo**

*¼ cup (60 g) mayonnaise*

*1 scallion, minced*

*1 tablespoon white miso*

*1 teaspoon rice vinegar*

*¼ teaspoon black pepper*

*1 tablespoon Sriracha®, for a spicier sauce (optional)*

NOTES FOR NEXT TIME:

1. **Prepare the beef:** Spread the beef cubes in an even layer on a large plate. Freeze until the meat is very firm and edges are starting to harden but still pliable, about 25 to 35 minutes.

2. **Grind the beef:** Working in two batches, pulse half of the beef in a food processor until ground into 1/16-inch pieces, about 20 pulses. Transfer to a plate. Repeat with remaining beef. Pick through the ground beef to remove any long strands of gristle or large chunks of fat (for short ribs, this will typically be about 4 ounces).

3. **Form the patties:** Divide the ground beef into two equal portions. Gently shape each portion into a patty about ¾-inch thick and 4 inches in diameter. The patties should weigh roughly 6 ounces each. Sprinkle both sides of the patties with salt and pepper. Use a spatula to handle them gently.

4. **Cook the patties:** Heat the vegetable oil in a 12-inch nonstick or cast iron skillet over high heat until just smoking. Carefully transfer patties to the skillet and cook without moving them for 3 minutes. Flip patties gently and continue to cook for another 2 minutes until the second side is well browned.

5. **Finish cooking:** Off the heat, cover the skillet and let the patties sit to finish cooking to desired doneness:
   - **Medium-rare:** Let sit for about 2 minutes (internal temp: 125°F / 52°C).
   - **Medium:** Let sit for 3 minutes (internal temp: 130–135°F / 54–57°C).
   - **Medium-well:** Let sit for 4 minutes (internal temp: 140–145°F / 60–63°C).

6. **Rest the burgers:** Transfer the patties to a plate, tent with aluminum foil, and let rest for 5 minutes.

7. **For the sauce:** In a small bowl, whisk together mayonnaise, scallion, miso, rice vinegar, pepper, and optional Sriracha® if using. Taste and adjust seasoning. I add a teaspoon of lime juice if using Sriracha.

8. **Assemble:** Place the burger patties on the bottom buns, spread a generous amount of scallion-miso mayo over patties, and cap with the top buns. Serve immediately.

# Crispy Lamb Pita

One of our favorite neighborhood spots was Christos, a cozy Greek restaurant where we would gather after the boys' baseball games. We always sat at the bar-top table, tired but happy, replaying the game's highlights over a comforting meal. No visit was complete without the flaming saganaki appetizer—our boys' faces lighting up as we all shouted "Opa!" in unison with the server when the cheese was set ablaze. Then came the main event: a plate piled high with lamb gyro meat, warm pita, and a spread of fresh toppings. This crispy lamb pita brings back those memories, but in a way that's perfect for two. Instead of traditional slow-roasted meat, we streamline the process by using ground lamb, achieving the same crispy edges by pan-frying the spiced meat.

**What you need:**

- ½ lb (225 g) ground lamb
- ½ teaspoon dried oregano
- ½ teaspoon dried rosemary
- ½ teaspoon ground cumin
- ½ teaspoon kosher salt, plus more to taste
- Zest of ½ lemon, about 1 teaspoon
- 2 cloves garlic, grated (use a microplane)
- 2 teaspoons olive oil, divided
- ½ cup (75 g) seedless cucumber, quartered and chopped
- ⅓ cup (60 g) tomato, chopped, about 1 small tomato
- 1 tablespoon diced red onion
- 1 tablespoon red wine vinegar
- ½ cup (120 g) plain Greek yogurt
- 2 pitas, warmed
- Chopped dill, for serving (optional)

 **NOTES FOR NEXT TIME:**

1. **Prepare the lamb:** In a medium bowl, mix the ground lamb with oregano, rosemary, cumin, salt, lemon zest, garlic, and 1 teaspoon olive oil. Work everything together with your hands or a spoon until well combined. Cover and refrigerate for at least an hour, or overnight for deeper flavor.

2. **Make the cucumber salad:** While the lamb marinates, combine the chopped cucumber, tomato, red onion, red wine vinegar, and the remaining teaspoon of olive oil in a small bowl. Season with a pinch of salt, toss to coat, and refrigerate until ready to serve.

3. **Cook the lamb:** Heat a 10-inch nonstick or well-seasoned cast iron skillet over medium-high heat. Add lamb mixture, pressing it down with a spatula to form a thin, even layer. Let it cook undisturbed for about 4 minutes, until the bottom is deeply golden and crispy.

4. **Break and crisp the meat:** Use your spatula to cut the lamb into manageable portions, then flip them over. Cook for another minute, then break the lamb into bite-sized pieces, stirring and flipping occasionally, until crispy and cooked through, about 4 more minutes. Remove from heat.

5. **Assemble the pitas:** Spread a few tablespoons of Greek yogurt down the center of each warm pita. Pile on the crispy lamb and top with the cucumber salad. Sprinkle with fresh dill, if using.

6. **Serve and enjoy:** Fold up the pita, take a bite, and savor all the flavors—just like those post-game dinners at Christos, minus the flaming cheese (but feel free to yell "Opa!" anyway).

# Grilled Portobello Burger
## with Whipped Feta and Mediterranean Relish

Take your burger night up a notch and grill a meaty portobello cap, slather on a layer of whipped feta, and pile high with my Mediterranean relish recipe (pg.218) from my week-long boot camp at the Culinary Institute of America. It's a fresh, savory, and satisfying vegetarian burger that feels just as indulgent as the classic.

**What you need:**

- ⅓ cup Mediterranean relish (pg.218)
- 2 tablespoons whipped feta (pg.24)
- 2 portobello mushrooms (4 to 5 inches in diameter), stems and gills removed
- ¼ cup extra-virgin olive oil
- 1½ tablespoons red wine vinegar
- 1 garlic clove, minced
- Salt and Pepper
- ½ cup baby arugula
- 2 kaiser rolls, split

 NOTES FOR NEXT TIME:

1. **Prepare mushrooms:** Using tip of paring knife, cut ½-inch crosshatch pattern on tops of mushroom caps, ¹⁄₁₆ inch deep. Combine oil, vinegar, garlic, ½ teaspoon salt, band ¼ teaspoon pepper in 1-gallon zipper-lock bag. Add mushrooms, seal bag, turn to coat, and let sit for at least 30 minutes or up to 1 hour. Meanwhile make the Mediterranean relish and the whipped feta

   •**For a charcoal grill:** Open bottom vent completely. Light large chimney starter filled with charcoal briquettes (6 quarts). When top coals are partially covered with ash, pour evenly over grill. Set cooking grate in place, cover, and open lid vent completely. Heat grill until hot, about 5 minutes.

   •**For a gas grill:** Turn all burners to high, cover, and heat grill until hot, about 15 minutes. Turn all burners to medium-high.

2. **Prepare grill:** Clean and oil cooking grate and heat grill.

3. **Grill:** Remove mushrooms from marinade, reserving excess. Place mushrooms, gill side up, on grill. Cook (covered if using gas) until mushrooms have released their liquid and are charred on first side, 4 to 6 minutes. Flip and continue to cook (covered if using gas) until mushrooms are charred on second side, 3 to 5 minutes.

4. **Relish it:** Transfer mushrooms to platter, gill side up, and divide Mediterranean relish evenly among caps, packing down with hand. Return mushrooms to grill, relish side up, and cook, covered, until heated through, about 3 minutes.

5. **Finishing touches:** Return mushrooms to platter and tent with aluminum foil. Grill rolls cut sides down until lightly charred, about 1 minute. Spread whipped feta on bun bottoms and top each with 1 mushroom. Divide arugula evenly among burgers, then cap with bun tops. Serve.

Grilled Portobello | 84 | 86 | Tuna Cheese Melt

87 | Smashed Chicken Sandwich

# Tuna Cheese Melt

Crunchy, creamy, and perfectly gooey, these tuna melts are made for cozy lunches or easy weeknight dinners. We skip the skillet in favor of the oven, assembling the melts on buttery, untoasted bread so everything crisps up golden while the filling warms and cheese melts. Best of all, the oven method means both sandwiches are ready at once—no juggling batches, just a quick flip halfway through and lunch is served.

**For the tuna filling**

1 can (5 ounces / 140 g) solid white tuna in water, drained and flaked

2 tablespoons mayonnaise

2 tablespoons finely chopped onion

2 tablespoons chopped bread-and-butter pickles

2 tablespoons minced celery

1½ teaspoons Dijon mustard

1 teaspoon lemon juice

¼ teaspoon black pepper

**For the sandwiches**

⅛ teaspoon table salt

4 slices hearty white sandwich bread, multigrain, or ciabatta, thickly sliced

3 tablespoons unsalted butter, melted

2 slices (2 ounces / 55 g) deli sharp cheddar cheese or Gruyère,

2 slices (2 ounces / 55 g) deli cheese such as provolone, fontina, or American

NOTES FOR NEXT TIME:

1. **Make the tuna salad:** Before preheating the oven, adjust the oven rack to the middle position. Preheat oven to 425°F (220°C). Combine all ingredients in medium sized bowl. If time is short, make ahead and refrigerate up to 3 days.

2. **Assemble sandwiches:** Line rimmed baking sheet with aluminum foil. Melt your butter in the microwave and brush 1 side of each slice of bread with melted butter. Place 2 slices of bread, buttered side down, on prepared sheet. Top each slice with 1 slice of cheddar, one-quarter of tuna salad, 1 slice American cheese, and 1 remaining slice of bread, buttered side up.

3. **Make it a melt:** Bake sandwiches until golden brown on top, about 8 minutes. Flip sandwiches using a fish spatula and continue to bake until golden brown on second side and cheese is melted, 5 to 8 minutes longer. Let cool for 5 minutes. Cut in half and serve.

**TABLE TALK TIPS:** For the best results, do not use chunk light tuna here. You can substitute one (6.7-ounce / 190 g) jar of Tonnino Tuna Fillets in Olive Oil, if desired.

There are 5 favorite cheeses that I would give the honor of gracing my tuna cheese melt:

1. **American cheese** – and yes, I am calling it cheese. It's the meltiest and creamiest of the bunch and is the one you will find on my tuna melt.

2. **Cheddar** – deli slices of cheddar melt very well and bring a sharp quality that adds complexity to our cheese melt.

3. **Gruyere** – it's slightly sweet, salty, nutty, and brings a beautiful pull to the sandwich.

4. **Fontina** – the flavor of this Italian cow's milk cheese is not far from a milk provolone. It melts extremely well.

5. **Provolone** – grab the deli-sliced provolone, you will love how it melts and the mild tang it adds to your tuna melt.

# Smashed Chicken Sandwich
## with Mint Mojo Sauce

Get ready to meet your new go-to sandwich! This smashed chicken sandwich with mint mojo sauce is the definition of a flavor-packed, quick-fix meal with a fresh, farm-to-table twist. The real magic? It's all in the sauce—fresh, zesty, and full of minty goodness that elevates every bite. The inspiration came from cherry tomato gems at my local food co-op—vibrant reds, oranges, and yellows—that not only pack a punch of flavor but add beautiful color to this sandwich.

**What you need:**

- 2 chicken thighs, skin on, bone removed
- ¼ cup (60 mL) extra-virgin olive oil
- Salt and freshly ground black pepper
- 2 sandwich rolls, toasted (such as brioche or ciabatta)
- ½ cup (30 g) romaine lettuce, sliced into thin ¼-inch (6 mm) strips
- ½ cup (75 g) cherry tomatoes, quartered
- ¼ cup (60 mL) mint mojo sauce (Pg.222)
- Mayonnaise

**NOTES FOR NEXT TIME:**

1. **Prepare chicken:** Grab your chicken thighs and give them a good ol' smash! Wrap 'em in plastic wrap, and with a rolling pin, let out any stress—it's smash time! Starting in the center of each thigh, pound evenly out toward the edges, until ½-inch thick throughout.

   Toss chicken into a bowl and season with salt, pepper, and ¼ cup olive oil, about ¼ a cup. Get in there and flip those thighs around to make sure they're fully coated. Set them aside while you whip up that awesome mint mojo sauce.

2. **Pan fry:** Heat up your pan until it's nice and hot – a splash of water should bead on the surface. Toss in chicken, skin side down, and press it with something heavy (like the lid of a Dutch oven or whatever you've got that'll give it a good press). Let it cook until skin is brown and seriously crispy, about 3-4 minutes.

   Flip chicken, cook the other side for about another 3 minutes. Add a couple of spoonfuls of that magical sauce and give the pan a little swirl. Once it's looking and smelling amazing, remove from heat and drizzle a bit more sauce over the chicken.

3. **Time to build your sandwich!** Grab your bun and slather on some mayo. Pile on those beautiful cherry tomatoes (don't forget to sprinkle them with a little salt), and add some crisp lettuce. Then lay your juicy, saucy sliced chicken thigh on top. Finish with an extra drizzle of that sauce for good measure.

**TABLE TALK TIPS:** If you are unsure if the chicken is done, use an instant-read thermometer and check that internal temperature of the thigh reads 165 degrees F.

# Croque Monsieur Sandwich
## (Ultimate Hot Ham and Cheese)

Imagine yourself on the patio of a Parisian bistro, savoring a leisurely lunch of a Croque Monsieur alongside a simple salad. This iconic French sandwich, with its golden, melty cheese and savory ham tucked between slices of crusty bread, is truly "tout simplement divin"—as the French would say! On one of our trips to Paris, I fell in love with this classic sandwich. It's like a grilled cheese, but elevated with French flair: Dijon mustard, creamy béchamel sauce, and perfectly toasted sourdough. Over time, I have worked to recreate that memory at home, and I think I've finally nailed it. This dish is a go-to for a lovely lunch or a delightful brunch for two.

**For the béchamel sauce**

*1 tablespoon unsalted butter*

*1 tablespoon all-purpose flour*

*1 cup (240 mL) half-and-half or whole milk*

*⅛ teaspoon kosher salt*

*⅛ teaspoon freshly ground black pepper*

*⅛ teaspoon freshly grated nutmeg*

**For the sandwiches**

*4 slices sourdough bread (or any crusty bread)*

*1 tablespoon unsalted butter, melted*

*Dijon mustard, for spreading*

*4 ounces (115 g) Emmental, gouda, or Monterey Jack cheese, grated, about 1 ⅓ cups*

*4 ounces (115 g) deli ham or prosciutto*

*½ cup (120 mL) béchamel sauce*

**For garnish**

*Pinch of fresh thyme, chopped*

*1 tablespoon fresh chives, snipped*

1. **Make the béchamel sauce:** Melt butter in a medium saucepan over medium heat. Whisk in flour and cook, stirring constantly, until combined and golden, about 1 minute.

   Slowly add the half-and-half, whisking thoroughly to prevent lumps. Cook for 4–5 minutes, whisking frequently, until the sauce thickens to a spreadable consistency. Season with salt, pepper, and nutmeg. Remove from heat and let cool.

2. **Assemble the sandwiches:** Preheat oven to 425°F (220°C) and adjust the rack to the middle position. Line a rimmed baking sheet with aluminum foil or parchment paper.

   Brush one side of two slices of bread with melted butter and place them, buttered side down, on prepared sheet. Lightly spread Dijon mustard on each slice.

   Sprinkle half the grated cheese on mustard-covered slices. Top with ham, then add another layer of grated cheese, reserving 2 tablespoons for later.

   Place remaining bread slices on top, pressing gently. Spread 3–4 tablespoons of béchamel sauce over the top slice of each sandwich. Sprinkle reserved cheese evenly over the béchamel.

3. **Bake and serve.** Bake the sandwiches for 8–10 minutes, or until golden brown and bubbly on top. Remove from oven, cut each sandwich in half, and sprinkle with thyme and chives. Serve immediately and enjoy the French charm of this classic dish.

**TABLE TALK TIPS:** The béchamel sauce can be made up to one day in advance. Cover with plastic wrap directly on the surface and refrigerate.
**For serving:** Feel free to cut off the crusts or slice into bite-sized portions for a more elegant presentation.

 NOTES FOR NEXT TIME:

**Perfect Pot Roast**
Pg.114

**Pear & Prosciutto Stuffed Pork Loin** Pg.103

**Greek Baked Ziti**
Pg. 100

## Butcher's Favorites, Cook's Pride

*"You don't have to cook fancy or complicated masterpieces — just good food from fresh ingredients."*

– Julia Child

# Beef Wellington

Beef Wellington is the kind of meal that feels like a love letter—elegant, indulgent, and perfect for a date night. But when cooking for two, the traditional recipe can feel like a bit much. We set out to streamline the process without compromising the charm or sophistication that makes this dish so special.

### What you need:

5 ounces (142 g) cremini mushrooms, trimmed and halved

2 (8-ounce / 227 g each) center-cut filet mignons, 2 inches (5 cm) thick, trimmed

Kosher salt and freshly ground black pepper

2 teaspoons vegetable oil

2 tablespoons unsalted butter

1 tablespoon shallot, minced

1 garlic clove, minced

2 teaspoons minced fresh thyme

1 ½ tablespoons Madeira

1 (9 ½ x 9-inch / 24 x 23 cm) sheet store bought puff pastry, thawed

1 teaspoon Dijon mustard

2 slices prosciutto

1 large egg, lightly beaten

Green peppercorn sauce (pg.227)

1. **Finely chop mushrooms:** Position your oven rack to the upper-middle level and preheat your oven to 400°F (200°C). Line a rimmed baking sheet with parchment paper. In a food processor, pulse mushrooms until finely chopped, about 13–15 pulses, scraping down the sides as needed.

2. **Sear the filets:** Pat the filets dry with paper towels and season generously with salt and pepper. Heat the oil in a 10-inch non-stick skillet over medium-high heat until shimmering and just beginning to smoke. Sear the filets for about 2 minutes per side, until well-browned. Transfer to a plate lined with paper towels to rest.

3. **Make the duxelles:** In the now-empty skillet, melt butter over medium-high heat. Add the chopped mushrooms, shallot, garlic, thyme, ¼ teaspoon of salt, and ⅛ teaspoon of pepper. Cook, stirring frequently, until the mixture is browned and most of the moisture has evaporated, about 10 minutes. Stir in the Madeira and cook for another 2 minutes. Let the mixture cool completely. (If making ahead, refrigerate the duxelles in an airtight container for up to 3 days.)

4. **Assemble the Wellington:** On a lightly floured counter, roll the puff pastry into an 11-inch (28-cm) square, then cut into 4 equal squares.

   Place 2 pastry squares on the prepared baking sheet. In the center of each square, place a slice of prosciutto, leaving about a ½-inch border of pastry on all sides. Spread the duxelles evenly over the prosciutto, leaving a 1-inch border of prosciutto visible on all sides. (If the duxelles are cold, microwave briefly to soften before spreading.)

   Place a filet on top of the mushroom-coated prosciutto. Spread ½ teaspoon of mustard over the top of each filet. Stretch the remaining pastry squares over the filets, aligning the edges with the bottom pastry squares. Use your hands to gently shape the pastry around filets, ensuring a snug fit.

# Beef Wellington *(continued)*

1. **Seal and chill the packets:** Pinch the edges of the top and bottom pastry squares together to seal, then trim the excess pastry, leaving a ½-inch border around the filet. Crimp edges evenly using your fingers. Refrigerate the packets, uncovered, for 1 hour to chill.

2. **Bake the Wellington:** Brush the tops and sides of the pastry packets with beaten egg. Bake until the filets reach an internal temperature of 110°F (43°C), about 18–20 minutes. Transfer the baking sheet to a wire rack and let the Wellingtons rest—10 minutes for medium-rare or 20 minutes for medium. (The puff pastry acts as an insulator and will continue cooking the steaks as they rest.)

3. **Plate Wellingtons:** And serve immediately with green peppercorn gravy (pg.227).

~~~

**TABLE TALK TIPS:** Scaling down the portion size while preserving the grandeur was no easy task. We ditched goose liver pâté (you won't miss it, we promise), focused on eliminating extra moisture from the mushroom duxelles, and embraced the ease of frozen puff pastry. It turns out that ready-made pastry works like a dream, wrapping the beef in an "oven" that keeps everything perfectly sealed and cooking evenly during its rest.

~~~

Speaking of resting, here's the key: Pull those puff pastry packets out of the oven when the meat registers 110°F (43°C). The insulated pastry keeps the filets cooking as they rest, and with our suggested times, you'll nail your desired doneness. For accuracy, opt for 2-inch-thick filets, which cook evenly and fit snugly inside their pastry shells.

**A FEW TIPS FOR SUCCESS:** Thaw your puff pastry properly—either overnight in the fridge or for 30 minutes to an hour on the counter—and don't chill the assembled Wellingtons for longer than an hour, or the pastry might turn soggy.

**SERVING SUGGESTIONS**: If you'd like to take this dish to the next level, consider serving it with my green peppercorn sauce—it's creamy, peppery, and the perfect complement to the buttery puff pastry and tender beef (found on pg. 227). Complete the meal with Creamed Spinach (pg.157).

 **NOTES FOR NEXT TIME:**

# Spiedies

Spiedies are the soul of summer grilling in Binghamton, N.Y., and the surrounding areas where my friend Juli lived as a child. Passed down from her mom, this recipe captures the heart of this local favorite—a simple yet irresistible sandwich that is all about the marinade. Think of it as Italian dressing gone gourmet: tangy, herbaceous, and ready to infuse skewered chunks of lamb, pork, beef, venison, or chicken with incredible flavor.

The secret to great spiedies is patience—marinating for 24 to 36 hours (or just 10 to 12 hours if using chicken) ensures the meat is deeply seasoned and charred to perfection. After grilling, the meat gets tucked into a soft sub roll, finished with a drizzle of fresh marinade, olive oil, or hot sauce. For a little extra flair, add a squeeze of lemon over Italian bread or serve over rice. This is the kind of dish that turns an ordinary cookout into a celebration for two.

### Spiedies

¾ to 1 lb. (340–450 g) lamb, beef, pork, venison, or chicken, cut into 1-inch (2.5 cm) cubes (Note: I used lamb shoulder)

2 soft sub rolls or sliced Italian bread

### Marinade

¼ cup (60 ml) red wine vinegar

¼ cup (60 ml) canola oil

¼ cup (60 ml) dry white wine

1 teaspoon fresh basil, rolled and chopped (chiffonade)

1 teaspoon fresh oregano leaves

1 teaspoon parsley leaves, chopped

¼ teaspoon freshly ground black pepper

1 clove garlic, smashed (or 1 teaspoon garlic powder)

**1. Make the marinade:** In a large bowl, whisk together the wine vinegar, canola oil, white wine, basil, oregano, parsley, pepper, and garlic.

# Spiedies (continued)

1. **Marinate the meat:** Add meat cubes to the bowl and stir to coat, or transfer everything into a large resealable plastic bag (Juli's mom's favorite method). Seal tight and refrigerate for 24 to 36 hours (only 10 to 12 hours for chicken). Don't rush this step—this is where all that flavor magic happens.

2. **Prepare the skewers:** When you're ready to grill, remove the meat from the marinade and thread it onto skewers. If using wooden skewers, soak them in water for about 30 minutes beforehand so they don't burn. Use a knife to sharpen the bottom ends to make threading easier. Pack meat close together on the skewers and season with a good pinch of salt and pepper.

3. **Preheat your grill:**
   - **For a charcoal grill:** Light your charcoal and let it burn until the coals are covered with gray ash. Leave about one-third of the grill free of coals so you have a cooler zone to move skewers if they start to char too quickly. You should barely be able to hold your hand over the hot side for more than a couple of seconds—then you know it's ready.
   - **For a gas grill:** Preheat to high heat. That's it—easy!

4. **Grill the skewers:** Place the skewers directly over the hottest part of the grill. Let them sear, undisturbed, for 3 to 4 minutes, then use kitchen tongs to turn them over. Continue turning every couple of minutes, letting the edges get beautifully crisp and caramelized, for another 5 to 7 minutes total.
   - **For charcoal grill:** If the meat starts to char too quickly, move it to the cooler side and close the lid to finish with a gentle smoky roast.
   - **For gas grill:** Just turn down the heat slightly or move the skewers to a cooler part of the grill if needed.

5. **Rest and serve:** When the meat is cooked through and juicy, remove the skewers from the grill and let them rest for a few minutes. Slide the meat off onto soft sub rolls or slices of Italian bread. Drizzle with olive oil, squeeze over some lemon, or add a dash of hot sauce—just like they do in Binghamton. Grab a roll and dig in.

**TABLE TALK TIPS:** The meat can be marinated up to 36 hours in advance (or 10 to 12 hours for chicken). You can also prep the skewers a few hours before grilling—just keep them covered in the fridge until you're ready to fire things up. I like to use lamb shoulder for spiedies. It's flavorful, well-marbled, and easy to cube up into tender, juicy pieces perfect for the grill.

**SERVING SUGGESTIONS:** Serve these with fresh corn on the cob and a simple, crisp coleslaw. My go-to is a bag of shredded cabbage and carrots tossed with Rudolf's Cole Slaw® Dressing. To make it extra special, I sprinkle the slaw with toasted pine nuts and a few grinds of fresh black pepper.

# Small Glazed Ham

Buying a smoked, spiral-cut, bone-in ham sounds like a great idea—until you realize the smallest one is about nine pounds, guaranteeing a week of ham-filled meals and a few mystery bags lost in the freezer, only to be rediscovered during a deep clean-out. But what if you could have all the flavor of a perfectly glazed ham, without the leftovers taking over your life?

For a dinner-for-two-friendly option, look for a boneless, smoked, unsliced or pre-sliced ham under three pounds. The trick is finding a quality one—some boneless hams are reassembled bits of ham, jelled together and canned. Instead, look for one cured in natural juices and smoked over hardwoods for the best flavor and texture. Once you've found the right ham, all that's left is a simple glaze and an easy oven bake that keeps it juicy and flavorful.

### What you need:

3 lbs (1.4 kg) or less, fully cooked boneless smoked ham

3 garlic cloves

4 ounces (115 g) mango chutney – e.g., Major Grey Mango Chutney®

¼ cup (60 g) Dijon mustard

½ cup (100 g) light brown sugar, packed

Zest of ½ orange

2 tablespoons freshly squeezed orange juice

**SERVING SUGGESTIONS:** When I think of baked ham, I think of scalloped potatoes (pg.174) for a recipe that cooks in under an hour!

**LEFTOVER IDEAS:** If you have just a little left over, put it to good use—try the Croque Monsieur on pg. 88 for a delicious next-day meal.

1. **Bake ham:** Preheat oven to 325°F (165°C).. Remove ham from packaging, and netting from ham (if applicable). Place on a rack in a baking pan, add package drippings and ¼ cup water to bottom of pan. Cover pan tightly with aluminum foil to retain moisture and bake for 16-20 minutes per pound, Bake until a meat thermometer registers 135°F (57°C).

2. **Make the glaze:** Meanwhile, mince the garlic in a food processor fitted with steel blade. Add the chutney, mustard, brown sugar, orange zest, and orange juice, and process until smooth.

3. **Ready to serve:** Remove ham from oven, uncover and pour the glaze over the ham; increase the heat to 400°F(200°C) and bake for 15-20 minutes longer until the glaze is well browned but not burned. Serve hot or at room temperature.

# Passover Brisket
## (My Friend's Mother's Recipe)

My friend's mother's Jewish Brisket is one we all should know how to make. This Passover brisket recipe uses budget friendly pantry items and combined with low-and-slow cooking techniques, which transforms this inexpensive cut of meat into a tender, juicy, melt-in-your-mouth experience. As my friend Pam, says *"Roast a day or two ahead of when you want to serve; it tastes even better the next day!"*

**What you need:**

- 1 lb. (450 g) flat-cut brisket, trim any excess fat
- 1 cup (240 ml) white wine, or more
- 1 large white onion, sliced into ½-inch (1.3 cm) rings
- ¼ cup (60 ml) A-1® steak sauce
- ¼ cup (60 ml) Worcestershire sauce
- ¼ cup (60 ml) Heinz 57® Steak Sauce
- ½ teaspoon garlic powder
- ½ teaspoon onion powder
- ¼ package Lipton's dry onion soup mix (approx. 0.25 oz / 7 g)
- Freshly ground black pepper, to taste

1. **Layer and season:** Spray baking dish with PAM® cooking oil. Layer sliced onion on the bottom of the glass baking dish. Add just enough white wine to the bottom of the pan so onions are slightly submerged. Place the brisket on top of the onions and sprinkle with onion soup mix, onion powder, garlic powder and pepper. Evenly spread A-1, Heinz 57, and Worcestershire sauces on top of meat.

2. **Roast in oven:** Cover and tightly seal with aluminum foil and bake at 275°F (135°C) for 4 – 5 hours. Test doneness by using a fork. The fork should go in easily and meat should start to pull apart as you lift it out of the pan.

3. **Rest, rest, rest:** Let the brisket rest covered for at least 30 minutes before carving. Once the brisket is carved, put back in the gravy and spoon gravy between the slices. Serve right out of the baking dish.

**MAKE AHEAD:** This brisket is best when served the next day. You'll want to cool it down whole in its juices and refrigerate. Remove the pan from refrigerator and let it come up to room temp. To reheat: Preheat oven to 275°F (135°C). Slice brisket into thin slices against the grain and place them back in the baking dish, along with the onions. Spoon sauce in between the slices and cover the pan tightly with aluminum foil. Heat the brisket until it's warmed through, about 45 to 60 minutes.

 **NOTES FOR NEXT TIME:**

# Greek Baked Ziti
## (with Lamb and Eggplant)

When the boys were still home, one of our go-to spots was Christo's, a cozy Greek restaurant just down the road. I always ordered their baked moussaka—layered, comforting, and full of flavor—but I'll admit, making the traditional version at home felt like more work than I wanted on a weeknight. That's where this Greek Baked Ziti comes in. With tender lamb, roasted eggplant, and plenty of creamy, cheesy goodness, it captures all the heart and soul of a Greek casserole in a simplified, small-batch version just right for two.

**For the eggplant and lamb**

¾ pound (340 g) medium-sized eggplant/aubergines, about 1–2 eggplants, cut into 1-inch (3 cm) cubes

½ pound (225 g) ground lamb (Not a fan of lamb? Use 93% lean ground beef.)

1 small onion, halved and thinly sliced

¼ cup (15 g) fresh oregano leaves, roughly chopped

2 tablespoons extra-virgin olive oil

2 tablespoons tomato paste

3 garlic cloves, thinly sliced

½ tablespoon ground cinnamon

1 teaspoon ground allspice

¼ teaspoon red pepper flakes

Kosher salt and freshly ground black pepper, to taste

15 ounces (425 g) canned tomato sauce

1 teaspoon roasted chicken Better Than Bouillon®

2 tablespoons flat-leaf parsley, roughly chopped

**Béchamel and pasta**

2 tablespoons unsalted butter

2 tablespoons all-purpose flour

1 garlic clove, minced

½ teaspoon table salt

¼ teaspoon grated nutmeg

⅛ teaspoon freshly ground black pepper

4 cups (960 ml) whole milk

4 ounces (115 g) ziti, about 1¼ cups

4 ounces (115 g), kasseri cheese, shredded, about 1 cup, divided, (Kasseri unavailable? See Table Talk Tips)

1 large egg, lightly beaten

**For the topping**

¼ cup (35 g) feta cheese, roughly crumbled

2 tablespoons pine nuts

1 tablespoon flat-leaf parsley, roughly chopped

Pinch red pepper flakes

1. **Roast the lamb & eggplant mixture:** Preheat oven to 450°F (240°C). In a baking dish, combine eggplant, lamb, onion, oregano, olive oil, tomato paste, garlic, cinnamon, allspice, and red pepper flakes. Season with salt and pepper. Bake for 15 minutes, then break up the meat with a wooden spoon. Bake another 15 minutes.

2. **Build the sauce:** Stir in tomato sauce, chicken bouillon, and parsley. Return to the oven and bake until thickened and bubbly, about 30 minutes. Set aside.

3. **Prepare the béchamel & pasta:** While the lamb mixture bakes, melt butter in a large saucepan over medium heat. Add flour, garlic, salt, nutmeg, and pepper; cook, stirring constantly, until golden, about 1 minute. Gradually whisk in milk, bring to a boil, then stir in ziti. Simmer, stirring frequently, until al dente, about 15 minutes.

4. **Assemble and bake:** Turn oven down to 400°F (205°C). Spray a second loaf pan with vegetable oil spray and place on a rimmed baking sheet. Use a spider skimmer (a long handle and a wire-mesh basket resembling a spider's web) to transfer pasta to the prepared loaf pan, leaving excess béchamel in the saucepan. Stir ⅓ cup kasseri cheese into the pasta and press into an even layer.

5. **Finishing touches:** Whisk the remaining kasseri and egg into the béchamel. Spread meat sauce over the pasta and top with

béchamel. Sprinkle with remaining kasseri, feta, pine nuts, parsley, and red pepper flakes. Bake until golden and bubbling, about 15–20 minutes. Let cool for 15 minutes before serving.

**TABLE TALK TIPS:** If kasseri cheese is unavailable, substitute a mixture of ¾ cup grated Pecorino Romano and ¾ cup shredded provolone, adding ½ cup (instead of the ⅓ cup of kasseri) to the ziti, ½ cup to the béchamel, and the remaining to the top of the béchamel.

Pear and Prosciutto Stuffed Pork Loin | 103

104 | Fruit Cake Stuffed Pork Loin

Hollace's Family Bolognese Recipe | 107

108 | Left-over Bolognese Lasagna

# Pear and Prosciutto Stuffed Pork Loin

On our 10th wedding anniversary, Mark and I left the kids with my mom and dad and spent ten unforgettable days in Tuscany. One evening, after dinner at a vineyard restaurant, we struck up a conversation with a German couple seated nearby. By the end of the meal, we had pushed our tables together, shared a bottle of Tuscan wine, and swapped travel stories. They told me about a local woman who welcomed guests into her home to teach traditional country-style cooking, and the very next day I found myself in her kitchen learning to make a stuffed pork loin. I may not remember her name, but I'll never forget that meal—or the generosity that led me to it. This version has been updated slightly for our table, but it still carries the warmth and rustic flavors of Tuscany.

**What you need:**

- 1 Bosc pear, cored and chopped into ½-inch (1.3 cm) pieces
- 1½ tablespoons grated Parmigiano Reggiano
- ¼ cup (30 g) panko breadcrumbs
- ½ teaspoon crushed fennel seeds
- ¼ cup + 1 teaspoon (65 ml) extra-virgin olive oil, divided
- 12 ounces (0.7 lb / 340 g) pork loin
- 2 tablespoons fig spread (found by specialty cheeses)
- 4 slices prosciutto
- Salt, to taste
- Freshly ground black pepper, to taste
- 2 rosemary sprigs, to tuck under the string outside of the pork loin
- 1 cup (240 ml) dry white wine or use a mix of ½ cup apple cider (cloudy apple juice) plus ½ cup dry white wine.

 NOTES FOR NEXT TIME:

1. **Brine and Butterfly the pork loin** (see pg.106 for step-by-step instructions)

2. **Prepare the filling:** Mix together the chopped pears, grated Parmigiano Reggiano, breadcrumbs, and fennel seeds. Add about 1 teaspoon extra virgin olive oil to help the filling come together. If it is too dry add more olive oil.

3. **Stuff:** Pat pork dry with paper towels. Spread fig spread over the loin. Shingle the prosciutto down the center of the loin. Spread the pear stuffing evenly over the prosciutto, leaving a ½-inch border on the short edges of the pork loin, as it will be easier to roll it. Roll the pork tightly into a cylinder (from short edge to short edge) and tie it with kitchen twine at 1-inch intervals. If you have them, tuck a few rosemary sprigs under the string, it will release its wonderful aroma while cooking.

4. **Sear the pork:** Now grab a pan big enough to hold the pork—I usually go for a enameled Dutch oven. Drizzle in enough olive oil to coat the bottom generously (about 1 to 2 tablespoons). Heat over medium until it's shimmering.

   Once the oil is ready, carefully lay pork loin in the pan. Let it sizzle and sear until that first side is golden brown, about 3 to 4 minutes. Then grab two wooden spoons (or something similar) and gently turn it over. No forks here; we're keeping all those precious juices locked inside. Repeat until all four sides are browned, about 3 minutes on the next side, then 2 minutes for the last two. We are looking for that perfect golden crust all around.

5. **Cook low and slow:** When your pork looks beautifully golden, pour in a cup of white wine (or a mix of half apple cider and wine). It's going to sizzle like crazy that's exactly what we want. Let it bubble away for a few seconds, then pop a lid on the pot. Turn the heat down as low as it'll go. Now, let the pork simmer gently for about 30 minutes. Peek in every 10 minutes to make sure there is still some liquid on the bottom of the pan. You might need to add more wine or cider to keep the pan juices from burning.

## Stuffed Pork Loin *(continued)*

1. **Rest, rest, rest:** Turn off the heat but leave the pork right where it is, lid on, for at least an hour. Seriously, don't skip this step! The residual heat in the pan will keep cooking the pork to juicy, tender perfection. Patience is key here.

2. **Serve it up:** When you're ready to slice and serve, you've got options. If you're looking for neat, thin slices, let the pork cool completely then stash in the fridge overnight—it's so much easier to slice cold. If you want it now (and who could blame you?), just go for it, but slice carefully.

3. **Make gravy:** This step is optional but I do like to turn pan juices into a gravy. Follow the step 8 in the Fruitcake Stuffed Pork Loin (pg. 105). As you follow the gravy instructions, consider using apple cider, some apple brandy and butter, but skip the cream.

4. **Reheating tips:** To warm up slices without drying them out, don't reheat the pork itself. Instead, warm up a serving dish. I place my serving dish in the oven and then heat the oven to 350°F (175°C). After about 15 minutes, remove the serving dish from the oven, lay the slices on it. Now reheat the gravy and pour over the top. Turn down oven to 275°F (135°C). Cover the pan tightly with aluminum foil. Heat until it's warmed through, about 30 minutes.

## Fruitcake Stuffed Pork Loin

Fruitcake gets a bad rap. It's dense, full of candied fruit, and often the butt of holiday jokes. But as fruitcake fans will tell you, the best ones are "seasoned"—matured for months to deepen their flavor and make them easier to slice. As skeptical as I was, this misunderstood holiday classic became the star of a recipe that won me over. When a fellow member of my church described this fruitcake stuffed pork roast, I thought, "Fruitcake? In a savory dish? No way." But I decided to give it a try. The fruitcake's sweetness pairs beautifully with the pork and as they roast together, the flavors meld into something magical. And the bourbon-cider gravy? Absolutely spectacular—rich, tangy, and the perfect finishing touch.

### What you need:

- 1 tablespoon + 1 teaspoon chopped onion
- 1 garlic glove, minced
- 1 ½ teaspoons olive oil
- 1 ½ cups store-bought fruit cake, crumbled
- 12 ounces (0.7 lb / 340 g) pound pork loin roast, boneless, with fat cap
- 1 ½ teaspoons dried thyme
- 2 sprigs of fresh thyme, to tuck under the string outside of the pork loin
- ½ cup (120 ml) good apple cider
- ½ cup (120 ml) white wine
- 2 tablespoons bourbon + 2 Tablespoon bourbon for sauce
- 2 tablespoons honey
- 1 tablespoon butter
- 1 teaspoon cornstarch
- 3 to 4 tablespoons heavy whipping cream.

1. **Brine and Butterfly the pork loin (see pg.106 for step-by-step instructions) Prepare the filling:** Heat a skillet over medium-high heat and add olive oil. Cook the onion and garlic, stirring frequently, until softened but not browned. Remove the skillet from heat and mix in the fruitcake thoroughly. Set aside.

2. **Stuff:** Pat the pork dry with paper towels. Season with 1 ½ teaspoons of thyme. Spread the fruitcake mixture evenly over the pork, leaving a ½-inch border on all sides. Roll the pork tightly into a cylinder (from short end to short end) and tie it with kitchen twine at 1-inch intervals. Tuck a few thyme sprigs under the string on the outside of the pork, it will release its wonderful aroma while cooking.

3. **Sear the pork:** Okay, now grab a pan big enough to hold the pork—I usually go for a enameled Dutch oven. Drizzle in enough olive oil to coat the bottom generously. Heat it up over medium until shimmering.

    Once the oil is ready, carefully lay pork loin in the pan. Let it sizzle and sear until that first side is golden brown, about 3 to 4 minutes. Then grab two wooden spoons (or something similar) and gently turn it over. No forks here; we're keeping all those precious juices locked inside. Repeat until all four sides are browned, about 3 minutes on the next side, then 2 minutes for the last two. We are looking for that perfect golden crust all around.

4. **Cook low and slow:** Pour ½ cup each of apple cider and white wine into the pot around the pork. In a small dish, combine 2 tablespoons bourbon and honey. Brush the mixture lightly over the pork, reserving some for basting. Sprinkle the remaining thyme over the top. Let it bubble away for a few seconds, then pop a lid on the pot. Turn the heat down as low as it'll go. Now, let the pork simmer gently for about 30 minutes. Baste with the bourbon mixture every 10 minutes, adding more apple cider to the pan if necessary to prevent drippings from burning.

5. **Rest, rest, rest:** Turn off the heat but leave the pork right where it is, lid on, for at least an hour. Seriously, don't skip this step! The residual heat in the pan will keep cooking the pork to juicy, tender perfection.

6. **Make the gravy:** After the pork has rested, remove from pan and set aside on a cutting board or baking sheet. Bring the pan drippings to a boil. Cook until reduced to ½ cup, then lower the heat to medium-low. Stir in butter until melted. Add 1 tablespoon bourbon, stirring until the sauce thickens. If needed, create a cornstarch slurry (1 teaspoon cornstarch mixed with 1 teaspoon water) and add to the gravy, stirring until smooth. If the gravy becomes too thick, thin it with apple cider, 1 tablespoon at a time. Once the desired consistency is reached, remove from heat and stir in cream.

7. **Serve it up:** When you're ready to slice and serve, you've got options. If you're looking for neat, thin slices, let the pork cool completely then stash in the fridge overnight—it's so much easier to slice cold. If you want it now (and who could blame you?), just go for it, but slice carefully.

8. **Reheating tips:** To warm up slices without drying them out, don't reheat the pork itself. Instead, warm up a serving dish. I place my serving dish in the oven and then heat the oven to 350°F (175°C). After about 15 minutes, remove the serving dish from the oven and lay the slices on it. Now reheat the gravy and pour over the top. Turn down oven to 275°F (135°C). Cover the pan tightly with aluminum foil. Heat until it's warmed through, about 30 minutes.

 **NOTES FOR NEXT TIME:**

## Brining a pork loin

*2 cups water*

*3 tablespoons salt*

*1/4 cup dark brown sugar*

*1 bay leaves*

*1 tablespoon peppercorns*

*2 springs thyme*

*2 sprigs rosemary*

1. Mix water, salt, and brown sugar in a saucepan, stirring to dissolve salt and sugar. Add bay leaf, peppercorns, and thyme; bring to a boil. Reduce heat to low and simmer brine for 5 minutes. Let brine cool to room temperature. Place pork roast into a large nonreactive bowl, pour brine over pork, and cover; marinate in refrigerator for 2 to 3 hours. Brining for 4 hours or longer may make the roast too salty for some. Rinse the pork roast and pat dry before you butterfly and stuff.

## How to butterfly a pork loin

1. Remove the pork from brine ( I recommend only 2 to 3 hours of brine time), rinse and pat dry. We want a thin long strip of pork. To do this, place the pork loin on a cutting board. Starting about ½-inch (1.27 cm) from the bottom of the roast (think thin!), make a horizontal cut, stopping ½-inch (1.27 cm) before reaching the edge.

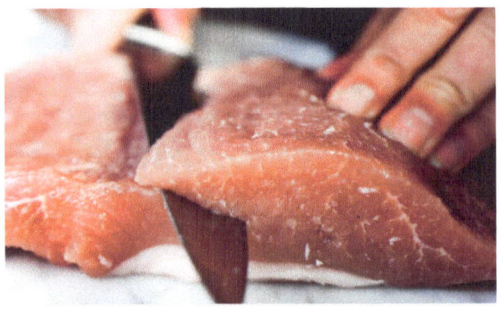

2. Open the flap and make another horizontal cut into the thicker side.

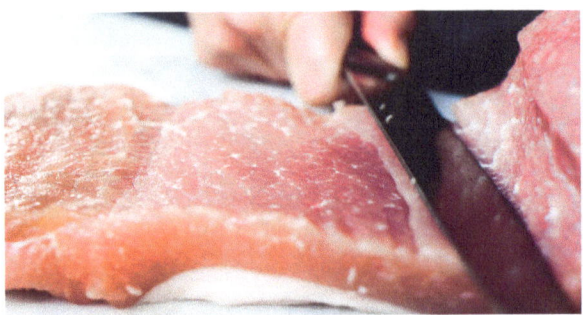

3. Again, stopping ½-inch (1.27 cm) before the edge.

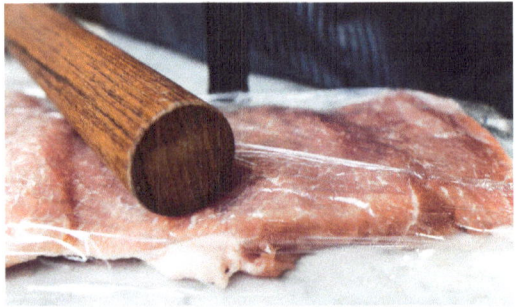

4. Lay the meat flat like opening a book. If the thickness is uneven, cover with plastic wrap and gently pound with meat pounder or rolling pin until ½-inch (1.27 cm) thick throughout. Now you are ready to stuff.

# Hollace's Family Bolognese Recipe

Every spoonful of this bolognese tells a story of the Mancino family—a Sicilian tradition lovingly passed down through generations and shared with me by my dear friend Hollace. This recipe isn't just a dish, it's an all-day symphony of flavors that rewards patience with a rich, velvety sauce. The secret? Building layers of flavor through careful browning, deglazing, and hours of lazy simmering. Trust me, it is worth every minute , even when it seems like an all-day project. Make the full batch. It is perfect for a hearty dinner for two tonight and freezes beautifully for future meals. And don't forget to save some for the Leftover Bolognese Lasagna on page 108.

**What you need:**

- 1 tablespoon olive oil
- 3 tablespoons butter, plus 1 tablespoon (14 g) for tossing the pasta
- ½ cup (75 g) chopped onion
- ⅔ cup (90 g) chopped celery
- ⅔ cup (70–75 g) chopped carrot
- 4 garlic cloves, minced
- 8 ounces (225 g) ground beef (80% lean; 20% fat provides excellent flavor and juiciness)
- 4 ounces (115 g) mild pork sausage, casings removed
- Salt, to taste
- Freshly ground black pepper, to taste
- 1 cup (240 ml) whole milk
- ⅛ teaspoon grated from a whole nutmeg
- 1 cup (240 ml) dry white wine
- 1¼ cups (310 g) imported Italian plum tomatoes, cut up with their juice
- 8 ounces (225 g) of pasta like a pappardelle or another thick flat noodle.

1. **Sauté the base:** Heat olive oil and 3 tablespoons butter in a heavy-bottomed pot over medium heat. Add chopped onion and cook, stirring occasionally, until it becomes translucent. Toss in the chopped celery and carrot, stirring to coat the vegetables well. Cook for about 4 minutes until fragrant. Stir in garlic and cook for about 1 minute.

2. **Brown the beef:** Add the ground beef and pork, a generous pinch of salt, and a few grinds of black pepper. Use the back of a wood spoon to crumble the meat as it cooks. Stir well and cook until meat loses its raw, red color.

3. **Add the milk:** Pour in the milk and let it simmer gently, stirring frequently, until it's completely absorbed. Be patient, this will take about 1 hour. Grate in ⅛ tsp of the nutmeg and stir to incorporate.

4. **Deglaze with wine:** Add the wine and let it simmer until fully evaporated, about 45 - 60 minutes. Stir in tomatoes, ensuring everything is well coated. When tomatoes start to bubble, reduce heat to lowest setting. Let the sauce simmer uncovered for at least 3 hours. Stir occasionally and add ½ cup of water or more wine as needed to prevent sticking. By the end, the sauce should be thick, with the fat separating from the meat. Stir the fat back into the sauce. Taste to adjust the salt if needed.

5. **Finishing touches:** Add an extra tablespoon of butter to the sauce for a silky finish. Toss sauce with cooked, drained pasta and serve with freshly grated Parmesan.

**TABLE TALK TIPS:** This dish is an all-day labor of love. When I say "simmer," I really mean give it at least an hour—sometimes more. I've included timing estimates in each step, but the real secret is patience. Slow simmering builds deep, layered flavors you just can't rush, so pour a glass of wine, put on some music, and let the kitchen do its magic.

# Leftover Bolognese Lasagna (17- ish layers!)

A few years ago my son Zach sent me a photo of the famous 40-layer lasagna from L'Ardente in Washington D.C., a show-stopping creation with endless layers of pasta, short ribs, truffle cheese and a béchamel sauce. I've never had the chance to taste it myself, but that picture alone was enough to inspire me to create a version of my own. While I wasn't about to tackle 40 layers, I did discover that leftover bolognese makes the perfect shortcut for a rich, flavorful lasagna. Using a loaf pan keeps this recipe small-batch and just right for two, while a truffle-kissed béchamel sauce gives it that luxurious flavor. If you can find a cheese like Il Foreteto Boschetto al Tartufo, go for it—but a splash of white truffle oil in the sauce will also do beautifully.

### Béchamel sauce

1 tablespoon unsalted butter

1 tablespoon all-purpose flour

1 cup (240 ml) half-and-half or whole milk

⅛ teaspoon kosher salt

⅛ teaspoon freshly ground black pepper

⅛ teaspoon freshly grated nutmeg (or ground, if in a pinch)

### Lasagna filling

2 cups (480 g) bolognese sauce (see pg. 107)

5 oven-ready lasagna noodles (no-boil)

1½ cups (140 g / ~5 ounces) white truffle cheese, such as Il Foreteto Boschetto al Tartufo

(Note: If unavailable, substitute with gruyère cheese and add ½ teaspoon white truffle oil to the béchamel to mimic the truffle flavor in the sauce.)

 NOTES FOR NEXT TIME:

1. **Make the béchamel sauce:** Melt the butter in a medium saucepan over medium heat. Whisk in flour and cook, stirring constantly, until combined and golden, about 1 minute.

   Slowly add the half-and-half, whisking thoroughly to prevent lumps. Cook for 4–5 minutes, whisking frequently, until sauce thickens to a spreadable consistency. Season with salt, pepper, and nutmeg (and truffle oil, if using). Remove from heat and let cool. Taste and adjust seasoning with more salt or nutmeg.

2. **Assemble the lasagna:** Preheat oven to 375°F (190°C). Spread ⅓ cup bolognese sauce over the bottom of a traditional sized (8-in x 5-in) loaf pan, breaking apart large chunks of meat. Lay 1 noodle in the pan, spread another ⅓ cup of sauce over the noodle, sprinkle with ¼ cup truffle cheese, and lay another noodle over the cheese. Now repeat sauce, cheese, noodle layering 3 more times. Place another ⅓ cup of sauce over the 5th noodle in the pan, sprinkle with ¼ cup truffle cheese, then pour half of the béchamel over the top. Push the béchamel to the edges of the top noodle.

3. **Bake:** Cover pan tightly with aluminum foil that has been sprayed with vegetable oil spray. Place the pan on a baking sheet to catch any drips. Bake until sauce bubbles lightly around the edges, 35 - 40 minutes. Remove foil and continue to bake until hot throughout and the cheese is browned in spots, about 10 minutes.

4. **Rest and serve:** Let cool for 20 minutes before cutting to serve. Gently rewarm the remaining béchamel sauce over low heat. Spoon a puddle of sauce in the middle of each serving plate and place the lasagna on top of the sauce and serve!

obe Flank Steak | 110  112 | Asian Flat Iron Steak
Sausage and Fennel | 113  114 | Perfect Pot Roast

# Adobo Flank Steak
## with Roasted Summer Corn and Black Bean Relish

Grilled flank steak paired with roasted sweet corn and black bean relish is one of my all-time favorite summertime duos. When the warm weather rolls in and the corner produce stands start popping up around the neighborhood with piles of just-picked sweet corn, I know it's time to fire up the grill. This recipe brings together two of my go-to summer flavors: smoky, tender flank steak marinated in adobo, and a charred corn and black bean relish that's just as good spooned over the steak as it is scooped up with tortilla chips.

It's a dish I've made again and again—especially when the boys are home. We enjoy this meal often when the summer evenings allow us to dine on the patio. The adobo steak recipe was first shared with me at a dinner party hosted by dear friends Martha and Greg, and the relish is a variation of a salsa my friend Juli always keeps on hand for get-togethers. Juli's Texas roots shine through in the bold, bright flavors—and let's just say, when she brings a salsa to the table, it's guaranteed to become your next keeper recipe.

**Steak**

½ teaspoon black peppercorns

½ teaspoon cumin seeds

1 whole clove

1 chipotle chili in adobo sauce

1 tablespoon cider vinegar

1½ teaspoons fresh thyme leaves

1 teaspoon brown sugar

½ teaspoon kosher salt

1 garlic clove, peeled

¾ pound (340 g) flank steak, trimmed

Cooking spray

**Salad**

1 cup (160 g) fresh corn kernels, about 2 ears

3 tablespoons vegetable oil, divided

¾ teaspoon salt, divided

½ teaspoon ground cumin

3 tablespoons lime juice

1 tablespoon cider vinegar

¼ cup (40 g) red onion, chopped

2 plum tomatoes, chopped

1 jalapeño pepper, seeded and chopped

½ red bell pepper, seeded and chopped

1 teaspoon garlic, minced

1 can (15 oz / 425 g) black beans, rinsed and drained

1 avocado, peeled and diced

1 tablespoon cilantro leaves, chopped

**1. Start with the steak marinade:** We're going to toast a quick spice blend to bring out some extra flavor. Grab a small nonstick skillet, toast the first 3 ingredients over medium heat for 45 seconds, just until it smells amazing and toasty. Keep an eye on it so it doesn't burn.

Pour toasted spices into a spice grinder or clean coffee grinder and pulse until everything is finely ground. If you don't have a grinder, a good mortar and pestle will work too—just use a little elbow grease.

Next, pull out one chipotle chile from a can of chipotle peppers in adobo sauce, just one—you can transfer the rest of the chilies and sauce to a freezer container and freeze for another use. In a blender or with a stick blender and tall container, combine that chile with your freshly ground pepper mixture, vinegar, thyme, sugar, salt, and garlic. Blend it all up until it's smooth, scraping down the sides as needed.

2. **Marinate overnight:** Pour this mixture into a zip-top bag and add your flank steak—about ¾ to 1 pound is perfect for two. Seal the bag and give it a good massage so steak is well coated. Pop it in the fridge and let it marinate for 24 hours.

3. **Time to grill:** When you're ready to cook, take the steak out of the marinade and discard the extra. Cook steaks until well browned and the meat registers 125°F (52°C) for medium-rare, about 5 to 7 minutes per side. Transfer to a cutting board, cover loosely with foil, and let rest for 5–10 minutes.

   •**If pan-searing steaks:** Heat 2 tablespoons oil in 12-inch nonstick or cast-iron skillet over medium-high heat until just smoking. This is important so it can develop a flavorful crust on the outside before it's overcooked on the inside.

   •**If grilling steaks:** Turn all burners on gas grill to high, close lid, and heat grill until hot, 10 to 15 minutes. Grill steak covered for 4 to 6 minutes on first side and 3 to 5 minutes on second side.

4. **Now for the roasted corn and black bean relish:** Grab a cast-iron or non-stick skillet and heat 1 tablespoon oil over medium-high heat—just until the oil starts to shimmer. Add corn kernels and sprinkle with ¼ teaspoon of salt. Spread out in an even layer—and here's the important part—let them sit undisturbed for about 3 to 5 minutes. You want them to get that beautiful, deep char. Once caramelized, transfer them to a big mixing bowl.

5. **Whisk the dressing:** In a small jar with a tight-fitting lid, add ground cumin, lime juice, vinegar, the remaining 2 tablespoons oil, and ½ teaspoon of salt. Shake it up until it's well combined. Taste and adjust seasoning.

6. **Get 'er done:** Add cilantro, onion, tomatoes, jalapeno, bell pepper, garlic, and beans to the roasted corn, mix well. Toss with the dressing; mix well. Add avocado, toss gently to combine. Serve over steak. You can serve immediately or refrigerate up to 6 hours.

 **NOTES FOR NEXT TIME:**

# Asian Flat Iron Steak

Summers on the "Island" are our favorite way to unwind, soaking in the breeze off Lake Minnetonka and catching the sunset over the water. As longtime members of the Minnetonka Yacht Club, we savor packing up a simple but delicious dinner to enjoy al fresco. With access to the grill, this steak recipe was born—an easy yet flavorful meal perfect for outdoor dining.

**What you need:**

**Marinade & steak**

¼ cup (60 ml) soy sauce

¼ cup (60 ml) dry sherry

2 tablespoons honey

1 tablespoon sesame oil

1 tablespoon minced fresh ginger

1 tablespoon minced garlic, about 1–2 cloves

½ teaspoon crushed red pepper flakes

1 flat iron steak or flank steak, about 8–10 oz / 225–280g

**Garnish**

1 tablespoon toasted sesame seeds

1 green onion, thinly sliced

**Greens**

1 bunch baby arugula

4–6 cherry tomatoes, halved

2 teaspoons olive oil

1 tablespoon lemon juice

Salt and fresh ground pepper

1. **Make the marinade:** In a small bowl, whisk together soy sauce, sherry, honey, sesame oil, ginger, garlic, and red pepper flakes.

2. **Marinate the steak:** Place the flat iron steak in a zip-top bag or shallow dish and pour the marinade over it. Seal or cover and refrigerate 3 to 6 hours.

3. **Grill the steak:** Preheat a grill or cast-iron skillet to high heat. Remove the steak from the marinade and pat dry. Grill 4 minutes per side for medium-rare or adjust to your preferred doneness.

4. **Rest and serve:** Let the steak rest for 5 minutes, then slice against the grain. Sprinkle with toasted sesame seeds and sliced green onions.

5. **Toss your greens:** While steak rests, mix arugula with a drizzle of olive oil in a bowl, adding a squeeze of lemon juice and a little salt and pepper. Toss in cherry tomatoes and serve the salad alongside your steak.

**TABLE TALK TIPS:** Flat iron steak is my favorite cut—it's richly marbled, incredibly tender, and grills beautifully. When I can't make it to the farmers' market, flank steak is my runner-up. Both cuts soak up this flavorful marinade, creating a juicy, savory bite. A hot grill or cast-iron pan gives the steak a delicious crust, and letting it rest before slicing keeps it perfectly tender.

 NOTES FOR NEXT TIME:

# Sausage and Fennel Rigatoni

In our house, this Sausage and Fennel Rigatoni is affectionately known as "Ski Pasta." There's just something about coming in from a snowy day—rosy-cheeked, chilled, and hungry—that makes a hearty bowl of pasta feel like the ultimate comfort. The sweet Italian sausage paired with a creamy tomato sauce and the subtle licorice note of fennel creates a flavor combination that's both cozy and craveable. My boys love it so much it's become a non-negotiable part of every ski trip.

**What you need:**

1 ½ tablespoons good olive oil

1 ½ cups (150 g) small fennel, chopped

¾ cup (100 g) yellow onion, chopped

½ pound (225 g) sweet Italian sausages, casings removed

1 teaspoon minced garlic (1 clove)

½ teaspoon whole fennel seeds, crushed

¼ teaspoon crushed red pepper flakes

1 tablespoon (15 g) tomato paste

1 teaspoon kosher salt, to taste

½ teaspoon freshly ground black pepper, to taste

½ cup (120 ml) dry white wine

1 (14-ounce / 400 g) can diced tomatoes, basil and garlic flavored including juice

½ cup (120 ml) heavy cream

⅓ cup (80 ml) half-and-half

¼ cup (15 g) chopped fresh parsley leaves

½ cup (50 g) freshly grated Italian Parmesan cheese, divided

8 ounces (225 g) rigatoni pasta

**SERVING SUGGESTIONS:** And for the perfect pairing? Serve a simple green salad tossed in a jam jar Vinaigrette (pg. 224)

1. **Prepare the base:** Heat olive oil in a large, heavy pot or Dutch oven over medium heat. Add chopped fennel and onion. Sauté for 7 minutes, stirring occasionally, until tender and fragrant.

2. **Cook the sausage:** Add the sausage to the pot. Use the back of a wooden spoon to crumble it into small pieces. Cook for 7 to 8 minutes, stirring occasionally, until the sausage is browned and cooked through. Aim for a fine, even texture.

3. **Season and build the sauce:** Stir in garlic, crushed fennel seeds, red pepper flakes, tomato paste, 1 teaspoon kosher salt, and ½ teaspoon black pepper. Cook for 1 minute until fragrant. Pour in diced tomatoes with their liquid and the white wine. Bring the mixture to a boil.

4. **Add cream and simmer:** Stir in the heavy cream and half-and-half. Reduce heat to low and let sauce simmer gently for 20 minutes, stirring occasionally, until it thickens slightly.

5. **Cook the pasta:** While the sauce simmers, bring a large pot of water to a boil. Add 2 tablespoons salt and the rigatoni. Cook according to the package directions until al dente. Drain well.

6. **Combine pasta and sauce:** Add cooked rigatoni to the sauce, stirring to coat pasta evenly. Cook over low heat for 5 minutes to allow pasta to absorb the flavors of the sauce. Off the heat, stir in parsley and ¼ cup of Parmesan cheese. Divide pasta into shallow bowls and serve hot. Pass the remaining ¼ cup Parmesan at the table for topping.

 **NOTES FOR NEXT TIME:**

# Perfect Pot Roast

Every cook should have a go-to recipe to make a melt-in-your-mouth pot roast with root vegetables perfectly every time. Here, the classic 17th century French boeuf á la mode gets an update, maintaining its status as an elegant dish a cut above a simple pot roast. To do this we include root vegetables, red onion, mushrooms, and a whole head of garlic, cooking it low and slow in a rich, red-wine and beef broth gravy. It's so good it is worthy to serve as a Sunday night dinner or for a date night.

**What you need:**

2 pounds (900 g) grass-fed boneless beef top blade roast or chuck roast

Fine sea salt and freshly ground black pepper, to taste

2 tablespoons canola oil

2 tablespoons unsalted butter

1 medium red onion, quartered

2 carrots, peeled and cut into 2-inch (5 cm) pieces

2 celery stalks, cut into 2-inch (5 cm) pieces

1 small rutabaga, peeled and cut into 12 pieces

1 head garlic, top trimmed to expose the cloves

3 tablespoons tomato paste

1 bay leaf

1 sprig fresh rosemary

¾ cup (180 ml) red wine, preferably Cabernet

2 cups (480 ml) beef broth or stock

Garnish

Prepared horseradish sauce (optional – pg. 220)

**SERVING SUGGESTIONS:** Serve with mashed potatoes or a simple green salad.

1. **Getting started:** Adjust oven rack to middle position and preheat oven to 300°F (150°C). Thoroughly pat roast dry with paper towels and sprinkle generously with fine sea salt and freshly ground black pepper.

2. **Sear roast:** In a large Dutch oven or other heavy oven-proof pot with a lid, heat oil over medium high heat until shimmering but not smoking. Add the meat and sear until a dark crust forms, reducing heat if fat begins to smoke, 3 to 4 minutes per side. Transfer to a plate; set aside.

3. **Sauté the vegetables:** Reduce heat to medium and add the butter to the now empty pan. Melt butter, add all vegetables and the garlic, stirring frequently and scraping the bottom of the pot until vegetables start to color, about 8 to 10 minutes

4. **Make a pan gravy:** Add tomato paste and cook, stirring frequently until it darkens slightly, about 5 minutes. Add bay leaves, rosemary, and wine, cooking until liquid is reduced to a thick gravy, stirring constantly. This should take about 5 to 7 minutes.

5. **Bake slow and low:** Return roast and any accumulated juices to pot; add broth until halfway up sides of roast. Bring liquid to simmer over medium heat, place foil over pot and cover tightly with lid (this makes for easy clean up). Transfer pot to oven. Turn the roast after 1 hour. Continue to cook until the pot roast is very tender and starts to fall apart. Begin checking the doneness at 2 hours.

6. **Let it rest:** Transfer roast to carving board, tent with foil to keep warm. Let it rest for at least 10 minutes. Let liquid in the pot settle for about 5 minutes, then use a wide spoon to skim fat off the surface. Discard bay leaves and rosemary stems. Squeeze any garlic cloves remaining in their skins into the sauce and discard the skins.

7. **To carve:** Using a chef's or carving knife, cut meat against the grain into ½-inch-thick slices, or pull apart into large pieces. To serve, lay slices of pot roast in a shallow bowl along with the vegetables and a generous amount of cooking liquid ladled over the top. Dollop with a teaspoon of prepared horseradish sauce.

# Sunday Supper Pork Ragu

There's something magical about a rich, slow-cooked ragu that fills your home with warmth and enticing aromas on a chilly winter day. This pork ragu is one of my all-time favorites for Sunday supper.

**What you need:**

- 1 to 1½ pounds (450–680 g) boneless pork shoulder roast
- 1 small onion, chopped
- 1 small fennel bulb, chopped
- 1 garlic clove, minced
- Salt and freshly ground black pepper, to taste
- 1 tablespoon olive oil
- 1 tablespoon unsalted butter
- 1 (28-ounce / 794 g) can whole tomatoes, with juice
- 1 cup (240 ml) red wine
- ⅛ teaspoon red pepper flakes
- 3 sprigs fresh thyme
- 3 sprigs fresh oregano
- 1 teaspoon whole fennel seeds, crushed with mortar and pestle
- 1 tablespoon hot sauce (optional, for smokiness; I use Sriracha®)
- 8 ounces (225 g) pappardelle pasta
- Freshly grated Parmesan cheese, for serving

1. **Getting started:** Preheat oven to 325°F (163°C). Generously season the pork shoulder with salt and pepper.

2. **Sear the pork:** In a 3-quart Dutch oven, heat olive oil and butter over medium-high heat until butter melts but doesn't burn. Add the pork roast and sear on all sides until browned, about 8-10 minutes total. Transfer pork to a plate. Add chopped onion and fennel to the Dutch oven and sauté until softened, about 5-7 minutes. Stir in the minced garlic and cook for an additional minute until fragrant.

3. **Build the sauce:** Add the canned tomatoes (with their juice), red wine, fennel seeds, red pepper flakes, thyme, oregano, and hot sauce to the pot. Stir to combine and bring the mixture to a boil.

4. **Braise the pork:** Return seared pork to the pot, ensuring the liquid comes about ⅓ of the way up the roast. Cover and transfer pot to preheated oven.

5. **Cook low and slow:** Braise the pork in the oven for 3-4 hours, turning it every hour. If the liquid reduces too much, add a bit more water or wine to maintain the right level of moisture. The pork is ready when it is tender and falls apart easily.

6. **Shred pork:** Remove pork from the pot and place it on a cutting board. Using two forks, shred the meat into bite-sized pieces. Return shredded pork to the pot and stir it into the sauce. Adjust seasoning with additional salt and pepper if needed.

7. **Cook pasta:** Cook the pappardelle and divide between bowls. Ladle the pork ragu over pasta and top with Parmesan. Serve immediately.

# Hachis Parmentier

Hachis Parmentier is the French take on Shepherd's Pie—or, as a Midwesterner like me might think of it, a minced lamb (or ground beef) casserole topped with creamy mashed potatoes. It's a family favorite in our house and one the boys always request when they're home. I first discovered this comforting dish in a charming pub in the Cotswolds, and ever since, it has been a keeper. My version carries a little Irish twist: a splash of stout in the filling, which adds malty depth and makes every bite rich and hearty.

**TABLE TALK TIPS:** You've got options when it comes to the liquid in this pie! For a classic take, use ½ cup beef bone broth. Often, I will reach for Better Than Bouillon®—just mix ½ teaspoon concentrate base with ½ cup water. If you'd like to give it an Irish pub twist, swap the broth for a stout like Guinness. Either way, you'll get a rich, hearty filling that makes this dish shine.

**For the filling**

1 tablespoon olive oil

¾ cup onion, chopped

1 small carrot, trimmed, peeled, chopped, about ¼ cup / 30 g

1 small celery stalk, trimmed, chopped

1 garlic clove, smashed and peeled

1 teaspoon fresh rosemary leaves, minced

1 teaspoon fresh thyme leaves, minced

1 teaspoon tomato paste

½ pound (225 g) 85% lean ground beef or ground lamb

½ pound (225 g) pork sausage, mild, casings removed if necessary

½ cup (120 mL) stout beer like Guinness, or substitute beef bone broth

1 bay leaf

Salt and freshly ground pepper, to taste

**For the potato topping**

1 pound (450 g) Yukon Gold potatoes, peeled

1 sprig fresh rosemary

¼ cup (60 mL) whole milk

2 tablespoons heavy cream

1½ tablespoons unsalted butter, at room temperature, plus ½ tablespoon butter cut into bits

Salt and freshly ground pepper, to taste

¼ cup (30 g) gruyère, Comté, or emmentaler, grated

1 tablespoon freshly grated Parmesan cheese (optional)

1. **To make the filling:** Put a heavy bottomed skillet like a cast iron skillet (8 or 10 inches) or a small 2 quart Dutch oven, over medium heat and pour in olive oil. When hot, add onion, carrot, and celery to the pan. Sprinkle vegetables with ¼ teaspoon salt and ⅛ teaspoon pepper. Sauté just until translucent and soft, about 3 minutes. Add garlic, rosemary, thyme, and tomato paste, stirring to mix everything together. Sauté for about 30 seconds just until the garlic begins to take on some color.

2. **Cook the meat:** Now add the ground beef and sausage, breaking up the clumps of meat and cooking until the beef and sausage are just pink. Add bay leaf. Stir in ½ cup of stout and bring to a boil. You want just enough stout in the pan to moisten the filling and to bubble up gently wherever there is a little room. If you think you need more, add just a smidgen. Season with salt and pepper, especially pepper. Cover with lid or tightly with aluminum foil and set aside while you prepare the potatoes. You can make the dish to this point up to a few hours ahead, cover the casserole with foil and refrigerate.

3. **To make the topping:** Put the potatoes and rosemary sprig in a large pot of generously salted cold water and bring to a boil. Cook until the potatoes are tender enough to be pierced easily with the tip of a knife or tines of a fork, about 20 minutes, drain them well.

    Meanwhile, center a rack in the oven and preheat to 400°F (200°C). Warm the milk and cream. Remove rosemary sprig and mash the potatoes using a potato masher or a hand blender, until just smooth. Using a wooden spoon or a sturdy spatula, stir in the milk and cream, then blend in the 1½ tablespoons of butter. Season to taste with salt and pepper.

4. **Ready to bake:** Remove bay leaf from filling and then spoon the potatoes over the filling, spreading them evenly and making sure they reach to the edges of the pot. Sprinkle the grated gruyere, Comté or emmental over the top of each pie, dust with the Parmesan, and scatter the bits of butter. Bake for 30 minutes or until the filling is bubbling steadily and the potatoes have developed a golden-brown crust.

 **NOTES FOR NEXT TIME:**

# Wine Braised Short Ribs

This braised short rib recipe will always hold a special place in my heart—it was the very first dinner-party-worthy dish I created on my own. The inspiration came when a dear friend convinced me to co-host a fundraising dinner party for our Minnetonka public school foundation, where the boys went to school. I wanted a recipe that felt elegant yet deeply comforting, and these short ribs delivered. Slowly braised in red wine until they're fall-off-the-bone tender, they became not only a crowd-pleaser that night but also one of my signature dishes.

**What you need:**

1 tablespoon grapeseed or canola oil

2 bone-in English-style short ribs, bones 4–5 inches long (10–13 cm), 1–1½ inches thick (2.5–4 cm) of meat on top, trimmed

½ carrot, peeled and roughly chopped

½ celery stalk, roughly chopped

½ onion, roughly chopped

6 garlic cloves, peeled and cracked

1 tablespoon tomato paste

1 teaspoon all-purpose flour

1 cup (240 mL) red wine (preferably Cabernet Sauvignon)

3 cups (720 mL) beef broth

1 tablespoon unsalted butter, chilled and cut into 2 pieces

**Sachet / Bouquet Garni**

4 sprigs flat-leaf parsley

6 sprigs fresh thyme

2 bay leaves

1 teaspoon whole black peppercorns

1 leek, white and pale green part only, cut into 5-inch (13 cm) length and washed

1. **Getting started:** Adjust oven rack to lower-middle position and preheat oven to 325°F (163°C). Sprinkle ribs with salt and pepper. Set aside. Assemble Sachet (see Table Talk Tips).

2. **Sear ribs:** Using a Dutch oven, heat the tablespoon of grapeseed oil over medium heat until it shimmers. Sear short ribs on either side until caramelized and golden brown, about 5 minutes. Remove the meat from the pan.

3. **Sauté the vegetables:** Add carrot and celery to pan and cook 5 minutes over the same heat, just until lightly browned. Add onion and garlic, cooking until lightly browned and stirring occasionally as needed for another 5 minutes. Add tomato paste and flour and cook, stirring constantly, until paste begins to darken, about 45 seconds. Add wine, increase heat to high, and bring to boil. Cook until mixture is slightly thickened, about 3 minutes.

4. **Prepare braising liquid:** Stir in broth and add sachet packet (see the Table Talk Tips). Nestle short ribs into the pot, bone side up (ribs may overlap). Bring braising liquid to simmer, transfer pot to oven, and cook, covered, for 2 hours.

5. **Make sure to baste:** Remove pot from oven. Flip ribs meat side up so meat is above braising liquid. Return pot to oven and cook, uncovered, until fork slips easily in and out of meat, 1 to 1½ hours longer. For the last hour, baste short ribs every 15 minutes, leaving the lid off. You will know when ribs are done as the meat will be tender and almost falling off the bone.

6. **Strain braising liquid:** Transfer ribs to serving platter and tent with aluminum foil. Strain liquid through a fine mesh strainer into fat separator; discard solids and sachet packet. Allow liquid to settle for about 5 minutes.

7. **Make the gravy and serve:** Strain off fat and return defatted braising liquid to now-empty pot. Bring to boil over high heat and cook until reduced to 1 cup, 4 to 7 minutes. Reduce heat to low and whisk in butter one piece at a time. Season sauce with salt and pepper to taste. Pour sauce over meat and serve.

**TABLE TALK TIPS:** For the sachet, wrap parsley, thyme, bay leaves, leek, and peppercorns in a large square of cheesecloth and tie with butcher's twine. To thicken sauce, make a slurry of 1 tablespoon braising liquid to 1 tablespoon cornstarch. Serve over risotto (pg.221) or mashed potatoes.

# Prime Rib Roast
## with Fruit Compote and Horseradish Sauce

This show-stopping prime rib roast recipe is a gift from Chef Jared of the Erie Dining Club, with whom I had the pleasure of cooking alongside during a week-long Farm-to-Table Boot Camp at the Culinary Institute of America. On one unforgettable day, he whipped up this dish, and WOW—it was pure magic. I have reimagined it to suit a table for two. Featuring a perfectly roasted prime rib, a zesty horseradish sauce, and a sweet-tart fruit compote, this dish is a celebration of heirloom flavors brought into the modern kitchen.

**What you need:**

2 to 2.5 lbs (900–1,130 g), 2-rib roast of beef, with untrimmed fat cap, about ½ inch / 1.3 cm thick

Kosher salt, to taste

2 teaspoons vegetable

Freshly ground black pepper, to taste

2 tablespoons Flaky salt

1 cup(237 ml) broth or white wine

1 tablespoon butter

**For serving**

Horseradish sauce (pg.220)

Fruit compote (pg.220)

1. **Salt the roast:** Truss the meat using 2 lengths of kitchen twine, if your butcher has not already done this. Using a sharp knife, cut slits spaced 1-inch apart into surface layer of fat using a crosshatch pattern and being careful to cut down to, but not into meat. Rub 2 tablespoons salt over entire roast and into slits. Transfer to a quarter sheet baking sheet or large plate and refrigerate, uncovered, at least 24 hours and up to 96 hours. Now this is very important: before roasting, allow the roast to come to room temperature for 1–2 hours. The roast will look dry and turn a bright red from the salt (this is what we want).

2. **Sear and slow roast:** Preheat oven to 200°F (93°C) and position a rack in the middle. Using a 12-inch heavy bottomed skillet like a cast iron skillet, heat oil over high heat until just smoking. Sear sides and top of roast until browned, 6 to 8 minutes total (do not sear side where roast was cut from bone). Transfer roast, fat side up, to wire rack set in rimmed baking sheet and season with pepper. Let cool for 10 minutes. Roast until the meat registers 110°F (43°C), 1 to 2 hours.

3. **Rest and au jus:** Turn off oven and leave the roast inside until the internal temperature reaches 120°F (49°C) for rare, or 125°F (52°C) for medium-rare, about 30–90 minutes. Transfer to a cutting board, tent roast with foil, and let it rest for 30–60 minutes. Meanwhile, reserve any drippings to make an au jus. Pour off most of the fat from the pan, leaving a few tablespoons. Heat pan on the stove over high heat, add liquid (1 cup broth or wine) and scrape up the brown bits until reduced by half. Add 1 tablespoon butter.

4. **Reverse sear:** Adjust the oven rack to broiler position and preheat the broiler. Place roast on broiler pan. Remove foil and roll it into a ball to prop up the roast's fat cap. Broil the roast until the fat cap is browned and crisp, about 2–8 minutes. Slice roast on a large cutting board, ladle some pan juices over the roast, sprinkle with flaky salt and serve with fruit compote and horseradish sauce.

**TABLE TALK TIPS:** Remove the bones using a sharp knife, run it down the length of the bones, following the contours as closely as possible until meat is separated (or have your butcher do this). Truss the meat with two lengths of twine. My best advice is to buy a leave-in meat thermometer—this is your best bet to monitor the roast without opening the oven door unnecessarily. If you do have to open the oven door, do so as little as possible, removing roast from the oven while taking temperature. If roast has not reached the correct temperature in time range specified, heat the oven to 200°F (93°C), wait five minutes, then shut it off, and continue cooking the roast until it reaches desired temperature.

**Chicken Pot Pie**
Pg.142

**Baked Chicken
Parmesan Meatballs**
Pg.134

**Rhode-Island
Calamari**
Pg.133

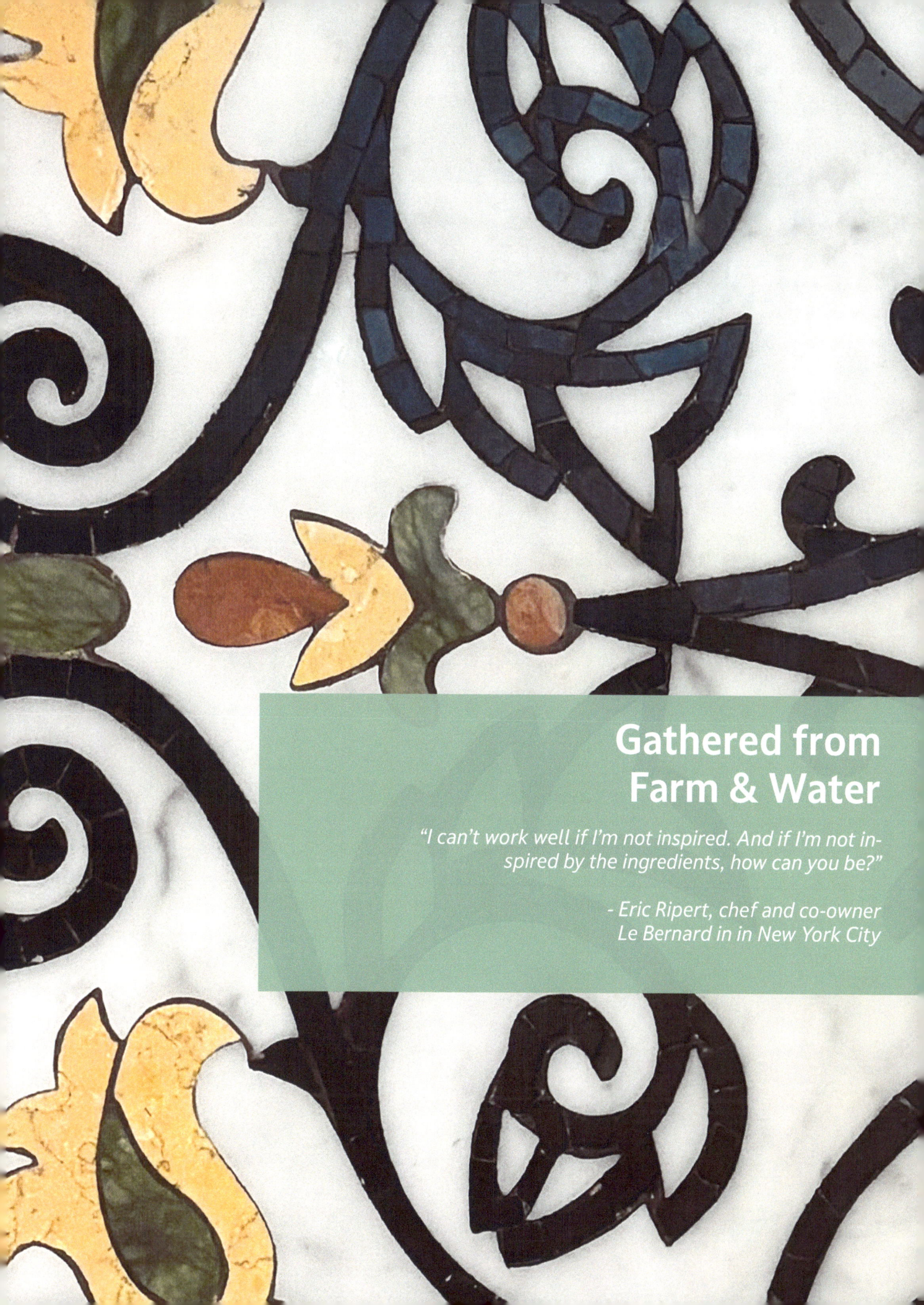

# Gathered from Farm & Water

*"I can't work well if I'm not inspired. And if I'm not inspired by the ingredients, how can you be?"*

*- Eric Ripert, chef and co-owner
Le Bernard in in New York City*

125 | [Chicken] | 126 | California Fish Tacos

Pasta Diavola | 127 | 128 | Sheet Pan Chicken Thighs

# Apricot Harissa-Glazed Chicken
## and Pearl Couscous

According to my friend Pam, every Jewish household cook has their version of Jewish Apricot Chicken. I am still dreaming about the apricot glazed chicken she served at book club. She said this flavorful dish was easy to make, so I decided to put my own spin on traditional Jewish Apricot Chicken.

**Apricot harissa glaze**

¾ cup (240 mL) apricot preserves

2 teaspoons packed brown sugar

1 tablespoon brandy or orange liqueur like Grand Marnier®, or lemon juice

2 teaspoons rose harissa

¼ cup (40 g) dried apricots, quartered

2 tablespoons currants

**Chicken**

½ teaspoon kosher salt, divided

¼ teaspoon black pepper, divided

1 tablespoon vegetable oil

2 skin-on chicken thighs

1¼ cups (300 mL) water

1¼ cups (230 g) pearl couscous (like Near East®)

¼ cup (30 g) shelled pistachios, toasted and chopped

1. **Getting started:** Adjust rack to middle position and heat the oven to 425°F (220°C).
2. **Make the glaze:** Whisk apricot preserves, sugar, brandy, and harissa together in a small bowl.
3. **Season and sear:** Season both sides of chicken with salt and pepper. Heat oil in a medium (8 to 10 inch) skillet that has a lid over medium-high heat until just smoking. In skillet, place chicken skin side down, cook until well browned and most fat has rendered, 8 to 10 minutes. Turn chicken and lightly brown second side, 2 to 3 minutes longer. If the oil starts to splatter, decrease the heat and cover the skillet with a lid.
4. **Sauce up the chicken:** Transfer chicken to 8 x 8 inch baking dish and set aside. Discard fat in skillet and add apricot-harissa mixture. Simmer vigorously over high heat, stirring constantly, until thick and syrupy, 3 minutes. Transfer 3 tablespoons harissa mixture to a second bowl and stir in dried apricots and currants; set aside. Brush remaining glaze over chicken and turn chicken skin side down.
5. **Finish in oven:** Bake 12 to 16 minutes until thickest part of thigh registers 160°F (70°C) on instant-read thermometer, turning chicken skin side up halfway through cooking. Transfer chicken to platter and let rest for 5 minutes. Meanwhile, transfer any glaze remaining in baking dish to a small serving bowl.
6. **Make the couscous:** Bring water to boil in saucepan over high heat. Stir in couscous, cover, and remove from heat. Let stand for 5 minutes. Stir in pistachios and reserved harissa-currant mixture. Serve chicken over couscous, pass extra glaze.

**TABLE TALK TIPS:** Rose harissa is one of my secret kitchen weapons! This North African chili paste gets a floral twist from rose petals, adding a sweet balance to its heat. I use Belazu® brand (buy online) for its punchy, well-rounded flavor, but if you're using a milder supermarket version, just add about 50% more.

 **NOTES FOR NEXT TIME:**

# California Fish Tacos For Two

California Fish Tacos—a simple, satisfying, fresh take on West Coast fish tacos. We're using mild but sturdy white fish, tossed in an ultrathin beer batter that fries up golden and crispy. A quick pickle of red onions and jalapeños adds color and spice, while some of that vinegary brine doubles as a light dressing for our cabbage. A creamy white sauce with a hint of lime and fresh cilantro ties it all together.

**Pickled onions**

½ small red onion, halved and thinly sliced

1 jalapeño, stemmed and sliced into thin rings

½ cup (120 mL) white wine vinegar

1 tablespoon lime juice

½ tablespoon sugar

½ teaspoon salt

**Cabbage**

1½ cups (90 g) shredded green cabbage (use a mandoline on setting 1 or a sharp knife)

2 tablespoons pickling liquid from pickled onions

¼ teaspoon salt

¼ teaspoon pepper

**White Sauce**

¼ cup (60 mL) mayonnaise

¼ cup (60 mL) sour cream

1 tablespoon lime juice

1 tablespoon milk

**Fish**

2–4 fillets (4–6 oz / 115–170 g each) skinless white fish (cod, haddock, or halibut), cut crosswise into 4 × 1-inch strips

Salt and pepper

⅓ cup (40 g) all-purpose flour

2 tablespoons cornstarch

½ teaspoon baking powder

½ cup (120 mL) beer (light lager works best)

2 cups (480 mL) peanut or vegetable oil

**For serving**

6 (6-inch / 15 cm) corn tortillas, warmed

½ cup fresh cilantro leaves

Green salsa (optional)

1. **Make the pickled onions:** Grab a small bowl and toss in the sliced onion and jalapeño. In a small saucepan, bring the vinegar, lime juice, sugar, and salt to a boil. Pour the hot mixture over the onions and jalapeños, then let them sit for at least 30 minutes.

2. **Prep the cabbage and white sauce:** In a medium bowl, combine the shredded cabbage with 2 tablespoons of the pickling liquid, salt, and pepper. Give it a quick toss with your hands to evenly coat. Set aside. Whisk together the mayo, sour cream, lime juice, and milk in a small bowl until smooth. Set aside.

3. **Batter and fry the fish:** Preheat oven to 200°F (93°C). Set a wire rack inside a rimmed baking sheet—this will help keep the fish crispy while you finish frying.
   Pat the fish dry with paper towels, then season with salt and pepper. In a medium bowl, whisk together the flour, cornstarch, baking powder, and a pinch of salt. Add the beer and whisk until smooth. Dip each piece of fish into the batter, coating evenly.

   Heat the oil in a Dutch oven or deep skillet over medium-high heat until it reaches 350°F (175°C). Carefully lower a few pieces of fish into the oil, dragging them along the surface before letting go to prevent sticking. Fry for about 2 minutes per side, until golden brown and crispy. Transfer to the wire rack and place in the warm oven. Repeat with remaining fish, making sure to let the oil return to 350°F (175°C) between batches.

4. **Assemble the tacos:** Lay out your warm tortillas and place a crispy piece of fish on each. Top with the pickled onions, cabbage, a drizzle of white sauce, and fresh cilantro. Serve immediately with a side of green salsa, if desired.

**TABLE TALK TIPS:** Store onions and white sauce in the fridge for up to 2 days.

# Pasta Diavola

Pasta Diavola is one of my favorite pastas to make, even when I am far from home. While in Emilia-Romagna, Mark, Zach, and I rented a small apartment and I visited Sfoglia Rina, a beloved pasta shop where tortellini is made fresh each morning. Arriving late, I managed to get just enough for two, and the owner kindly slipped in some homemade gnocchi as a gift. We ended up chatting about sauces. She laughed when I asked about an Alfredo Sauce ("who is Alfredo?") and the conversation inspired me to keep things simple. This spicy red sauce—my version of Pasta Diavola—was born.

**What you need:**

- 2–3 cloves garlic, smashed and peeled
- 3 tablespoons olive oil
- 1 small yellow onion, very finely chopped, about ½ cup / 75 g
- A pinch or two of red pepper flakes
- 1 tablespoon tomato paste
- 1 (14-ounce / 400 g) can plum tomatoes (San Marzano preferred) with juice
- 2–3 sprigs fresh basil
- 1 tablespoon butter
- 1 ½ teaspoons sugar
- 7 ounces (200 g) pasta (penne, rigatoni, or gnocchi)
- 1 (4-ounce / 133 g) ball burrata, room temperature

 **NOTES FOR NEXT TIME:**

1. **Make the sauce:** Put the garlic into a pot with the olive oil, then turn heat to medium and allow the oil to slowly warm until garlic is sizzling. The idea here is to infuse the oil and color the garlic. Add the onion, red pepper flakes, and tomato paste, cooking for 10 minutes until onion is tender and tomato paste turns brown. Cut up tomatoes in the can with a pair of scissors and add to the pot. Rinse out the can with a splash of water and add to the pot. Mix well, add a sprig of basil and bring to a gentle simmer. Leave sauce simmering for 20 minutes until it begins to thicken.

2. **Taste and adjust seasoning:** At this point, stir in the butter and sugar, taste and adjust the seasoning as necessary. This is where you might add more red pepper flakes or a bit more sugar to balance the acidity of the canned tomatoes. Sometimes I add a teaspoon of balsamic vinegar to avoid making it too sweet while balancing the acidity. Keep the sauce warm while cooking the pasta.

3. **Cook the pasta:** Now get your pasta going, Make sure water is properly boiling and well salted (1 tablespoon per 4 quarts (3.79 liters) water - will flavor the pasta nicely). Then add the pasta. When pasta is al dente, take out a mug of pasta water before draining the pasta; this will be used to adjust the consistency of the sauce. Drain the pasta and add to the pot of sauce. Add a drizzle of olive oil and give it a good stir. If sauce is too thick, add a splash of reserved pasta water. Keep adding until the sauce is silky and clings to the pasta.

4. **Finishing touches:** Spoon into bowls. Tear the burrata in half and place on top of the pasta. Season the burrata with flaky salt, a drizzle of olive oil, and a handful of torn basil leaves.

# Sheet Pan Chicken Thighs
## with Fresh Tarragon

If you're looking for a meal that tastes like it took hours but didn't, this Sheet Pan Chicken Thighs recipe is it. Marinated with fresh tarragon and garlic, roasted until the skin is golden and crisp, then finished with a rich tarragon cream sauce, this is a simple, fuss-free classic roasted tarragon chicken for two that delivers big flavor with minimal cleanup. It is a weeknight dinner that feels a little French, a little fancy, and completely doable.

**What you need:**

¼ cup finely chopped tarragon (leaves and tender stems) (~15 g)

1 garlic clove, finely grated or minced

1 tablespoon extra-virgin olive oil, plus more for drizzling

¾ teaspoon kosher salt, plus more as needed

¼ teaspoon ground black pepper, plus more as needed

2 bone-in chicken thighs, skin on (~1 lb / 450 g)

1 large onion, peeled and sliced (~1 cup / 150 g)

**Tarragon cream sauce**

½ cup heavy cream (120 mL)

¼ cup fresh tarragon leaves, roughly chopped (~5 g)

1 tablespoon Dijon mustard

½ cup dry white wine (120 mL)

1. **Start the marinade:** In a large bowl, stir together tarragon, garlic, oil, salt, and pepper. Add chicken thighs and toss to coat. Cover with plastic wrap and chill for at least 6 hours or up to overnight.

2. **Arrange on sheet pan:** Heat oven to 425°F (220°C). Spread onions out on a rimmed baking sheet, drizzle with oil, sprinkle with salt and pepper, then toss well. Clear spaces on the baking pan and place chicken thighs in the cleared spaces so the onions surround the chicken.

3. **Roast chicken:** Place in oven, tossing the onions after 15 minutes, until chicken is cooked through, onions are tender and chicken skin begins to turn a golden brown, 20 to 25 minutes.

4. **Make the tarragon cream:** Meanwhile, mix cream, tarragon and mustard in a bowl, and season well with salt and pepper. After 20 to 25 minutes, turn the oven down to 325°F (163°C), take out the sheet pan and pour a generous glass of white wine into the pan. Then pour the tarragon cream all over the chicken and place back in the oven for another 10 to 15 minutes. To judge when it's cooked, I check the deepest part of the thigh with a meat thermometer, looking for 160°F (71°C). If you don't have one, prod this spot with a skewer and ensure the juices run clear.

5. **Finishing touches:** Place chicken on a platter and let rest for 10 minutes, covered loosely with a bit of foil. Spoon onions around the chicken, pour any sauces left in the pan over the chicken and serve.

**NOTES FOR NEXT TIME:**

Low country boil | 130

131 | Can Pepi Fried Chicken

Baked Chicken Parmesan Meatballs | 132

133 | Rhode Island-Style Calamari

# Low Country Boil

When summer heat makes turning on the oven unthinkable, I turn to this no-fuss Low-Country Boil. Sweet corn from the market and shrimp from Fabian's Seafood—a family-run business from Galveston, Texas, that sells fresh Gulf shrimp out of a refrigerated truck behind a local gas station—make it extra special. It's all about simple prep, bold flavors, and plenty of fun. Serve it straight from foil packets or a big pan, with sauces on the side and a bowl for the shells—no special gear required!

**Seafood boil**

*½ pound (225 g) baby red potatoes, scrubbed and quartered*

*½ pound (225 g) large shrimp (16–20 count), in the shell, deveined*

*6 ounces (170 g) smoked kielbasa sausage, cut into 1-inch (2.5 cm) pieces*

*2 ears yellow corn, shucked and halved*

*2 teaspoons Old Bay seasoning*

*1 lemon, thinly sliced*

*¼ cup (60 ml) white wine*

*1 tablespoon minced parsley*

**Sauce**

*2 tablespoons prepared horseradish*

*1 teaspoon red wine vinegar*

*6 tablespoons ketchup*

*½ cup (120 ml) mayonnaise*

*1 ½ tablespoons sriracha*

**Creole remoulade**

*½ cup (120 ml) mayonnaise*

*1 tablespoon whole-grain mustard*

*1 ½ teaspoons Louisiana-style hot sauce*

*1 ½ teaspoons minced parsley*

*1 teaspoon Worcestershire sauce*

*1 teaspoon grated lemon zest plus 1 ½ teaspoons lemon juice*

*¼ teaspoon Old Bay® seasoning*

*Pinch of sugar*

*¼ teaspoon freshly ground black pepper*

1. **Parboil potatoes:** Grab a medium saucepan and toss in your potatoes. Cover them with cold water—about 4 inches above the spuds and set it on the stove over medium heat. Bring water to a simmer and let cook until potatoes are fork-tender. Once they're ready, use a spider strainer (a long handled wire-mesh basket) or a slotted spoon and scoop them out. Place into a bowl and let cool.

2. **Parboil corn:** Drop corn ears into the same pot of hot water and boil for just 2 minutes. Scoop the corn out and let it join the potatoes in the cooling bowl.

3. **To assemble foil packets:** Grab 4 large sheets of heavy-duty aluminum foil, about 18 inches each. Stack them into two double layers. Divide the potatoes, corn, shrimp, and sausage evenly between the two, placing in the center of each piece. Sprinkle 1 teaspoon of Old Bay seasoning over each pile and toss gently to coat everything. Top each pile with two slices of lemon and a generous splash (2 tablespoons) of wine. Now, fold up the edges of the foil tightly to form a packet.

4. **Or use a disposable aluminum pan:** Spread everything evenly in the pan. Sprinkle with Old Bay, toss to coat, and top with lemon slices and wine. Cover tightly with foil, sealing the edges like you mean it.

5. **Time to grill or bake in oven:** If you're cooking indoors, preheat oven to 450°F (232°C). Bake the packets for 15 minutes. *For outdoor grilling*, fire it up to high heat and preheat for 15 minutes. Place your foil packets/pan on a baking sheet (directly on grate) and cook for 12 to 15 minutes, flipping packets or tossing ingredients in the pan halfway through. You're looking for soft, tender corn and shrimp that are pink and perfectly opaque. Sprinkle with parsley and juice of half a lemon. Serve right out of the foil packet or pan but grab an extra bowl for discarding the corn cobs and shells.

6. **Prepare the sauces:** Meanwhile, place ingredients for each sauce in individual bowls and whisk until combined. If you want to make sauces ahead, they will keep in the refrigerator up to 3 days.

# Can Pepi Fried Chicken
## with Hot Honey

On a trip to Barcelona we discovered La Pepita, a cozy family-run spot opened by Sofia and Sergio in 2010. With its warm, lively atmosphere, it felt like a modern twist on a traditional tapas bar. The standout dish was their Fried Chicken Catalonia-style, surprisingly infused with green curry—one bite and we were hooked! Inspired by that unforgettable meal, this is my take on Can-Pepita Fried Chicken, an heirloom-worthy recipe you can make at home.

### Chicken Brine

- 1 ½ tablespoons kosher salt (Diamond Crystal®) or 2 teaspoons fine table salt
- 1 ½ tablespoons granulated sugar
- 2 whole chicken legs (or 2 drumsticks and 2 thighs)

### For Frying and Serving

- 1 quart (≈ 950 mL) peanut oil
- 1 cup all-purpose flour or Italian "00" flour
- 1 teaspoon kosher salt (Diamond Crystal®) or 1 teaspoon fine table salt
- 1 egg
- 2 tablespoons green curry paste, divided
- ¼ teaspoon cayenne pepper
- Store-bought hot honey (like Mike's Hot Honey®)

**TABLE TALK TIP:** "00" Flour: This finely milled Italian flour is typically used for pizza and pasta dough. Its powdery texture absorbs less oil during frying, keeping the crust crisp and dry. You can purchase it online or at specialty stores.

1. **Night before:** In a 3-quart container, combine 1 quart water with the salt and sugar. Whisk until dissolved. Divide the chicken legs into drumsticks and thighs by slicing through the knee joint along the white fat line (unless starting with pre-cut drumsticks and thighs). Trim any excess fat, then submerge the pieces in the brine. Cover and refrigerate for at least 24 hours and up to 36 hours.

2. **Get ready to fry:** Fill a large Dutch oven or heavy-bottomed pot with enough oil to come halfway up the sides. Attach a clip-on thermometer and heat oil to 325°F (≈ 163°C), over medium-high heat. Line one sheet tray with paper towels and set a wire rack in another sheet tray.

3. **Set up batter stations:** In a shallow dish like a pie plate, whisk together flour and salt. In a small bowl, mix 1 tablespoon green curry paste with 2 tablespoons water. Drizzle curry mixture into the flour and gently toss with your hands to create small clumps for a craggy coating.

   In a second wide shallow dish, beat egg with remaining 1 tablespoon green curry paste and cayenne pepper.

4. **Batter chicken:** Remove chicken from the fridge and pat dry with paper towels. Working one piece at a time, dip chicken into the egg mixture, then coat thoroughly in the flour mixture, pressing firmly to pack the coating. Shake off excess flour and set aside.

5. **Frying:** Carefully lower chicken pieces into the hot oil, working in batches to avoid overcrowding. Fry, flipping once, until golden brown and the internal temperature reaches 175°F (80°C), about 7-9 minutes per side.

   As each piece finishes frying, transfer it to paper towel-lined tray to blot excess oil. Then immediately move the chicken to a wire rack and let rest for 5 minutes or up to an hour (room-temperature fried chicken is excellent too). To serve, drizzle chicken with hot honey and enjoy!

•A note about Green Curry paste: I've used both Thai Kitchen® Green Curry Paste and Mekhala® Organic Thai Green Curry Paste, available at my local food co-op and Whole Foods. I especially love Mekhala's paste as they support women and provide opportunities to marginalized Burmese Shan youth.

# Baked Chicken Parmesan Meatballs

This recipe is my reimagining of the Italian-American classic, Chicken Parmesan, scaled perfectly for two. Inspired by a meatball recipe from my mother-in-law's Forks of the Delaware Garden Club cookbook, a cherished Easton, Pennsylvania collection where friends and neighbors shared their best dishes. I combined that nostalgia with memories of chicken Parmesan from Easton's family-owned Italian restaurants and gave it a modern twist with a no-fuss marinara. True to the original, Club crackers remain in the meatball mix for their unique texture. And, if you're feeling indulgent try burrata instead of mozzarella for an extra-creamy finish.

**The sauce**

2 ½ tablespoons extra-virgin olive oil, divided

2 to 3 garlic cloves, sliced thin

1 (14.5–15.0 ounce / 411–425 g) can crushed tomatoes

1 (8-ounce / 227 g) can tomato sauce

1 ⅛ teaspoons dried oregano, divided

¾ teaspoons table salt, divided

⅛ teaspoon red pepper flakes

**The meatballs**

11 Club® or Ritz® crackers

1 ¼ cups (4 ounces / 113 g) grated Parmesan cheese, divided

1 large egg, lightly beaten

1 teaspoon garlic powder

½ teaspoon fresh ground pepper

1 pound (454 g) ground chicken, (avoid "99% fat-free")

1 cup (4 ounces / 113 g) whole-milk mozzarella cheese or burrata, shredded

½ cup (30 g) panko bread crumbs

2 tablespoons torn fresh basil

1. **Prepare the marinara sauce:** Heat 1½ tablespoons oil in a large saucepan over medium heat until shimmering. Add sliced garlic and cook until lightly browned, about 1 minute. Stir in crushed tomatoes, tomato sauce, ⅛ teaspoon oregano, ⅛ teaspoon salt, and red pepper flakes. Bring the mixture to a simmer, then reduce heat to medium-low and cook, stirring occasionally until slightly thickened, 10 to 15 minutes. Remove from heat and cover to keep warm.

2. **Make the meatballs:** Adjust the oven rack to the middle position and heat oven to 350°F (175°C). Place the crackers in a 1 quart zipper-lock bag, seal the bag, and crush them into fine crumbs with a rolling pin (you should have about ½ cup crumbs).
   In a large bowl, combine the cracker crumbs, 1 cup Parmesan cheese, egg, garlic powder, black pepper, remaining 1 teaspoon oregano, and ½ teaspoon salt. Add the ground chicken and mix thoroughly with your hands meat mixture is well combined and has become tacky.

   Divide the mixture into 10 equal portions (about ¼ cup each). A rounded 3 tablespoon cookie scoop works well. When forming the meatballs, keep a small bowl of water nearby and wet your palms periodically to prevent the meat from sticking to your hands. Roll each portion into a ball and transfer to an 8 x 8-inch baking dish.

3. **Assemble and bake:** Pour prepared marinara sauce over the meatballs, then sprinkle with shredded mozzarella (or place torn burrata pieces over the top for a richer version). Bake until the meatballs register at least 160°F (71°C) and the mozzarella is melted and beginning to brown, 35 to 40 minutes. Let the dish cool for 15 minutes.

4. **Toast the panko topping:** While meatballs cool, combine the panko breadcrumbs, remaining 1 tablespoons oil, and remaining ⅛ teaspoon salt in a microwave-safe bowl. Microwave in 30-second intervals, stirring each time, until the panko is light golden brown, 1 to 3 minutes.

5. **Finish and serve:** Sprinkle the baked meatballs with the toasted panko mixture, the remaining ½ cup Parmesan cheese, and fresh basil leaves. Serve with crusty bread for sopping up the sauce.

# Rhode Island-Style Calamari

Inspired by our East Coast travels, this recipe celebrates Rhode Island's iconic calamari—lightly fried squid tossed with banana peppers. A tradition born in the 1950s, it blends Italian immigrant cooking with the bounty of the Atlantic, creating a dish that's simple, nostalgic, and full of flavor. Served with a spicy mayo dipping sauce, it's heirloom cooking for two.

**Calamari**

½ cup (120 ml) milk

1 teaspoon table salt

1 ½ cups (180 g) all-purpose flour

1 tablespoon baking powder

½ teaspoon pepper

1 pound (454 g) squid, bodies sliced crosswise into ¾-inch (2 cm) rings, tentacles trimmed

1 ½ cups (50 g) jarred sliced banana peppers

2 quarts (1.9 liters) vegetable oil, for frying

Lemon wedges, for serving

**Spicy mayo dipping sauce**

1 cup (240 ml) mayonnaise

2 tablespoons sriracha

2 teaspoons grated lime zest, plus 2 tablespoons lime juice

½ teaspoon smoked paprika

1. **Prepare the spicy mayo:** Before working with the squid, grab a small bowl and whisk together all dipping sauce ingredients. Cover and refrigerate until we are ready to serve.

2. **Gather tools:** Place a wire rack on a rimmed baking sheet. Set a second rack on another baking sheet and line it with a triple layer of paper towels. Preheat the oven to 200°F (93°C) to keep the calamari warm as we are going to fry in batches to avoid clumping.

3. **Set up dredging station:** In a medium bowl, whisk together the milk and salt. Almost all of the calamari recipes claim that soaking calamari helps keep the calamari tender during frying. In a separate bowl (I like using a pie plate), combine flour, baking powder, and pepper. I find that adding baking powder to the "dredge" lightens the texture of the coating.

4. **Dredge the squid:** Add the squid rings and tentacles to the milk mixture, tossing to coat. Let the squid soak briefly to help the dredge adhere and encourage even browning. Using a slotted spoon or your hands, remove half the squid from the milk, letting excess drip back into the bowl. Add the squid to the flour mixture and toss to coat evenly. Shake off any excess flour (this is important to avoid clumping during frying) and arrange the coated squid in a single layer on the unlined rack. Repeat with the remaining squid.

5. **Dredge peppers:** Toss 1 cup of banana peppers in the flour mixture, no need to pat dry as this will encourage the coating to adhere. Toss with your hands or a tongs to coat evenly. Shake off excess flour and arrange them alongside the squid. Let rest for 10 minutes to allow the coating to hydrate. Letting the dredged squid rest helps prevents a dusty film forming on the exterior and promotes even browning.

6. **Heat the oil:** While the coated squid and peppers rest, heat the vegetable oil in a Dutch oven over high heat to 350°F (175°C). Use a thermometer to monitor the temperature for consistent results.

7. **Fry the squid and peppers:** Fry in small batches to maintain oil temperature and achieve crisp results. For 1 pound of calamari, I work in two batches to avoid overcrowding, carefully adding half the squid and peppers to the hot oil. Fry for exactly 3 minutes, until golden brown and crisp. Using a slotted spoon or spider skimmer, transfer fried calamari and peppers to the paper towel-lined rack. Place the rack in the oven to keep warm while you fry the second batch. Return the oil to 350°F (175°C) and repeat with the remaining squid and peppers.

Arrange the calamari and peppers on a platter garnished with additional banana peppers. Serve immediately with lemon wedges and the spicy mayo dipping sauce on the side.

# Supper Club Cordon Bleu
## with Mushrooms, Leeks, and Prosciutto

Supper clubs are iconic in small towns across Wisconsin, and growing up my family often went to the Fireside Supper Club owned by our next-door neighbor. Friday nights meant a community fish fry, but as a kid I always skipped the fried fish in favor of the cheesy Chicken Cordon Bleu topped with a creamy white sauce—what I later learned was a French soubise. This reimagined version brings back that 1960s dinner party classic without the hassle of deep-frying. Rolled and baked with fontina, prosciutto, and a savory mushroom-leek stuffing, then finished with a golden panko crust and velvety soubise, it's supper club comfort made simple for two.

### Chicken

⅔ cup panko bread crumbs (~70 g)

1 tablespoon unsalted butter, melted

2 tablespoon vegetable oil, divided

5 oz white mushrooms, trimmed, wiped clean, and sliced thin (~140 g)

1 small leek, white part halved lengthwise, washed, and chopped, about ¾ cup, ~90 g

1 medium garlic clove, minced, about 2 teaspoons

¼ teaspoon fresh thyme leaves, chopped

1 teaspoon lemon juice

Fontina or gruyère cheese, cut into two 2½ inch × ½-inch sticks (~65 g total)

2 slices prosciutto or deli ham, about 4 oz / ~115 g

2 (6 - 8-oz / 170–225 g) boneless, skinless chicken breasts, trimmed

2 teaspoon Dijon mustard

**Soubise Sauce**

3 tablespoons unsalted butter

½ cup finely chopped onion (~75 g)

½ teaspoon kosher salt

1 tablespoon all-purpose flour

1 cup whole milk (~240 ml)

¼ cup sour cream (~60 ml)

¼ tsp black pepper

⅛ tsp grated nutmeg

1. **Prepare the panko coating:** Preheat oven to 400°F (200°C) and adjust the rack to upper-middle position. In an 8½ by 4½-inch loaf pan, toss the panko with melted butter until evenly coated. Bake 5-7 minutes, stirring halfway through, until golden brown. Let cool completely.

2. **Make the mushroom and leek filling:** Heat 1 tablespoon oil in a 10-inch skillet over medium-high heat, until shimmering. Add mushrooms and cook, stirring occasionally, until they release their moisture and turn golden brown, about 8-11 minutes. Add the remaining tablespoon oil along with the leek, cooking until softened, about 2-4 minutes. Stir in garlic and thyme, cooking another 30 seconds until fragrant. Add lemon juice and cook until fully evaporated. Transfer the mixture to a food processor and pulse about five times until roughly chopped.

3. **Assemble the cheese rolls:** Lay 1 slice prosciutto on a flat surface.. Spread ¼ cup of the mushroom mixture over the prosciutto, leaving a ½-inch border. Place a piece of fontina at one end and roll the prosciutto tightly around the cheese, tucking in the sides to fully enclose. Repeat with the second portion.

4. **Prepare and stuff the chicken:** Place each breast between two sheets of parchment paper and gently pound with a mallet to about ¼ to ½ inch thickness. Place a prosciutto-wrapped cheese roll 1 inch from the thicker and tightly roll chicken around it. Secure with toothpicks and set aside, seam-side down.

5. **Bread and bake the chicken:** Brush the outside of each chicken roll with 1 teaspoon Dijon mustard, then dredge in the toasted panko, pressing gently to help it adhere. Arrange the chicken, crumb side up, in the now-empty loaf pan. Bake 30-35 minutes, rotating pan halfway through, until internal temperature of the chicken reaches 160°F (71°C). Remove toothpicks before serving.

6. **Make the soubise sauce:** While chicken bakes, melt butter in a medium saucepan over medium-low heat. Add chopped onion and ½ teaspoon salt, cover, and cook for about 10 minutes, stirring occasionally, until onion turns translucent. Whisk in flour and cook for 1 minute, then slowly whisk in milk. Increase heat to medium-high and bring to a boil, whisking constantly until the sauce thickens, about 30 seconds. Remove from heat, whisk in sour cream, black pepper, nutmeg, and remaining ½ teaspoon salt. Cover and keep warm until ready to serve.

7. **To serve:** Ladle a generous spoonful of warm soubise sauce onto each plate, then place a baked chicken roll on top. Serve immediately and enjoy!

NOTES FOR NEXT TIME:

# Tuna Poke Bowl

Poke ("poh-KAY"), Hawaiian raw fish salad, became a favorite of mine after a spring break trip to Kauai with my boys. They had already nudged this Midwest small-town girl into trying sushi in Japan, so I happily dove into fresh poke from a local grocery fish counter—and loved it. My version is inspired by classic ahi shoyu poke: cubes of yellowfin tuna dressed with soy sauce, sesame oil, citrus, and a touch of chili crisp and topped with furikake and crispy shallots. Light, customizable, and full of bright flavors, it's a little taste of Hawaii made simple for two.

### Tuna poke marinade

1 rounded tablespoon spicy chili crisp

2 tablespoons ponzu sauce

1 ½ tablespoons oyster sauce

1 ½ teaspoons fresh lemon juice

1 ½ teaspoons fresh lime juice

2 tablespoons toasted sesame oil

2 tablespoons rice vinegar

2 cloves garlic, finely minced

1 tablespoon honey

¼ to ½ teaspoon wasabi paste, for heat (optional)

2 (4 oz / 115 g each) sashimi-grade tuna steaks, cut into ½-inch (1.3 cm) cubes

### Sushi rice

1 cup (200 g) sushi or short-grain rice, rinsed

1 ½ cups (360 ml) water

### Sushi rice seasoning

¼ to ⅓ cup (60–80 ml) rice vinegar, to taste

1 tablespoon granulated sugar

¼ teaspoon salt

1 tablespoon furikake rice seasoning

### Cucumber salad

½ English cucumber, thinly sliced and quartered

1 avocado, thinly sliced

1 small carrot, finely julienned

2 teaspoons sesame oil

1 tablespoon rice vinegar

Fresh cilantro, chopped

¼ teaspoon salt

### Fried shallot crumbs

2 tablespoons sesame oil

2 shallots, thinly sliced

⅓ cup (30 g) panko breadcrumbs

2 tablespoons sesame seeds, toasted

Salt, to taste

### Spicy mayo

⅓ cup (80 g) olive oil mayonnaise or light mayo

1 tablespoon sriracha (more to taste)

2 teaspoons soy sauce or tamari

1 teaspoon honey

Pickled ginger, for garnish (optional)

1. **Prepare the tuna poke:** In medium bowl, whisk together spicy chili crisp, ponzu sauce, oyster sauce, lemon juice, lime juice, sesame oil, rice vinegar, garlic, and honey. Taste and adjust seasoning. For more spice, add wasabi paste ¼ tsp at a time, whisking and tasting as you go.

    Slice tuna lengthwise, then cut into ½-inch cubes. Add to the marinade and toss to coat. Cover and refrigerate at least 1 hour (or up to overnight for deeper flavor).

2. **Cook the sushi rice:** Place rice in a fine-mesh strainer and rinse under running water until water runs clear, about 1½ minutes. Drain well and transfer to a small saucepan. Add water and bring to a boil over high heat. Reduce heat to maintain a gentle simmer, cover, and cook until water is absorbed, about 20 minutes. While rice is cooking, whisk together rice vinegar, sugar, and salt until dissolved. Remove rice from heat, fluff with a fork, add half the rice vinegar mixture; mix well. Add remaining rice vinegar mixture and furikake. Taste and adjust seasoning. Let the rice sit at room temperature, uncovered, about 20 minutes before using, allowing the vinegary seasoning to absorb.

3. **Make the cucumber salad:** While rice cooks, combine chopped cucumber, carrots, rice vinegar, and 2 teaspoons sesame oil in a bowl. Season with a pinch of salt, toss to coat, and refrigerate until ready to serve.

4. **Make fried shallot crumbs:** In skillet over medium heat, combine sesame oil and shallots. Cook, stirring frequently, until golden brown, about 4–5 minutes. Remove from heat and stir in panko breadcrumbs and sesame seeds. Season with salt and set aside.

5. **Make the spicy mayo:** In a small bowl, whisk together mayo, sriracha, soy sauce, and honey. Adjust seasoning to taste.

6. **Assemble the poke bowl:** Add a scoop of seasoned sushi rice to each bowl. Top with marinated tuna (including a little marinade for extra flavor). Arrange cucumber, avocado, carrots, and pickled ginger around the tuna. Sprinkle with crispy fried shallot crumbs.

7. **Finishing touches:** Drizzle with spicy mayo and garnish with fresh cilantro. Serve immediately and enjoy!

 **NOTES FOR NEXT TIME:**

# Harissa Baked Fish
## in Tomato Fennel Ragu

This recipe brings back memories of an unforgettable week sailing the Mediterranean with my dear friend, Lisa. She makes a fabulous tomato fennel ragu that she's been perfecting for years; a vibrant, layered sauce that highlights the best of these flavors. For added depth, I turned to my secret weapon: rose harissa. Just a spoonful adds a spicy, floral note that takes this ragu to the next level! My go-to fish here is halibut, but Lisa swears by sea bass—and she's right; it's absolutely divine! This dish is one you'll want to make again and again.

**What you need:**

*2 tablespoons olive oil*

*1 cup (150 g) yellow onion, diced*

*1 lb fennel, diced, about 450 g; yields ~1 cup*

*1 tablespoon chopped fennel fronds*

*½ teaspoon fennel seeds*

*2 cloves garlic, finely sliced*

*1 ½ tablespoons rose harissa (or 50% more depending on brand)*

*1 tablespoon tomato paste*

*1 (15-ounce / 425 g) can whole peeled tomatoes with juices*

*1 tablespoon packed brown sugar*

*1 preserved lemon, about 1.5 tablespoons*

*2 (4–6 oz / 115–170 g each) fillets of halibut, hake, cod, or seabass*

*Lemon Tahini Sauce, pg. 226*

**TABLE TALK TIPS:** Rose harissa is one of my secret kitchen weapons! This North African chili paste gets a floral twist from rose petals, adding a sweet balance to its heat. I use Belazu brand (buy online) for its punchy, well-rounded flavor, but if you're using a milder supermarket version, just add about 50% more.

1. **Season fish:** Lightly season fish with a rounded ⅜ teaspoon salt and set aside.
2. **Make harissa sauce:** In a wide and thick-bottom pot or Dutch oven, warm olive oil, then add the onion and fennel with a pinch of salt and cook until soft, about 2 minutes. Add garlic, frying for about a minute until the garlic is starting to turn brown, then add fennel seeds, tomato paste and harissa. Cook until tomato paste turns a deep brownish-red, stirring to keep it from sticking to the bottom of the pot. Pour in canned tomatoes and the juices. Rinse out the can with a splash of water and pour that in too. Add the sugar. Break up tomatoes with a wooden spoon and simmer for about 10 to 15 minutes to thicken the sauce.
3. **Prepare lemon:** Quarter and deseed preserved lemon, then chop into small pieces before adding to the sauce. Add the lemon one tablespoon at a time, tasting as you go to find the right balance. As lemons come in different shapes and sizes, you may need to adjust based on what amount is right for you. As you taste and adjust seasoning. For more spice, add a bit more harissa; as some harissa brands are more mild than others so you may need to increase the amount to your liking.
4. **Bake fish:** Nestle the fish into the tomato sauce, cover and cook for about 5 to 10 minutes, depending on thickness of the fillets, until just cooked.
5. **Finishing touches:** Gently lift out the fish and set aside somewhere warm (like your oven set on lowest setting). If the fish has released a lot of liquid during cooking and the sauce has become runny, increase the heat and let sauce bubble until thick. Taste and add salt if necessary.
6. **To serve:** Transfer fish to a serving dish, pour over the sauce, and finish with lots of tahini sauce and fresh fennel fonds. Serve immediately.

# Baked Halibut en Pappillote

Good things really do come in small packages! Baking halibut en papillote—sealed in parchment—locks in steam so the fish stays tender, moist, and full of flavor. I tried this technique after struggling to keep fish perfectly cooked in a pan, and it was a game-changer. I first discovered this elegant preparation at my college friend Kris's wedding reception in Chicago's historic Café Brauer, where halibut was served alongside mushroom ravioli in Alfredo sauce with peas—a meal so memorable it inspired me to recreate it at home for two.

### Halibut en Papillote

2 halibut fillets, 4–6 oz each (115–170 g), skin removed

¼ teaspoon freshly ground black pepper

½ teaspoon Aleppo pepper (or smoked paprika)

½ tablespoon kosher salt

2 ounces (60 ml) dry white wine

2 tablespoons unsalted butter

### Alfredo Sauce

¾ cup (180 ml) heavy cream

1 large egg yolk

1 tablespoon butter

1 small garlic clove, finely chopped

½ cup (50 g) finely grated Parmesan

Black pepper, to taste

**Mushroom ravioli and peas**

*10 ounces (280 g) fresh mushroom ravioli, pre-packed in the refrigerated section*

*1 tablespoon salt*

*½ cup (75 g) frozen green peas*

**NOTES FOR NEXT TIME:**

1. **Getting started:** Preheat the oven to 375°F (190°C).

2. **Halibut en Papillote:** Cut 12-inch parchment in a heart shape. by folding parchment paper in half lengthwise. Unfold heart and place fish on one half of the parchment fold. Season fish with salt, pepper and aleppo pepper or smoked paprika. Pour 1 tablespoon of white wine and place 1 tablespoon butter over each filet.

3. **Seal the packet:** Fold the other half over the top, then start at one end and make tight, overlapping diagonal folds along the open edge to create a semi-circular, airtight seal. Finish by tucking the final end underneath to secure it. Place the papillote on baking tray and bake 20 – 25 minutes.

   Meanwhile, bring 4 quarts of water in a covered stock pot or Dutch oven to a rolling boil.

4. **Creamy alfredo sauce:** While halibut bakes, whisk cream and egg yolk together in a large measuring cup until combined; set aside.

   In a medium saucepan, melt butter over medium-high heat. Add garlic and sauté until fragrant and sizzling, about 2 minutes. Slowly pour the cream-yolk mixture into the garlic butter, reducing heat immediately to medium. Cook, stirring frequently, until mixture is hot to the touch but not boiling, about 5 minutes.

   Whisk constantly, add in the Parmesan little by little and cook over medium heat, until cheese is melted. Continue cooking until sauce becomes creamy and thickened, stirring frequently, about 3 to 5 minutes. Season to taste with pepper.

5. **Ravioli and peas:** 2-3 minutes before you remove halibut from the oven, add 1 tablespoon salt and the ravioli to boiling water; cook pasta until al dente. Drain pasta and return to now empty stockpot. Drizzle with olive oil to prevent clumping. Meanwhile, heat peas in the microwave following package instructions.

6. **Finishing touches:** Divide ravioli among dinner plates or serving bowls; ladle alfredo sauce over ravioli, gently tossing to coat well. Open the parchment packet, using a spatula, gently slide the filet out and place on top of the bed of ravioli. Garnish with peas and drizzle with extra sauce, if desired.

# Chicken, Leek & Tarragon Pot Pie

There's something undeniably cozy about a pot pie—the golden, flaky crust giving way to a rich, creamy filling that feels like a warm hug on a chilly evening. This version, sized perfectly for two, takes its inspiration from classic French flavors, with leeks and tarragon adding a fragrant depth to tender, poached chicken. What makes this extra special? A homemade stock built right in. As the chicken thighs poach with aromatics, they create a deeply flavorful broth that becomes the base of the luscious sauce. And with a buttery puff pastry lid that crisps up beautifully in the oven, this dish delivers all the indulgence of a traditional pot pie without the fuss of rolling out dough.

**For the chicken:**

2 bone-in, skin-on chicken thighs

Olive oil, for frying

½ yellow onion (75 g), roughly chopped

1 celery stalk (50 g), roughly chopped

1 carrot (70 g), roughly chopped

2 bay leaves

1 tablespoon Kosher salt

**For the Pie:**

1 sheet store-bought puff pastry, thawed according to package directions

1 egg, beaten

Fennel seeds (optional)

1 celery stalk (50 g), halved lengthwise and sliced

½ pound leeks, white and light green parts only, sliced ½ inch thick, washed and dried, about 2 cups / 225 g

2 thick slices smoked bacon, chopped, about 2 oz / 55 g

1½ tablespoons butter

1½ cups (360 ml) poaching broth (from the chicken)

2 tablespoons all-purpose flour

¼ cup (60 ml) dry white wine or dry vermouth

¼ cup (60 ml) heavy cream

1 teaspoon Dijon mustard

½ teaspoon soy sauce

3 tablespoons fresh tarragon leaves, chopped

**For this recipe you will need two-14 ounce ramekins.**

1. **Poach the chicken:** Season chicken thighs generously with salt and let them rest for 30 minutes to 1 hour to allow the salt to penetrate. In a heavy-bottomed pot like a Dutch oven, heat 1 tablespoon oil over medium-low heat until shimmering. Sear chicken thighs until golden brown on both sides—this step builds deep flavor for the broth. Pour in enough water to cover the chicken, then add onion, celery, carrot, and bay leaves. Season with 1 tablespoon salt, bring to a simmer, cover, and cook for about 30 minutes until the chicken is cooked through. Remove chicken from the pot and let it cool on a cutting board. Once cool enough to handle, shred the meat and place the skin and the bones back in the broth. Continue to simmer the broth while you make the filling.

2. **Par-bake puff pastry pie crusts:** Adjust oven rack to middle position and heat oven to 400°F (200°C). Line a rimmed baking sheet with parchment paper. Unroll puff pastry dough onto the baking sheet. Use a 14-ounce oven-safe ramekin as a guide to cut out 2 rounds of dough. If your pastry sheet is too small, roll out the pastry to a size that will fit your ramekins. Then cut 3 vents in center of each crust. Whisk together egg with 1 teaspoon water. Brush pastry tops with egg wash and sprinkle with fennel seeds. Bake until crusts begin to brown and no longer look raw, about 10 minutes; set aside.

3. **Make the filling:** Strain 1 cup broth into a glass measuring cup (you can also use a fat separator with sieve top) and set aside. In the now empty broth pot, add the bacon and cook over medium heat until browned and crispy; add a bit of vegetable oil if your bacon begins sticking to the pan. Once crispy, remove bacon from pan and place on paper towel lined plate. Drain bacon fat from pan (keep all the

browned bits - this adds great flavor), then melt butter in the pan, using medium heat.

4. **Sauté the vegetables:** Add celery and leeks and sauté until leeks begin to soften, about 5 minutes. Sprinkle in flour, stirring gently to keep the leeks intact for texture, until slightly golden, about 1-2 minutes. Add dry vermouth along with ½ cup of the strained poaching broth, stirring gently to combine well. Cover and cook over medium-low heat until vegetables are tender, adding 1 cup of broth. The mixture may look lumpy at first—don't worry it will smooth out as you stir. Continue to cook until thickened. Remove from heat and stir in cream, shredded chicken, mustard, soy sauce, crispy bacon and fresh tarragon. Taste and adjust seasoning, if needed.

5. **Assemble & bake:** Divide the filling between the two ramekins. Place the ramekins on a foil lined baking sheet (to catch any drips) and bake 10 - 15 minutes, until filling is bubbling. Remove from oven and place the puff pastry rounds on top of the hot filling. Continue baking for 10 more minutes, until the crust is golden brown. Let pot pies rest for 10 minutes before serving.

 **NOTES FOR NEXT TIME:**

Spring Lasagna | 145    146 | Chicken Marsala

147 | Seared Salmon    148 | Six-Minute Seared Ahi Tuna Steaks

# Spring Lasagna

That first bundle of asparagus at the co-op is my cue that spring has arrived. This lasagna celebrates the season with tender asparagus, sweet peas, and spinach layered between pasta and a creamy, lemony white sauce. Baked in a loaf pan for three hearty servings, the noodles soften right in the oven—no pre-boiling required. Rustic yet a little decadent, it's full of bright flavor; perfect for those first warm days when daffodils dare to bloom.

**Vegetables & filling**

- 1 lb (450 g) asparagus, trimmed (tips and stalks separated)
- ½ lb (225 g) sweet Italian sausage, casing removed
- ½ teaspoon fennel seeds
- ¼ teaspoon red pepper flakes
- 2 tablespoon olive oil, divided
- ¼ cup (40 g) white onion, finely diced
- 1 garlic clove, minced
- 2 cups (60 g) fresh spinach (about 2 big handfuls)
- ¼ teaspoon Kosher salt
- 1 cup (150 g) peas, fresh or frozen
- 2 oz (60 g) fontina cheese, thinly sliced

**White sauce (Béchamel)**

- 3 tablespoons unsalted butter
- ¼ cup (30 g) all-purpose flour
- 2½ cups (600 ml) whole milk
- 1 bay leaf
- ¼ teaspoon freshly grated nutmeg
- 2 tsp lemon zest
- 1½ tablespoons fresh lemon juice
- ¼ cup (25 g) finely grated Parmesan cheese
- 2 oz (60 g) mild goat cheese
- ½ teaspoon salt, plus more to taste
- ¼ teaspoon freshly ground black pepper

**For assembly**

- 4 dried lasagna noodles (or no-boil or fresh)
- Thin lemon slices, about 2 slices (optional)

1. **Getting started:** Adjust oven rack to middle position and preheat the oven to 400°F (200°C). Lightly oil or butter a standard loaf pan (8½ x 4½ inches). Cut the tips off each asparagus spear and set aside. Slice remaining stalks into ½-inch pieces.

2. **Brown sausage:** In 10-inch skillet over medium heat, add the sausage, fennel seeds, and red pepper flakes. Cook, breaking up the meat with the back of a wooden spoon, until browned and no longer pink, about 6 minutes. Transfer to a paper towel-lined plate.

3. **Sauté aspargus:** In the same pan, add 1 tablespoon olive oil and chopped asparagus stalks. Cook until bright green and just tender, about 4 minutes. Remove and set aside. Add remaining 1 tablespoon olive oil, then gently cook garlic for 30 seconds, followed by onion. Sauté until translucent, about 3 minutes. Add spinach and ¼ tsp salt. Stir just until wilted. Remove from heat.

4. **Make white sauce:** In medium saucepan, melt butter over medium-low heat. Add flour and whisk until the mixture is smooth and golden, 2–3 minutes. Slowly pour in milk, whisking constantly. Add bay leaf and nutmeg. Cook, stirring frequently, until thickened, about 8–10 minutes. Remove from heat. Discard bay leaf, whisk in lemon zest and juice, Parmesan, goat cheese, ½ tsp salt, and pepper. Taste and adjust seasoning.

5. **Assemble the lasagna:** Spread about ½ cup white sauce in the bottom of the loaf pan. Add a noodle. Layer with half the asparagus, half the sausage, a few slices of fontina, and about ⅔ cup sauce. Top with another noodle, then spinach mixture, peas, ⅔ cup sauce. Top with third noodle, remaining sausage, a few more slices of fontina, and anothe ⅔ cup of sauce. Top with the final noodle, ⅓ cup of sauce, reserved asparagus tips, and lemon slices, if using.

6. **Bake, rest, serve:** Place loaf pan on a rimmed baking sheet. Cover with foil and bake 28 minutes. Remove foil and bake until golden and bubbling, 18–20 minutes more. Broil for a minute or two if you'd like more browning on top. Let lasagna rest for at least 10 minutes before slicing and serving.

# Chicken Marsala
## with Pancetta, Mushrooms and Shallots

Chicken Marsala is a timeless Italian dish that feels both comforting and elegant, especially when made for two. Mushrooms take the spotlight, with pancetta and roasted shallots adding savory depth to the silky Marsala sauce. Using authentic Sicilian Marsala wine brings out nutty vanilla notes, though a simple grape juice and vinegar blend makes a great substitute. Served with pasta, polenta or potatoes, it's a restaurant-worthy meal made cozy at home.

**What you need**

*2 (6 to 8 oz /170–225 g) boneless, skinless chicken breasts*

*2 tablespoons Dijon mustard*

*6 fresh sage leaves*

*2 oz (60 g) pancetta, diced*

*3 tablespoons olive oil, divided*

*1 tablespoon balsamic vinegar*

*4 oz (115 g) button mushrooms, halved*

*5 shallot cloves, cut in half*

*¼ cup (30 g) all-purpose flour or gluten-free all-purpose flour*

*¾ cup (180 ml) sweet Marsala wine*

*½ cup (120 ml) heavy cream*

*Salt and pepper, to taste*

**TABLE TALK TIPS:** Cooking without alcohol? Swap 3/4 cup Marsala wine with ¼ cup + 2 tablespoons white grape juice, 2 tablespoons sherry vinegar, and 1 tablespoon vanilla extract for a flavorful substitute.

 **NOTES FOR NEXT TIME:**

1. **Roast the shallots and mushrooms:** Preheat oven to 400°F (200°C). Toss shallots and mushrooms into a baking dish with 1 tablespoon olive oil and the vinegar. Roast 30 minutes, stirring several times.

2. **Prepare the chicken:** While shallots and mushrooms are roasting, place each chicken breast on a large sheet of plastic wrap, cover with second sheet.

   Starting in the center of each breast, pound evenly out toward the edges, taking care not to tear the flesh. Pound with meat pounder or rolling pin until ½-inch thick throughout. Spread 1 teaspoon mustard on one side of each breast and press 2 sage leaves into the mustard side of the breast.

3. **Cooking pancetta:** Heat 1 tablespoon oil in a large skillet and cook pancetta until it is crisp and lightly brown, about 4 – 5 minutes. Remove pancetta and set aside on paper towel to drain.

4. **Sautéing chicken:** Spread flour in shallow dish. Working with 1 breast at a time, dredge in flour to coat both sides, lightly shaking off any excess flour. In the empty pancetta skillet, add another tablespoon of oil and heat over medium-high heat until it begins to shimmer.

   Lay chicken in skillet and cook until well-browned on first side, about 4-5 minutes. Flip chicken, reduce heat to medium and continue to cook, about 3-4 minutes. Transfer to a plate and tent loosely with aluminum foil.

5. **Making the Marsala sauce:** Raise heat to medium-high, whisk in the Marsala, scraping up any browned bits. Add the cream and bring to a simmer, cooking until sauce is slightly thickened, about 3 minutes. Add remaining mustard and sage and give it a stir. Return chicken and half of the pancetta to skillet to reheat. Taste and adjust seasoning with salt and pepper.

6. **To serve:** Top chicken with pancetta, roasted mushrooms and shallots, spoon the sauce over the top.

# Baked Salmon
## with Oregon Cherry Glaze

Salmon feels fancy but is surprisingly effortless, especially with this cherry balsamic glaze. The glaze comes together in minutes—fresh cherries simmered with balsamic and black pepper for a tangy-sweet finish. I was inspired by a road trip through Oregon's Fruit Loop, where cherry stands lined roads and Columbia River salmon stands seem to be around every corner. The result is an elegant, no-fuss dinner with big flavor and easy cleanup.

**What you need:**

½ cup (75 g) red cherries or Rainier cherries, pitted and sliced into quarters — you can smash the cherry with the flat edge of a knife to easily remove the pit. Frozen cherries also work.

3 tablespoons light brown sugar

2 tablespoons balsamic vinegar

¼ teaspoon coarse salt

¼ teaspoon freshly ground black pepper

2 tablespoons dry white wine

2 salmon fillets, skin on, about 4 ounces (115 g) each

**NOTES FOR NEXT TIME:**

1. **Prepping the fish:** Adjust oven rack to the lowest position and line a rimmed baking sheet with parchment paper for easy clean up. Place the rimmed baking sheet on the oven rack and heat the oven to 500°F (260°C). For prepping the fish, make 4 or 5 shallow cuts about 1 inch (2.5 cm) apart along the skin side of each piece of salmon, being careful not to cut into flesh.

2. **Make the balsamic cherry glaze:** Place cherries, brown sugar, balsamic vinegar, salt, pepper, and wine in a saucepan and bring to a boil over medium/high heat, stirring to combine ingredients and dissolve sugar. Reduce heat to simmer and cook for 5-7 minutes, or until sauce has reduced and is thick enough to coat the back of a spoon. Remove from heat.

3. **Season and glaze fish:** Pat salmon dry with paper towels. Portion out about 2 tablespoons of glaze into a separate cup (to avoid cross contamination or glaze touching raw fish and then cooked fish) and brush glaze onto the salmon fillets, coating each one thoroughly. Season the fish with salt and pepper. Reduce oven to 275°F (135°C) and remove baking sheet. Place salmon skin side down on the hot parchment lined baking sheet. Roast until the thickest part of fillets registers 125°F (52°C), 9 to 13 minutes.

4. **Time to serve:** Remove from oven. Move fish to a serving platter and spoon remaining glaze generously over the fish.

**TABLE TALK TIPS:** I like to serve this on a bed of mashed potatoes. I boil my potatoes before I make the glaze, then I mash them while salmon is in the oven.

**LOCAL FLAIR:** Buy cherries from a local fruit stand and buy salmon from businesses committed to sustainable seafood (ASC-certified).

# Six-Minute Seared Ahi Tuna Steaks

This recipe comes from my dear friend Juli, who made it for us during a cabin weekend—one of those "up north" getaways that Mark and I never pass up. Cabin weekends with friends are the best, filled with laughter, good food, and stories that stretch late into the night. Juli's son Matt, who lives on the Gulf Coast of Texas, is an avid fisherman. He's always coming up with new ways to enjoy his fresh catch and this tuna recipe is one of his best. It's a keeper.

**What you need:**

2 ahi tuna yellowfin steaks, about 115 g each, 2.5 cm thick — see notes for thinner or thicker cuts)

2 tablespoons soy sauce

1 tablespoon toasted sesame oil (see notes)

1 tablespoon honey (see notes)

½ teaspoon kosher salt

¼ teaspoon black pepper

¼ teaspoon cayenne pepper (optional, but adds a nice kick!)

1 tablespoon canola or olive oil

Green onions, toasted sesame seeds, and lime wedges for serving (optional)

1. **Prep the tuna:** Pat tuna steaks dry with a paper towel—this helps get a good sear. Place on a plate or inside a zip-top bag.

2. **Make the marinade:** In a small bowl, whisk together soy sauce, toasted sesame oil, honey, kosher salt (skip this if marinating for more than an hour—see tips), black pepper, and cayenne if using. Make sure the honey dissolves completely. Pour marinade over the tuna, turning the steaks to coat evenly. Let them sit for at least 10 minutes (or up to overnight in the fridge for deeper flavor). If you want extra sauce for drizzling later, set aside a spoonful or two before adding the fish.

3. **Sear tuna:** Place a medium skillet (nonstick or cast iron) over medium-high to high heat. You want it hot—cast iron needs about 3-5 minutes to preheat, while nonstick takes about a minute. If your stove runs really hot, keep the heat at medium-high to prevent burning the marinade. Add canola or olive oil to the hot pan. Carefully lay in the tuna steaks and sear for:

    - **Very rare:** 30 seconds per side
    - **Medium-rare:** 1–1½ minutes per side (my favorite!)
    - **Medium-well to well:** 2–2½ minutes per side

    (Remember, stove temperatures vary, so trust your instincts—if the marinade starts to burn, lower the heat!)

4. **Time to serve:** Transfer tuna to a cutting board and slice into ½-inch thick pieces. Serve immediately with a sprinkle of green onions, toasted sesame seeds, and a squeeze of fresh lime juice if you like.

 **NOTES FOR NEXT TIME:**

**TABLE TALK TIPS:** Cooking time depends on thickness. If your tuna is thinner than 1 inch, keep it under a minute per side. If it's thicker, go for 2 minutes per side.

**Marinating tip:** If marinating for more than an hour, skip the kosher salt—it'll get too salty.

**Want to grill it instead?** High heat, about 1 minute per side.

**For a simple version:** Skip the honey and sesame oil and just use soy sauce.

**Carryover cooking is real!** Slice immediately for a more rare center, or let it rest for a couple of minutes if you like it more cooked through.

# Turkey Breast
## with Grandma's Stuffing

This Thanksgiving dinner menu may be scaled down in size, but certainly not in flavor. Turkey and stuffing are a perfect pair on the plate and we cook them together in one pan, not only cutting down on dirty dishes, but also creating a stuffing packed with savory poultry flavor.

As an homage to my grandmother's stuffing, we combine sage, onion, celery, wine, chicken broth and an apple for a flavorful turkey stuffing. Instead of small cubes of sandwich bread, we opted for larger chunks of ciabatta. The bigger pieces retained some chew even as they soaked up flavors from the turkey. We roast the turkey breast on top of the stuffing and when the breast is done, we'll pop just the stuffing back into the oven, crisping the top.

**Turkey**

¾ tablespoons kosher salt

½ tablespoon pepper

½ tablespoon minced fresh thyme leaves

3 pound (1.4 kg) bone-in split turkey breast, trimmed

**For the stuffing**

¼ cup (60 ml) extra-virgin olive oil

1 ½ cups (210 g) onion, chopped

1 ¼ teaspoons kosher salt, divided

1 ½ cups (150 g) celery stalks, chopped

2 garlic cloves, minced

½ cup (60 g) Granny Smith apple, chopped into ¼-inch (0.5 cm) pieces (unpeeled, if preferred)

1 ½ cups (360 ml) chicken broth

¼ cup (60 ml) dry white wine

1 large egg, lightly whisked

1 tablespoon unsalted butter

1 teaspoon poultry seasoning

1 tablespoon fresh sage, finely chopped

½ tablespoon fresh thyme leaves, minced

1 pound (450 g) ciabatta, cut into 1-inch (2.5 cm) cubes (about 10 cups) - If you can't find ciabatta, substitute another rustic, mild white bread. Avoid sourdough, as its flavor is too assertive.

**Mashed potatoes and gravy**

see Table Talk Tips for mashed potatoes and pg.221 for homemade gravy.

1. **Dry brine the turkey:** Combine salt, pepper, and thyme in a small bowl. Place turkey on large plate and pat dry with paper towels. Sprinkle all over with salt mixture. Refrigerate, uncovered for at least 2 hours, or up to 24 hours.

2. **Make the stuffing:** Adjust rack to lower-middle position and heat oven to 325°F (163°C). If you have a convection oven this is the time to use it! Spray 12- inch oven safe skillet or cast iron skillet with PAM® vegetable oil spray, then add oil to pan. Heat oil in skillet over medium heat until shimmering. Add onion and pinch of salt, cooking until onion becomes soft and translucent, about 5 minutes. Place celery in the pan and continue to cook until onion is golden brown, another 5 minutes. Add garlic and apple, cooking until garlic is fragrant, about 30 seconds.

   Remove skillet from heat, stir in broth, wine, butter, and lightly whisked egg, poultry seasoning, sage, thyme and remaining ¾ teaspoon salt, scraping up any brown bits. Add bread and, using tongs or your hands, toss until bread is evenly coated.

   Nestle turkey breast, skin side up into stuffing in center of roasting pan. Roast until thickest part of the breast registers 160°F (71°C), 1 ¼ to 1 ¾ hours.

# Turkey Breast *(continued)*

1. **How about some potatoes and gravy?** If making mashed potatoes, now is the time to peel, cut and boil the potatoes. See Table Talk Tips for instructions. For homemade gravy see pg.221 for ingredients and instructions.

2. **Finishing touches:** Transfer turkey to carving board, skin side up, and let rest uncovered, for at least 30 minutes, or up to 1 hour. Meanwhile, stir stuffing in the skillet. Return skillet to oven and cook until top of bread looks golden brown and evenly dry, about 10 to 15 minutes. Remove breast meat from bone and slice thinly crosswise. Arrange turkey over stuffing in skillet. Drizzle with gravy (pg.221), if desired. Serve, passing remaining gravy separately.

**TABLE TALK TIPS:** For mashed potatoes: 45 minutes before pulling the turkey breast from the oven, place 1½ pounds of potatoes cut into evenly-sized chunks in a large pot of cold water, so the water line sits about 1 inch above the potatoes. Add 1 teaspoon sea salt into the water. Bring water to a boil, reduce heat to medium-high to maintain the boil and continue to cook until fork tender, about 10 – 12 minutes. Drain water from pot and mash the potatoes to desired consistency. Fold in 1-2 tablespoons butter, about ¼ cup milk, 2 tablespoons sour cream and salt to taste. Keep warm in oven until ready to serve.

For a homemade gravy, try my recipe on pg.221

NOTES FOR NEXT TIME:

Roasted Beets
Pg. 158

Chive Popovers
Pg. 159

Apple and Winter
Squash Salad Pg. 173

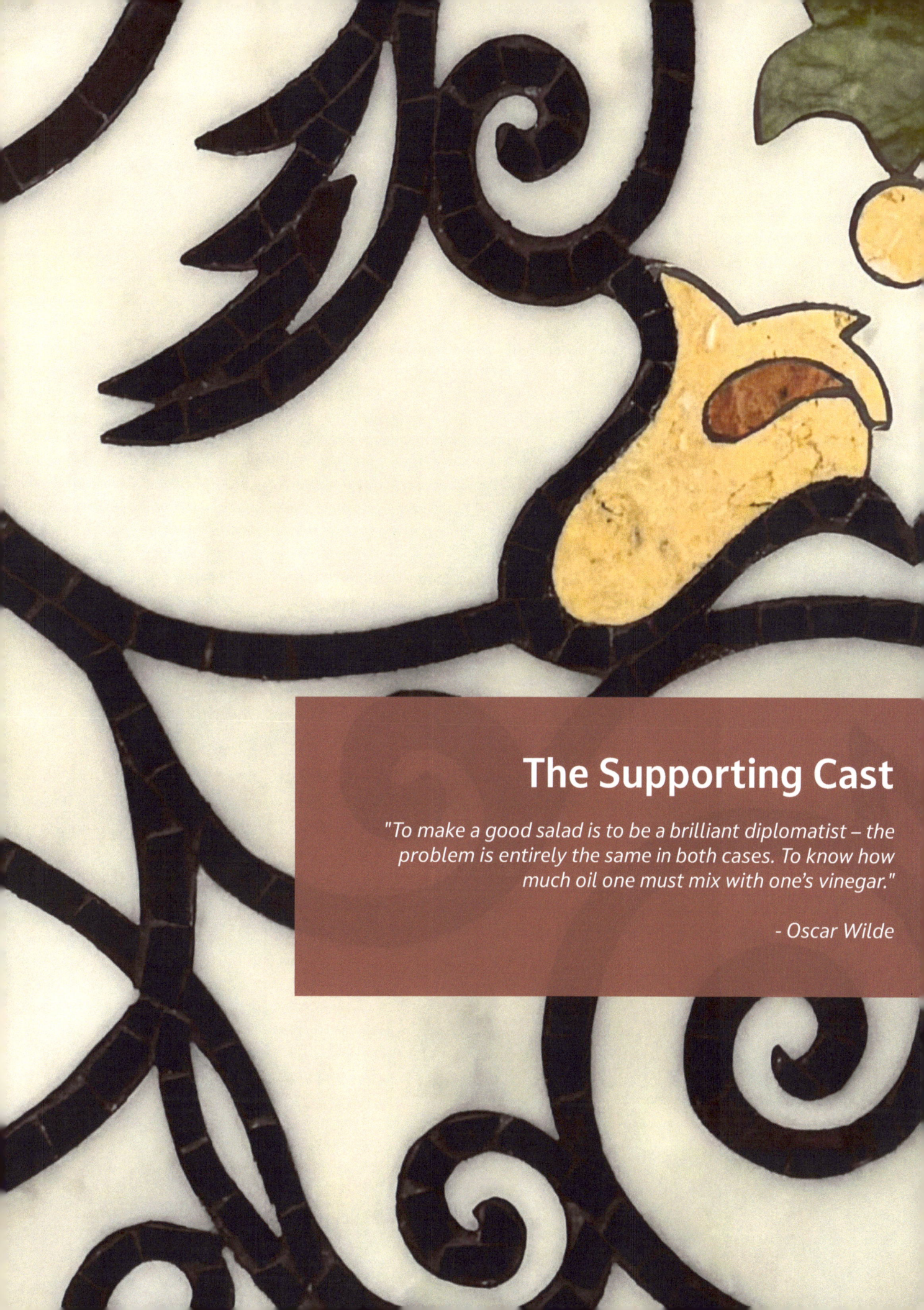

# The Supporting Cast

"To make a good salad is to be a brilliant diplomatist – the problem is entirely the same in both cases. To know how much oil one must mix with one's vinegar."

- Oscar Wilde

# Parmesan-Crusted Salmon Caesar Salad

I've always loved Caesar salad—especially my mom's version, with a dressing so good even the grandkids make it on their own. In this recipe, that same dressing works two ways; as the salad topper and as a quick marinade for the salmon. The trick is brining the salmon first—it only takes minutes, but it makes the fish buttery, tender, and perfectly seasoned. Add a crisp Parmesan crust and homemade croutons, and you've got a Caesar salad that feels both classic and a little extra special.

**For the brine**

2 tablespoons table salt

2 tablespoons sugar

1 quart (960 ml) cold water

**For the salad**

1 small baguette, torn into 1-inch (2.5 cm) chunks

1 teaspoon garlic powder, divided

Salt and freshly cracked black pepper

1 tablespoon olive oil or melted butter

½ cup (120 g) mayonnaise

1 tablespoon lemon juice

1 teaspoon coarse-ground Dijon mustard

1 teaspoon Worcestershire sauce

1 teaspoon fish sauce

¼ cup (25 g) finely grated Parmesan, plus extra for serving

2 skinless salmon fillets (4 to 6 ounces / 115 to 170 g each)

1 small head romaine lettuce, about ½ pound / 225 g, chopped into bite-sized pieces

1. **Brine the salmon:** In a large container, dissolve the salt and sugar in 1 quart of cold water. Submerge the salmon fillets and let stand at room temperature for 15 minutes. Remove from brine and pat dry with paper towels.

2. **Make the croutons:** Preheat the oven to 350°F (175°C) and place a rack 8 inches from the broiler. On a baking sheet, toss the torn baguette pieces with ½ teaspoon garlic powder, salt, pepper, and olive oil or butter. Spread in an even layer and bake for 10 to 12 minutes, tossing halfway through, until golden brown and crispy on the outside but slightly chewy inside. Transfer to a large bowl.

3. **Prepare the dressing & Parmesan coating:** In a medium bowl, whisk together mayonnaise, lemon juice, Dijon mustard, Worcestershire sauce, fish sauce, remaining ½ teaspoon garlic powder, and ½ teaspoon black pepper. Adjust seasoning if needed. In a small bowl, mix 2 tablespoons of the dressing with 2 tablespoons of grated Parmesan—this will be used to coat the salmon.

4. **Season salmon:** Lightly season salmon fillets with salt and pepper. Using a pastry brush, coat the fillets generously with reserved Parmesan dressing. Sprinkle the remaining 2 tablespoons Parmesan on top.

5. **Broil salmon:** Place fish skin side down, on a wire rack in a rimmed baking sheet lined with aluminum foil and broil for 3 to 5 minutes, until the surface is golden and bubbling. If it starts to smoke, move the pan to a lower rack. Continue cooking until the center registers 125°F (52°C) for medium-rare (about 6 to 9 minutes). Let the salmon rest for a few minutes.

6. **Assemble the salad:** In a large bowl, toss the romaine, croutons, and shallot with remaining Caesar dressing. Divide the salad between two plates. Using a fish spatula, remove the salmon from the skin and place a fillet on top of each salad. Finish with an extra sprinkle of Parmesan and serve immediately.

Supperclub Creamed Spinach Casserole | 157

158 | Apple Kohlrabi and Manchego Slaw

Roasted Beets | 158

159 | Chive Popovers

# Supperclub Creamed Spinach Casserole

Creamed spinach just feels like comfort, doesn't it? Rich, cozy, and a little nostalgic—like something you find at a supper club or classic steakhouse. My version adds a few twists: a pinch of red pepper flakes for warmth, Monterey Jack for extra meltiness, and a quick "beurre manié" (a fancy French paste of butter and flour) to keep it creamy without turning heavy. I love that you can make it with frozen spinach—super easy and still delicious—or swap in fresh if that's what's in your fridge. A golden panko topping gives it that irresistible crunch, and it's the perfect side for Beef Wellington (pg.93) or short ribs (pg.119).

**Spinach gratin**

1 (10-ounce / 285 g) package fresh baby spinach or frozen chopped spinach (do not thaw if frozen)

2 tablespoons unsalted butter, divided, plus more for buttering the baking dish

1 tablespoon all-purpose flour

1 tablespoon finely chopped shallot

1 garlic clove, minced

1 cup (250 ml) whole milk, half-and-half, or heavy cream

Freshly ground black pepper

¼ teaspoon celery salt

3 ounces (85 g) Monterey Jack cheese, cut into small cubes

¼ teaspoon crushed red pepper flakes

**Topping**

¼ cup (15 g) panko bread crumbs

2 teaspoons unslated butter, melted

1. **Getting started:** Preheat oven to 300°F (150°C). If using fresh spinach, skip ahead to the next step. If using frozen spinach, cook it according to the package instructions. Drain well, reserving about 1 cup of the cooking liquid (you won't need it all, but keep it just in case). Chop the spinach finely.

2. **Prepare your casserole dish:** Butter a shallow 2- to 3-cup baking dish or ramekin. In a small bowl, use a fork to mash 1 tablespoon softened butter with the flour to form a smooth paste (this is your beurre manié). Set aside.

3. **Cook the aromatics:** In a medium saucepan over medium heat, melt the remaining 1 tablespoon butter. Add the shallot and garlic and cook for 1 to 2 minutes until soft and translucent—but don't let them take on color. Keep it gentle here.

4. **Spinach time:** Add the spinach to the pan, turning with tongs to coat. If using fresh spinach, you may need to add it in batches. Don't worry if the pan seems dry at first—once the spinach starts to wilt, it'll release moisture. Cook until just wilted and heated through, about 4 minutes.

5. **Make it creamy:** Pour in ¾ up milk (or cream) and bring to a gentle simmer. Stir in the butter-flour paste, a few grinds of black pepper, celery salt, crushed red pepper flakes, and cheese. Stir until everything is melted and the sauce clings to the spinach, about 3 minutes. If the mixture looks too thick, you can stir in a splash of the reserved spinach liquid or more milk, 2 tablespoons at a time to loosen it slightly.

6. **Assemble and bake:** Spoon the mixture into the prepared baking dish. In a small bowl, toss the panko with 1 to 2 teaspoons melted butter. Sprinkle evenly over the top. Bake for 40 to 45 minutes, until the topping is golden and edges are bubbling slightly.

 **NOTES FOR NEXT TIME:**

# Apple Kohlrabi and Manchego Slaw

As soon as kohlrabi shows up at the market, I'm ready to make this slaw. It was inspired by a salad I first tried at Café Lurcat in Minneapolis—a simple mix of apple, Manchego, and chives that left a big impression. My version leans into that same crisp freshness, with kohlrabi matchsticks, sweet apple, nutty Manchego, and toasted pine nuts for crunch. Even though this recipe serves two, I've been known to eat the whole bowl myself—it's that good.

**What you need:**

- 1 tablespoon grapeseed oil, canola oil, or another neutral oil
- 1 tablespoon apple cider vinegar
- 2 teaspoons maple syrup
- 1 teaspoon Dijon coarse-grain mustard (country style)
- ¼ teaspoon fine sea salt
- ½ to ¾ medium apple, cored and cut into matchsticks
- ½ to ¾ medium kohlrabi or jicama, peeled and cut into matchsticks
- 2 tablespoons shallots, diced
- 2 tablespoons pine nuts, toasted and chopped
- 1.5 ounces (40 g) Manchego cheese, cut into 3-inch (7.5 cm) matchsticks
- 2 tablespoons finely chopped parsley, plus more for garnish
- Freshly ground black pepper

1. **Make the dressing:** In the bottom of a large bowl, whisk together oil, vinegar, maple syrup, mustard, and salt.
2. **Toss together and season:** Add the apple, kohlrabi, onion, pine nuts, cheese and parsley, and toss to coat. Season to taste with salt and pepper, garnish with additional parsley, and serve.

# Roasted Beets
## with Creamy Miso-Tahini Sauce

I love roasted beet salads, and this version was inspired by a dish I had at a Japanese restaurant in Jackson, Wyoming. The earthy sweetness of roasted beets pairs beautifully with the creamy tofu-tahini sauce, enhanced with a touch of miso for umami depth. A drizzle of ponzu adds brightness, while crispy potato chips and fresh mint create a contrast of textures.

**For the sauce**

- 1 block medium-(14–16 ounces / 400–450 g) firm tofu
- 2 tablespoons tahini
- 3 tablespoons white miso paste
- ½ cup (120 ml) broth, vegetable or chicken
- 1 tablespoon sugar
- ½ cup (120 ml) coconut milk

**For the beets**

- 1 cup (200 g) beets, trimmed, peeled, and cut into ½-inch (1.25 cm) wedges, about 2 medium beets
- 1 tablespoon olive oil
- ¼ teaspoon kosher salt
- Freshly ground black pepper, to taste
- 1 tablespoon ponzu sauce

**Garnish**

- Fresh mint leaves, chopped
- Lemon zest, finely grated
- Potato chips (optional)

**TABLE TALK TIPS:** If tofu isn't your thing, you can make a quick lemon-tahini sauce (pg.226) instead of the tofu-tahini sauce.

1. **Make the sauce:** Bring a small pot of water to a boil and add the block of tofu, ensuring it's fully submerged. Simmer 5 minutes, then drain and let cool slightly. In a high-speed blender, combine tofu, tahini, miso paste, broth, sugar, and coconut milk. Blend until smooth and creamy. Transfer to the refrigerator to chill.

2. **Roast the beets:** Preheat oven to 450°F (230°C) and position a rack in the middle. In a bowl, toss the beet wedges with a drizzle of olive oil, ¼ teaspoon salt, and ⅛ teaspoon pepper until completely coated. Spread them out on a baking sheet and roast 25–30 minutes, or until fork-tender. Let cool slightly.

3. **Assemble:** Toss roasted beets with the ponzu sauce. Spread a layer of the chilled tofu sauce on a serving plate. Pile the ponzu-dressed beets on top. Garnish with fresh mint, potato chips, and a sprinkle of lemon zest. Serve immediately and enjoy!

# Chive Popovers
## A Little Taste of Dayton's Magic

I still remember my first popover at Dayton's department store in Minneapolis—it felt like the fanciest treat in the world. Crisp and golden on the outside, tender and custardy inside, it was pure magic on a plate in the River Room, Sky Room, or Oak Grille. Dayton's may be gone, but every time I bake these popovers, I'm transported back to those special meals. This small-batch version makes just three—perfect for two, with one extra to savor tomorrow.

**What you need:**

- 2 large eggs
- 1 egg yolk
- ⅔ cup + 2 tablespoons (180 ml) whole milk
- 2½ tablespoons unsalted butter, melted
- ⅔ cup + 2 tablespoons (95 g) all-purpose flour
- Pinch of salt
- 2 tablespoons fresh chives, minced (optional)

1. **Getting started:** Crank up your oven to 400°F (200°C). Lightly coat three cups of a popover pan (or three pyrex custard cups) with nonstick spray. Stick the pan in the oven for at least 10-15 minutes to preheat—it's crucial for that big puff!

2. **Whisk eggs:** In a medium bowl, beat the egg with a whisk or mixer until frothy—like the bubbles on a cappuccino. Pour in milk and melted butter, mixing until smooth.

3. **Add dry ingredients:** Lower your mixing speed (or switch to a gentle whisk) and gradually add flour, salt, and chives, if using. Mix until just combined—try not to over mix. Let the batter chill for at least 15 minutes, up to 30 minutes. The longer the better!

4. **Pour into pan:** Carefully take the hot pan out of the oven. Divide batter evenly into three of the pre-heated cups, filling each just over halfway to ¾ full. Fill unused cups halfway with water to even out heat distribution.

5. **Bake:** Slide the pan into the oven and bake 30-35 minutes. Resist the urge to peek! Do not open the oven during the first 30 minutes of baking; if possible, use the oven window and light to monitor popovers.

6. **Serve 'em hot:** When your popovers are puffed and golden brown, transfer pans to a wire rack and cool 2 minutes. They should release from the pan easily—if not, gently coax them out with a butter knife.

# Roasted Vegetable Platter

When I first made this dish, life threw a curveball—Mark had a bike crash, and we spent the evening in the ER. Hours later, I came home to find the vegetables still beautiful and delicious, proof that roasted veggies are as resilient as they are versatile. Cut them a day ahead, roast a few hours before serving, then reheat or serve at room temperature—they'll always deliver. Garnish with pomegranate seeds, herbs, garlicky yogurt, or hot honey (or swap in tahini sauce for a vegan twist). Serve alongside grilled meat, tuck into tacos and sandwiches, or pile onto rice for a colorful veggie bowl.

### Roasted vegetables

1 small sweet potato, peeled and cut into ½-inch (1.25 cm) cubes

1 small zucchini, cut into thick slices, or ½ head purple, white, or orange cauliflower, cut into bite-sized florets

½ red bell pepper, cut into strips, or ½ pound (225 g) broccolini (about 1 stalk), trimmed and stalk quartered

2 spring onions or 2 shallots, cut into wedges

2 carrots, peeled, stems trimmed to leave a little green, and cut into long ½-inch (1.25 cm) batons

1 fennel bulb, trimmed but core left intact, cut lengthwise; reserve fronds for garnish

2 tablespoons olive oil

½ teaspoon kosher salt

¼ teaspoon black pepper

½ teaspoon rose harissa, smoked paprika, or ground cumin for earthy flavor

### Garlicky yogurt sauce

5 ounces (140 g) plain whole milk yogurt

1 small garlic clove, grated

1 teaspoon lemon juice

Pinch of salt

### Garnishes (choose your favorites!)

Pomegranate seeds

Toasted cumin seeds

Fennel fronds

Chopped fresh parsley, mint, or a mix of herbs — a good handful

Drizzle of pomegranate syrup

Sprinkle of rice vinegar

Tuscan Salt (pg. 225) or flaked sea salt

1. **Prep the vegetables:** Preheat your oven to 425°F (218°C) and line a large baking sheet with parchment paper for easy cleanup. In the bottom of a large bowl, whisk together olive oil, salt, pepper, and rose harissa, to create a flavorful base. Add your prepared vegetables and gently toss until everything is well coated—use your hands or a large spoon to make sure every piece gets some love. Spread vegetables out in a single layer on the parchment-lined baking sheet, making sure they aren't crowded. If needed, use two pans.

2. **Roast the vegetables:** Roast until they're golden and caramelized at the edges. Use this timing guide to help you stagger or remove veggies as they finish:
    - Zucchini or broccolini: 10 to 15 minutes
    - Red peppers, onions or shallots: 15 to 20 minutes
    - Fennel: 20 to 25 minutes
    - Cauliflower: 25 to 35 minutes
    - Sweet potatoes or squash: 30 to 35 minutes
    - Carrots: 30 to 40 minutes

    As each vegetable finishes roasting, transfer to a serving platter. You're aiming for tender centers with golden, slightly crispy edges.

    Want more color and a deeper char? Return all the veggies to the sheet pan once everything is roasted, and place under the broiler for 2 minutes—just watch closely so they don't burn.

3. **Make the yogurt sauce:** While the vegetables roast, stir together the Greek yogurt, grated garlic, lemon juice, and a pinch of salt in a small bowl. Taste and adjust—it should be bright, creamy, and just garlicky enough.

4. **Assemble and garnish:** Layer roasted vegetables on a serving platter in a way that shows off their colors and shapes. Drizzle with the garlicky yogurt. Go wild with garnish: scatter pomegranate seeds, sprinkle with rice vinegar, and tuck in fresh herbs like parsley or mint. Finish with a drizzle of pomegranate syrup and fennel fronds. Serve warm or at room temperature.

 **NOTES FOR NEXT TIME:**

**TABLE TALK TIPS:** This dish is flexible, make-ahead friendly, and downright stunning. You can roast them a few hours before serving, and reheat them for 7 to 15 minutes at 350°F (177°C) to 400°F (204°C) - they are very forgiving, Another option is to serve them at room temperature. .

**SERVING SUGGESTIONS:** Serve with grilled meats or spoon into a warm tortilla for veggie tacos, or serve over rice for a simple, satisfying meal.

# Bookclub Quinoa Chicken Salad

In our book club, this Quinoa Chicken Salad is practically a rite of passage—every new member gets introduced to it like a secret handshake. Fresh, bright, and just the right mix of hearty and healthy, it's the dish that always keeps the table happy. I usually lean on a rotisserie chicken for ease, but if you want to go all out, try cooking your own with my homemade stock recipe—you'll get tender chicken and a freezer stash of broth for later. For Minnesota cooks, Ferndale Market's organic chicken makes this salad taste even more special.

### Salad

- 1 cup (170 g) quinoa, rinsed and drained
- 2 ounces (55 g) slivered almonds, toasted
- 1 bunch green onions, thinly sliced, about ½ cup / 50 g
- ½ cup (15 g) fresh parsley, chopped
- ½ cup (75 g) red seedless grapes, halved
- ½ Granny Smith apple, cubed about 60 g
- 1 cup (140 g) cubed cooked chicken breast — rotisserie chicken or roasted chicken breast from the deli works well. Ask for a thick slice, about ½ inch / 1.25 cm and cube it at home.
- ½ cup (75 g) red bell pepper, diced (optional)

### Dressing

- 2 tablespoons apple cider vinegar
- 3 tablespoons good quality olive oil
- Juice and zest of 1 lemon
- 1 tablespoon honey
- 1 garlic clove, crushed or finely chopped
- ¼ teaspoon kosher salt
- ¼ teaspoon freshly ground black pepper
- 1–2 teaspoons curry powder to taste
- 1 teaspoon cumin

**TABLE TALK TIPS** *(from a book club member):* Put apple cubes in resealable plastic bag, add ⅛-¼ c fresh lemon juice and shake to cover - reduces discoloration.

1. **Cook the quinoa:** Combine quinoa and 1 ¾ cups water (415 ml) in a medium pot. Bring to a boil, cover, and reduce heat. Simmer 15 minutes. Remove pot from heat and let it sit, covered, 10 minutes more. Remove lid and fluff with a fork. Set aside and let it cool to room temperature

2. **Whisk the dressing:** In a small bowl, whisk together vinegar, lemon, honey, garlic, salt, pepper, curry and cumin until well combined. Slowly drizzle in the oil while whisking continuously, until the dressing is fully blended and smooth.

3. **Mix the quinoa salad:** In a large salad bowl, gently toss the quinoa and the rest of the salad ingredients together with about half of dressing - just enough to coat everything nicely. This quinoa salad can be made a day ahead if you want to get a jump on things. Just pop it in the fridge until you're ready to serve.

4. **Assemble and serve:** When you're ready to eat, lay a bed of mixed greens on a large platter or individual plates., Drizzle greens with just enough dressing to lightly coat. Pile quinoa mixture over the greens. Drizzle remaining dressing over the top.

 NOTES FOR NEXT TIME:

Spicy Cucumber Salad | 165      166 | Artichoke and Ricotta Flan

Lagoon Wild Rice Salad | 167      169 | Deviled Egg Salad

# Spicy Cucumber Salad

CSA season always meant coming home with a canvas bag brimming with farm-fresh veggies and a folded newsletter from Spring Hill Farm. For decades, Mark and I have belonged to a CSA, and every summer we found ourselves swimming in cucumbers—more than we could ever imagine finishing. It became a fun little race to use them up before the next week's share arrived and that challenge is exactly how we stumbled on this recipe.

This Spicy Cucumber Salad came from one of those newsletters—a single sheet of paper, but always filled with produce notes and recipe gold. I've been making it ever since. The secret is slicing the cucumbers paper-thin (I use my mandoline on the number 2 setting) and salting them first so they stay perfectly crisp in that sweet-and-spicy dressing. A handful of crushed peanuts adds crunch and depth, making it a quick, bold, and refreshing dish that feels just right on a summer night.

**What you need:**

- ¾ pound (340 g) English cucumber, peeled, halved lengthwise, and thinly sliced; (use a mandoline on setting #2 if you have one)
- 1 teaspoon kosher salt
- ¼ cup (60 ml) unseasoned rice vinegar
- ¼ (60 ml) cup water
- 1 ½ tablespoons sugar
- Pinch of red pepper flakes (about ⅛ teaspoon, or more if you like a kick)
- 1 tablespoon shallot, minced
- 1 tablespoon dry-roasted peanuts, chopped

 **NOTES FOR NEXT TIME:**

1. **Salt and drain the cucumbers:** Start by piling your cucumber slices into a colander set over a plate or in the sink. Sprinkle them with salt and gently toss with your hands to make sure the salt reaches all the slices. Let them sit for about 1 hour—this step helps draw out excess moisture and keeps your cucumbers crisp.

2. **Make the dressing:** While the cucumbers are draining, pour rice vinegar, water, sugar, and red pepper flakes into a small saucepan. Bring to a boil over medium-high heat. Once it bubbles, turn heat to low and let it simmer, uncovered, until liquid reduces to about 3 tablespoons, around 10 minutes. Remove from heat and let it cool completely. Stir in shallots.

3. **Dry them off:** After cucumbers have drained, spread a few layers of paper towels on the counter. Lay cucumbers out in a single layer, then top with more paper towels. Let them sit for 5 minutes, pressing down gently a few times with your hands to absorb even more moisture. Rinse to remove lingering salt and pat them dry.

4. **Assemble the salad:** Add your cucumbers to the cooled dressing in the saucepan (or transfer both into a bowl), and toss until every slice is glossy and well coated with dressing.

5. **Finish and serve**: Divide salad between two small plates or shallow bowls. Now, for the crunch: sprinkle with the crushed peanuts. I usually grab my mortar and pestle for this step, but a small resealable bag and a rolling pin also work perfectly. Give them a light bash and scatter over the top just before serving.

# Artichoke and Ricotta Flan

Mark and I have traveled to Italy a number of times and each trip reminds me why it's one of my favorite culinary destinations. Food there isn't just about eating—it's about honoring the land, family, and traditions woven into every meal. Whether chatting with a shopkeeper about the sharpness of pecorino, swapping stories with a trattoria server, or rolling out pasta during a cooking class, I'm always listening and looking for inspiration.

This artichoke and ricotta flan was born from those travels, where I saw fresh ricotta being made and noticed how often it shared the stage with artichokes on Tuscan menus. The flan is light and delicate, yet full of flavor, making it a natural partner for grilled meats, a simple roasted chicken, or even a crisp green salad for brunch. To give it an extra Tuscan touch, I like to serve it with a chilled glass of Vermentino—the citrusy notes play beautifully against the richness of ricotta and the earthiness of artichokes.

**What you need:**

- 4 canned whole artichoke hearts, rinsed and drained
- 2 garlic cloves
- ¾ (180 g) cup ricotta
- ¼ cup (25 g) Pecorino Romano, grated
- 1 large egg
- ¼ teaspoon salt
- ⅛ teaspoon black pepper
- 1 tablespoon panko breadcrumbs
- Butter, to grease the pan
- 1 tablespoon sliced raw almonds

 **NOTES FOR NEXT TIME:**

1. **Make a purée:** Place artichokes and garlic into a blender and blend into a smooth purée. I often grab my stick blender to blend in a medium mixing bowl. Transfer the purée to a mixing bowl. Add the ricotta, grated pecorino romano, and beaten egg. Season with salt and pepper and stir everything together until well combined.

2. **Prepare flan dish:** Grease two - 12-ounce (355 ml) ramekins or an oval baking dish about 7 inches by 1½ inches high (18 × 4 cm) and dust with panko breadcrumbs, making a thin layer on the bottom of the dish. Pour artichoke and ricotta mixture into the prepared ramekin, spreading it out evenly. Sprinkle the top with more breadcrumbs and drizzle with a little extra virgin olive oil or garlic confit oil (pg.229).

3. **Bake flan:** Bake in a preheated oven at 400°F (200°C) for about 50 minutes. In the last 10 minutes of baking, scatter sliced almonds on top and bake until the flan turns a beautiful golden brown. Once baked, let the flan cool for at least 30 minutes before serving. This resting time helps the flavors come together and makes slicing easier.

**TABLE TALK TIPS:** If you're not serving it right away, no worries! The flan keeps well in the fridge for up to a day. Simply reheat before serving.

# Lagoon Chicken Wild Rice Salad

This recipe was given to me by a dear friend who served it one unforgettable night at book club. We all immediately demanded the recipe! I've scaled it down to serve two (but trust me, you might want to double it for leftovers).

### Chicken

1 boneless, skinless chicken breast, about 6–8 ounces / 170–225 g or use leftover rotisserie chicken

¾ cup (180 ml) unsweetened apple juice

### Salad

1 cup (150 g) cooked wild rice

1–2 tablespoons real maple syrup

Salt and freshly ground black pepper, to taste

¾ cup (115 g) seedless grapes, halved (red, green, or a mix—dealer's choice!)

¼ cup (30 g) chopped celery

½ apple, unpeeled and chopped (Granny Smith, or mix a tart green and a sweet red like Honeycrisp or Pink Lady)

¼ cup (40 g) fresh blueberries

⅜ cup (45 g) slivered toasted almonds (a scant ½ cup), divided

¼ cup (35 g) chopped water chestnuts, about half a small can

### Dressing

½ cup (120 g) mayonnaise

¼ teaspoon seasoned salt (such as Jane's Krazy Mixed-Up Salt!)

Pinch of cinnamon, about ⅛ teaspoon

1–2 teaspoons apple juice or milk, if dressing is too thick

### Garnishes (optional)

3 tablespoons dried cranberries or dried cherries, for a pop of tartness

Spinach leaves or mixed greens, to serve

1. **Cook the chicken (skip this step if using rotisserie chicken):** In a small saucepan, bring the apple juice to a simmer. Gently lower the chicken breast in, cover, and cook about 15 minutes (or until your fork slides in like butter). Drain, let cool, and dice into bite-sized chunks.

2. **Prep the rice and cranberries:** Turn the rice into a colander, and rinse with cold water until water runs clear. Move rice into a pot and cover with 4-inches cold water. Set pot over a high flame, bring to a boil, reduce heat, cover the rice and simmer until the kernels open slightly, about 20-22 minutes. Drain off all but ¼ inch of water. Toss in cranberries, if using, and return to the stove, cover and set over a low flame. Cook until cranberries plump up, about 5 minutes, and season with maple syrup, salt and pepper. Set aside.

3. **Assemble the salad base:** In a medium mixing bowl, combine the wild rice, halved grapes, chopped celery, diced apple, blueberries, half of the slivered almonds, and water chestnuts. Gently toss together.

4. **Whip up the dressing:** In a small bowl, stir together mayo, seasoned salt, and cinnamon until smooth. Give it a taste test. Adjust as needed (more salt or cinnamon). If too thick, add 1 teaspoon apple juice or milk. Pour the dressing over the salad and gently fold in until everything's well-coated. Sprinkle remaining almonds over the salad and fold them in. Use the rest to garnish the top.

5. **To serve:** Spoon the salad onto a bed of spinach leaves or mixed greens. Alternatively, just dive in with a fork straight from the bowl. No judgment.

**TABLE TALK TIPS:** A note about wild rice: if you can get your hands on real, hand-harvested wild rice, do it! This beautiful, variegated rice cooks in just 15 to 20 minutes and has a rich, nutty flavor—totally worth seeking out at farmers' markets or your local food co-op. Most hand-harvested wild rice in the U.S. comes from Minnesota lakes and is picked by hand, often by Native Americans. If you're using cultivated wild rice, that works too—just plan for about twice the cooking time.

# Deviled Egg Salad

I first met deviled eggs in a Nebraska church basement, where no summer luncheon was complete without a tray of them. But instead of fussing with piping bags, I chop everything together into a no-fuss deviled egg salad. This version leans Southern, with a splash of Tabasco and a touch of Dijon for that punchy tang. Pile it between two slices of white bread for a retro sandwich or scoop it up with crackers for an easy table-for-two light lunch.

**What you need:**

- 4 large eggs, hard-boiled
- ¼ cup (60 g) mayonnaise
- 1 tablespoon Dijon mustard
- 1 teaspoon Tabasco® sauce
- ½ teaspoon kosher salt (such as Diamond Crystal®), plus more to taste
- ¼ teaspoon black pepper, plus more to taste
- 1½ teaspoons rice wine vinegar
- 2 tablespoons minced celery
- 2 tablespoons dill relish
- 1 tablespoon minced scallions or chives
- ¼ teaspoon paprika
- Toasted bread or crackers for serving

1. **Hard-boil the eggs:** Bring 12 cups (2.8 L) water to a boil in a large saucepan over high heat. Fill a large bowl halfway with ice water.

2. **Cool the eggs:** Using a spider skimmer or slotted spoon, gently lower eggs into the boiling water. Once the last egg is in, start the timer for 13 minutes. Transfer eggs to the ice bath and let cool 5 minutes.

3. **Peel the eggs:** Gently tap each egg on the counter to crack the shell all over. Peel from the wider end, making sure to loosen the membrane between the shell and egg white. Run the egg under gentle water while peeling to help remove any stubborn bits.

4. **Make the egg salad:** Use a pastry cutter to chop the eggs, mayonnaise, Dijon mustard, Tabasco®, salt, and black pepper in a bowl until the egg whites are cut into rough ¼ inch (6 mm) pieces. If you don't have a pastry cutter, finely chop the eggs with a knife and mix. Stir in rice wine vinegar, celery, dill relish, scallions, and paprika. Taste and adjust seasoning with more salt and black pepper, if needed. Spoon egg salad on to toasted bread to make sandwiches or serve with crackers for a quick snack.

 **NOTES FOR NEXT TIME:**

Maple Roasted Carrots | 170

171 | Supper Club Wedge Salad

Roasted Celery Root | 172

173 | Apple and Winter Squash Salad

# Maple Roasted Carrots
## and Maple Glazed Pepitas

Looking for a holiday side that's as easy as it is eye-catching? These maple-roasted carrots bring all the cozy vibes, served over a creamy rosemary white bean purée and finished with maple-glazed pepitas and jewel-like pomegranate arils. They're festive, colorful, and fancy-looking—yet simple to make. Proof that carrots can absolutely steal the show.

**For roasted carrots**

1 pound (450 g) long carrots, cut into long ½-inch (1.3 cm) batons, peeled and stems trimmed to leave just a little bit on the end

1 tablespoon olive oil

1 tablespoon maple syrup

½ teaspoon kosher salt

2 tablespoons chopped fresh parsley, for garnish

¼ cup (40 g) pomegranate arils, for garnish

Pinch of red pepper flakes

Flaked sea salt, for garnish

**For pepitas**

¼ cup (30 g) raw pepitas

1 teaspoon olive oil

2 teaspoons maple syrup

Kosher salt

**For bean purée**

1 cup (170 g) warmed cooked cannellini beans or other white beans, drained

1 tablespoon extra-virgin olive oil

2 teaspoons lemon juice

1 garlic clove, grated or minced

Pinch of cayenne

¼ teaspoon fennel seeds, toasted and crushed

1 teaspoon chopped rosemary

Salt and pepper

1. **Roast carrots:** Preheat oven to 450°F (230°C). Start by tossing the carrots with maple syrup, oil, and a ½ teaspoon salt on a parchment-lined baking sheet. Spread carrots out in a single layer—they need some breathing room to roast evenly! Place pan in the oven.

2. **Glaze pepitas:** While carrots are roasting, grab a small bowl and toss raw pepitas with a 1 teaspoon olive oil, 2 teaspoons of maple syrup, and a sprinkle of salt. This little maple coating will make them deliciously crunchy and flavorful.

3. **Roast pepitas:** After the carrots have had their 7 minutes of roasting time, pull the pan out and gently slide carrots to one side, making space for the pepitas on the other half. Spread out the pepitas and return pan to the oven for another 5-8 minutes, until the carrots start to brown but still have a slight bite, and the pepitas turn a light golden brown around the edges.

4. **Let 'em cool:** Once they're done, take everything out and let it cool. If you're prepping ahead, you can make this up to 6 hours in advance—just assemble the dish right before serving!

5. **Whip up a tasty white bean puree:** Start by tossing beans, olive oil, lemon juice, garlic, a pinch of cayenne, and fennel seeds into a food processor, or grab your hand blender. Blend until everything's nice and smooth. Transfer to a bowl and sprinkle in some chopped rosemary, plus a little salt and black pepper. Give it a few minutes to let all those flavors mingle, then taste and tweak the seasoning if you like.

6. **Time to serve:** Spread the creamy white bean puree across the bottom of a serving platter. Toss the carrots with parsley and a sprinkle of red pepper flakes on the baking sheet to add a little kick. Arrange the carrots over the puree, then top it all off with a handful of extra herbs, crunchy pepitas, and pomegranate airls. Finish with a pinch of flaked salt, and you're ready to dig in!

# Supper Club Wedge Salad
## with Green Goddess Dressing

The wedge salad was one of the few salads I adored as a kid growing up in the Midwest. At our local supper club, it felt like a showstopper every time it landed on the table—crisp iceberg lettuce, creamy dressing, and just the right amount of drama. There's something wonderfully nostalgic about its unapologetic simplicity, yet it still manages to feel indulgent and refreshing all at once. This version keeps that same spirit but with an added little glow-up. I slice a single iceberg wedge into two mini mountains of crunch, then swap the sharp bite of raw onion for quick-pickled shallots and fresh chives. Plum tomatoes add sweet, bacon a savory crisp. And the dressing? A creamy, green goddess–style blue cheese blend with fresh herbs that feels classic yet totally fresh.

### Pickled Shallots

3 tablespoons red wine vinegar

1 tablespoon sugar

1 shallot, sliced thin

### Dressing

⅓ cup (80 mL) light mayonnaise

4 tablespoons whole milk

1 teaspoon lemon juice

2 tablespoons chopped chives

2 tablespoons chopped basil

2 tablespoons chopped parsley

¼ cup (30 g) crumbled blue cheese

¼ teaspoon salt

### Salad

3 slices thick-cut bacon, cut crosswise into ½-inch-wide (1.25 cm) pieces

½ head iceberg lettuce (about ½ pound / 225 g), stem trimmed, chilled

½ plum tomato, cored and cut into ¼-inch (6 mm) pieces

2 ounces (60 g) blue cheese, crumbled

2 tablespoons fresh chives, cut into ½-inch (1.25 cm) lengths

1. **Pickle the shallots:** Combine vinegar and sugar in a small bowl and microwave until sugar dissolves and vinegar is steaming, about 30 seconds. Add shallots and stir to combine. Cover and let cool completely, about 30 minutes. Drain shallots and discard liquid (can cover and refrigerate for up to 1 week). Pop two shallow bowls in the refrigerator to chill.

2. **Make the dressing:** While the shallots pickle, add mayo, milk, lemon juice, 2 tablespoons chopped chives, basil, parsley, blue cheese, and salt to a blender. Blend until smooth. If needed, add another ½ teaspoon lemon juice and 1 tablespoon milk. Season to taste with salt and pepper. Chill until ready to serve (can cover and refrigerate for up to 1 week).

3. **Fry the bacon:** Cook the bacon in a 10-inch skillet over medium-low heat, stirring occasionally, until the fat is rendered and the bacon turns deep golden brown but still has a slight chew, 10 to 12 minutes. Adjust the heat as necessary to avoid browning too quickly. Transfer the bacon to a paper towel-lined plate to drain. Discard the fat or save it for another use.

4. **Assemble the salad:** Halve the lettuce through its core, then cut one of the halves into two wedges, keeping the core intact. Store the other half for another use - like a slip of a leaf between the folds of a BLT. Arrange the wedges, rounded side down, in the chilled bowls. Drizzle 3 tablespoons of dressing over each wedge, using a spoon to help it cascade down the sides. Top with tomato, crumbled blue cheese, and bacon. Garnish with pickled shallots and the remaining chives. Season generously with freshly ground black pepper and serve with extra dressing on the side.

 **NOTES FOR NEXT TIME:**

# Roasted Celery Root
## with Romesco and Miso Tahini Sauce

Slow-roasting celery root in olive oil with garlic and citrus makes it taste like it's been secretly buttered, soft and irresistible. To keep things lively, I pair it with smoky romesco (thank you jarred roasted peppers) and a creamy miso–tahini bean sauce that feels way fancier than it is. Everything can be made ahead, which means tomorrow's roasted veggies or sweet potatoes just got an upgrade. Serve it as a satisfying vegetarian main or let it play sidekick to roasted chicken.

### For the roasted celery root

- ⅓ cup plus 2 teaspoons (95 mL) olive oil, divided
- 1 lemon — zest shaved into 3 strips, then juiced
- 3 whole garlic cloves, peeled
- 2 teaspoons cumin seeds, roughly crushed, divided
- ½ teaspoon kosher salt
- 1 medium celery root peeled and cut into 6–8 wedges, about about 1 lb / 450 g

### For the romesco sauce

- Scant ¾ cup (170 g) jarred roasted red bell peppers
- ¼ cup (35 g) whole blanched almonds, toasted
- 2 teaspoons sherry or red wine vinegar, plus more to taste
- 1 teaspoon honey
- ½ teaspoon smoked paprika
- ½ teaspoon kosher salt
- ⅛ teaspoon cayenne pepper

### For the miso tahini sauce

- 1 (14.5-ounce / 411 g) can white beans (Great Northern, cannellini, or navy), rinsed, drained, and warmed
- ½ lemon, juiced
- 2 tablespoons quality tahini
- 3 tablespoons white miso paste
- ½ cup vegetable or chicken broth (120 mL)
- 1 tablespoon honey
- 1 teaspoon of the remaining crushed cumin seeds

*Chopped fresh parsley, for garnish*

1. **Roast the celery root:** Heat oven to 400°F (200°C) and adjust rack to middle position. Layer two 16x12-inch (40.6 cm x 30.5 cm.) sheets of foil inside a quarter sheet pan or 9x13-inch (22.9 cm x 33 cm) baking dish. In the center, combine ⅓ cup olive oil, lemon zest strips, lemon juice, garlic, 1 teaspoon cumin seeds, and ½ teaspoon salt. Add celery root wedges and toss to coat. Fold foil tightly to seal. Roast for 1 hour to 1 hour 20 minutes, rotating pan halfway, until a skewer meets little resistance. Carefully open foil and let steam escape. Let cool 15 minutes.

2. **Make the miso-tahini sauce:** Meanwhile, in a high-speed blender, combine warm beans, lemon juice, tahini, miso paste, broth, honey, and 1 teaspoon crushed cumin. Blend until smooth. Chill until ready to serve.

3. **Make the romesco sauce:** Toast almonds in a dry skillet over medium heat, stirring often, about 3 minutes. Measure out 3 tablespoons of the oil from the foil packet. Add oil, garlic cloves, and lemon peel to a clean blender. Add bell peppers, honey, toasted almonds, vinegar, paprika, cayenne, salt, and black pepper. Blend until smooth. Taste and adjust seasoning with vinegar and salt.

4. **Brown the celery root:** Heat remaining 2 teaspoons oil in a nonstick skillet over high heat until shimmering. Add celery root wedges and cook, turning occasionally, until golden and caramelized on all sides, 6–8 minutes. Transfer to a serving plate.

5. **Assemble and serve:** Spoon about two-thirds of the romesco over the browned celery root. Add dollops of tahini sauce between the wedges. Sprinkle with chopped parsley and remaining almonds. Serve with extra sauces on the side.

# Apple and Winter Squash Salad
## with Crispy Parmesan and Maple Hazelnut Vinaigrette

This salad was inspired by a stroll through the Mill City Farmers Market in Minneapolis, where local farmers' harvests sparked ideas for bringing fall flavors to the table. Sweet apples, nutty farro, and tender roasted squash rest on a bed of spinach, with a sprinkle of Parmesan added at the last minute for a salty, crispy edge. A hazelnut vinaigrette ties it all together—nutty, light, and just a little unexpected.

### Salad

1½ cups (240 g) cooked and drained farro, rye berries, or hulled barley

1 small winter squash, about 1 pound / 450 g, peeled, seeded, and cut into 1-inch (2.5 cm) pieces

¼ cup (60 mL) hazelnut oil, divided

Salt and freshly ground black pepper, to taste

¼ cup (25 g) finely grated Parmesan cheese

¼ cup (30 g) hazelnuts, toasted

### Dressing

1 tablespoon apple cider vinegar

1 tablespoon maple syrup

1 teaspoon Dijon mustard

1 teaspoon finely chopped shallots

### Mix 'ins

2 green onions, trimmed and sliced into ⅛-inch (3 mm) pieces

½ medium tart apple, cored and cut into ½-inch (1.3 cm) dice

2 tablespoons dried cranberries

1. **Prep the farro**: Arrange a rack at the bottom of your oven and set it to 400°F. Toss about 1 cup of uncooked farro into a pot, add enough water to cover by about four inches. Set pot over high heat and bring to a boil. Once it's bubbling away, lower heat and let simmer gently until farro is tender, somewhere between 25 and 45 minutes. Give it a little taste test if you're unsure. Drain and set aside.

2. **Roast the squash:** Scatter cubed winter squash on a sheet pan, drizzle with 2 tablespoons hazelnut oil, and give it a light sprinkle of salt and pepper. Slide the pan onto the bottom oven rack and let squash roast undisturbed for 15–20 minutes. We want a nice golden brown on the bottoms, so after 15 minutes, check a few pieces in the middle of the pan (the edges brown a bit faster).

3. **Make crispy Parmesan:** Sprinkle squash with Parmesan, and scatter hazelnuts across the pan. Pop it back in the oven until squash is tender, the Parmesan is melted and golden in spots, and those hazelnuts are toasty. Watch them carefully—hazelnuts can go from perfect to too toasty quickly! When the skins begin to crack and they smell fragrant, about 5 minutes, you're good to go. Let the pan cool a few minutes so the Parmesan can crisp up nicely.

4. **Whisk up the dressing:** In a small bowl, whisk together vinegar, maple syrup, mustard, and shallots until well combined. Slowly drizzle in 2 tablespoons hazelnut oil while whisking continuously, until the dressing is fully blended and smooth.

5. **Mix the farro salad:** Add sliced green onions, apples, and cranberries to the drained farro, then toss with about half of the dressing—just enough to coat everything nicely. This farro salad can be made a day ahead if you want to get a jump on things. Just pop it in the fridge until you're ready.

6. **Assemble and serve:** When you're ready to eat, lay a bed of spinach on a large platter (or individual plates, if you're feeling fancy), pile the farro mixture over the greens, then top with the roasted squash. Drizzle the remaining dressing over the top. Finish with a sprinkle of those toasted hazelnuts for a little crunch and extra flavor.

# Skillet Scalloped Potatoes for Two

Scalloped potatoes were a staple in my Grandma Sagehorn's Nebraska farm kitchen. I can still picture her well-used metal baking pan—dented, seasoned from years of use—as she carefully layered in thinly sliced potatoes, then slid the pan into the oven to bake low and slow until the top was bubbling and golden. When I want that same creamy, cheesy comfort—but scaled down for just the two of us—I turn to my 8-inch skillet. By starting the potatoes on the stove top, we give them a head start, then finish in the oven for that same rich, casserole-style finish in under 30 minutes. It's the flavor I grew up with, made weeknight-friendly.

**What you need:**

- ½ cup (50 g) mild cheddar cheese, shredded (~2 ounces)
- 1½ teaspoons cornstarch, divided
- ½ cup (50 g) Parmesan cheese, grated (~1 ounce)
- 1 teaspoon vegetable oil
- ½ cup (75 g) onion, finely chopped (white, yellow, or shallots)
- 1 garlic clove, minced
- 1 teaspoon fresh thyme (or ¼ teaspoon dried thyme)
- ⅓ cup (80 mL) chicken broth (or ½ teaspoon Better Than Bouillon dissolved in ½ cup / 120 mL water)
- ⅓ cup (80 mL) heavy cream
- 12 ounces (340 g) russet potatoes, peeled and sliced ¼-inch (0.6 cm) thick
- ½ teaspoon salt
- ½ teaspoon freshly ground black pepper

1. **Before you begin:** Prepare and assemble all ingredients before slicing the potatoes or they will begin to turn brown. Adjust the rack to upper middle position and preheat your oven to 425°F (220°C).

2. **Starch up the cheese:** In a small bowl, toss cheddar cheese with 1 teaspoon of cornstarch. In a second bowl, toss ½ teaspoon of cornstarch with the Parmesan.

3. **Starting with the stovetop:** Heat the vegetable oil in an 8-inch cast iron skillet. Add chopped onion and cook until soft and translucent. Stir in garlic and thyme, and cook for about 30 seconds. When you begin to smell the garlic and thyme, stir in the broth, cream, potatoes, salt and pepper. I always add a bit more cream to make sure the potatoes are swimming in liquid. Now simmer the potatoes until they are almost tender or al dente – they should be a "firm" tender and not "break apart easily" tender. This may take about 10 minutes.

4. **Bake the potatoes:** Remove the skillet from the stove top and stir in the cheddar mixture. I like to press the potatoes into an even layer using a wooden spoon to remove any air pockets. Now sprinkle the top evenly with Parmesan. Bake until the top is golden brown and the cheesy cream is bubbly hot, about 12 minutes.

**SERVING SUGGESTIONS:** When I think of scalloped potatoes, I think of baked ham (pg.97).

 **NOTES FOR NEXT TIME:**

Acai Bowl
Pg.184

Lemon-Blueberry French Toast
Pg.181

Herb-pot & Garlic Souffle
Pg.179

## Morning Gatherings For Two

"Brunch is cheerful, sociable, and inciting. It is talk-compelling. It puts you in a good temper, it makes you satisfied with yourself and your fellow beings."

— Guy Beringer, who coined the term "brunch" in 1895

# Herb-Pot and Gruyere Soufflés

I'm not much of a breakfast-or-brunch girl, but when I do make brunch, this is my sure-fire win—it always makes me feel like a kitchen rock star when they puff up golden in the oven. These Herb-Pot and Gruyere Soufflés are light, luscious, and full of flavor, especially in summer when your pots of herbs are overflowing—snip some chives, basil, and a little minced garlic, or wild garlic if you have it. Paired with a crisp green salad and lemon vinaigrette, you've got a fresh, effortless brunch for two.

**What you need:**

- 2 tablespoons butter, plus more for greasing the ramekins
- 3 tablespoons finely grated Parmigiano Reggiano
- ¼ cup (30 g) all-purpose flour
- ¾ cup (180 ml) whole milk
- ¼ cup (30 g) gruyère cheese, grated
- ¼ teaspoon freshly grated nutmeg, about ½ whole nutmeg
- 1 teaspoon Dijon mustard
- ½ cup (about 15 g) chopped wild garlic, or a mix of 1 heaping tablespoon finely chopped chives, ½ teaspoon fresh chopped basil, and ½ teaspoon minced garlic
- 2 extra-large eggs, separated
- ¼ teaspoon kosher salt or Tuscan salt (pg.225)

1. **Getting started:** Grease three 8-ounce ramekins generously with butter, making sure to get every nook and cranny. This helps the soufflés rise evenly. Sprinkle one tablespoon Parmesan into each ramekin, then tap out the excess. Wipe rim clean with a paper towel. Line them up on a baking sheet for easy handling later. Adjust oven rack to the lower third of oven, then preheat to 390°F (190°C)

2. **Start the base:** Melt 2 tablespoons butter in medium saucepan over low heat. Once it's melted and bubbly, stir in flour. Cook this mixture gently for a couple of minutes until it smells nutty and turns golden—this is key to keep your soufflé from tasting floury. Gradually pour in milk, whisking constantly to keep lumps at bay. Once it's all in, keep whisking until mixture thickens into a smooth, creamy sauce, about 2-3 minutes.

3. **Make it cheesy:** Take the pan off the heat and stir in gruyère, grated nutmeg, Dijon mustard, and your handful of chopped wild garlic. If you can't find wild garlic, chives and herbs will work perfectly. Add a ¼ teaspoon salt, and a crack of black pepper, about ¼ teaspoon. Taste and adjust seasoning. Let mixture cool for a minute or two.

4. **Add the eggs:** Separate eggs, putting whites in a large, clean bowl. Stir yolks into the cooled sauce one at a time. Using an electric mixer (or elbow grease), beat egg whites until they form stiff peaks. You'll know they're ready when you can hold the bowl upside down and nothing moves—yes, really!

5. **Fold eggs into cheese batter:** Take a third of whipped egg whites and gently stir them into the cheese mixture to lighten it up. Then, carefully fold in the rest of the whites in two batches, using a spatula and a soft, scooping motion. Try not to knock out too much air—you want to keep things light and fluffy. Err on the side of having some white streaks in the batter from the egg whites - this will help you keep the air in the whites. Divide mixture evenly between your prepared ramekins, filling them almost to the rim. Pop them into the oven and bake 15-20 minutes. No peeking! You want them to rise undisturbed. When the soufflés are puffed and golden, remove from oven and serve right away with a simple green salad. The soufflés will deflate slightly as they cool - so serve while hot!

**TABLE TALK TIPS:** Make sure your egg whites, beaters and mixing bowl are completely clean and free of any grease, or the whites won't whip properly. Use 8-ounce ramekins—two to three depending on how much you fill them.

Lemon Blueberry French Toast | 181

182 | Chilaquiles with Mushrooms

Eggs in Purgatory | 183

184 | Easy Sausage and Spinach Egg Bake

# Lemon Blueberry French Toast

Summers with my grandparents in a tiny Nebraska town of 300 are some of my sweetest memories. My grandmother was a fantastic cook, and her simple French toast with maple syrup was legendary at our big family breakfasts. Years later, one of my recipe testers, Vicki, suggested adding a blueberry-stuffed French toast—her inspiration came from a Minnesota State Fair recipe card. Inspired by both her creativity and my grandmother's breakfasts, I've reimagined it here as French toast topped with homemade blueberry jam and lemon whipped cream, brightened with a swirl of lemon curd. Oh my heavens, it's one delicious breakfast—especially with cinnamon bread, brioche, or challah.

**For the French toast**

¼ cup (60 ml) milk

¼ cup (60 ml) heavy cream

2 large eggs

½ teaspoon vanilla extract

¼ teaspoon ground cinnamon

1 teaspoon brown sugar

4 to 6 slices cinnamon bread (about 2.5 cm thick) or day-old brioche/challah

1 tablespoon butter

1 tablespoon vegetable oil

Maple syrup, for serving

**Lemon curd whipped cream**

Note: You can use store bought lemon curd and add the heavy whipping cream to the curd.

1 egg

1 egg yolk

⅓ cup (67 g) sugar

¼ cup (60 ml) fresh lemon juice from about 2 lemons

1/16 teaspoon kosher salt (a small pinch)

1½ tablespoons unsalted butter, cubed

¾ cup (180 ml) heavy whipping cream, cold

**Toppings (optional)**

Blueberry jam or preserves

Fresh blueberries

1. **Prepare the lemon curd (or use store-bought and skip to step 2):** In a medium saucepan, whisk together the egg, yolk, sugar, and salt until smooth. Slowly whisk in the lemon juice. Cook over medium heat, stirring constantly, until the mixture thickens and coats the back of a spoon (about 5 minutes). Remove from heat and stir in the butter until melted. Strain the curd into a bowl and cover surface with plastic wrap to prevent a skin from forming. Refrigerate until chilled.

2. **Whip the cream:** In a large bowl, whip the heavy cream to stiff peaks using a whisk or stand mixer with the whisk attachment. Loosen lemon curd by stirring gently with a spatula. Fold the curd into the whipped cream, preserving as much volume as possible. Use immediately or store in refrigerator for up to one week.

3. **Prepare the custard:** In a medium bowl, whisk together milk, cream, eggs, vanilla, cinnamon, and brown sugar until smooth. Pour mixture into a shallow dish.

4. **Dredge bread:** Set a griddle, large nonstick skillet, or well-seasoned cast iron pan over medium heat. Dip each slice of bread into the custard, allowing it to soak but not fall apart. Let any excess drip off.

5. **Prepare griddle:** Add butter and oil to the pan. Once melted and shimmering, place the soaked bread in the pan. Cook until golden brown on one side (about 2–4 minutes), then flip and cook the other side until golden (about 2 minutes more). Repeat with remaining slices, adding more butter to the pan, as needed.

6. **Serve hot:** Top with maple syrup, blueberry jam, and a dollop of lemon curd whipped cream.

**TABLE TALK TIPS:** For a stunning presentation, spread a thin layer of blueberry jam over each slice of French toast before adding the lemon whipped cream and lemon zest.

# Chilaquiles with Mushrooms

Chilaquiles (pronounced chee-lah-KEE-lays) are a classic Mexican comfort food, made by tossing crispy tortillas in a rich chile sauce and topping them with eggs, chicken, or a swirl of crema. Rooted in Aztec cuisine, the dish began as a clever way to transform leftover tortillas into something warm and nourishing. Over time, it became a beloved breakfast staple, with every family adding their own twist—red or green sauce, eggs or meat, crunchy or softened chips. What I love most is how chilaquiles embody the heart of Mexican home cooking: resourceful, hearty, and full of bold flavor.

**What you need:**

*6 corn tortillas, cut into 8 wedges each*

*2 tablespoons vegetable oil*

*Salt, to taste*

*¼ pound (115 g) cremini mushrooms, sliced about ¼-inch (6 mm) thick*

*1 tablespoon olive oil*

*2 tablespoons shallots, minced*

*1 garlic clove, minced*

*½ cup (120 ml) store-bought tomatillo salsa*

*2 tablespoons sour cream*

*1 ounce (28 g) queso fresco*

*2 eggs (optional)*

*2 tablespoons cilantro, for garnish*

*⅛ teaspoon Kosher salt, as needed*

1. **Turn tortillas into chips:** Adjust the racks to upper-middle and lower-middle positions, then heat oven to 425°F (220°C). Grab two rimmed baking sheets and spread out tortillas evenly. Drizzle each sheet with 1 tablespoon of oil and sprinkle with ⅛ teaspoon of salt. Give them a good toss until they're evenly coated. Pop them into the oven, stirring them around occasionally to make sure they get nice and golden, about 15 to 20 minutes. Rotate the sheets halfway through so they bake evenly. Keep the oven on—we'll use it again to melt cheese at the end!

2. **Sauté mushrooms:** Grab a 10-inch cast iron skillet or oven safe skillet with lid and heat 1 tablespoon olive oil over medium-high heat. Once it's hot, toss in mushrooms and cook until they're slightly browned, about 3 to 5 minutes. Add shallots and let them soften for about a minute. Then, toss in garlic and let it cook until fragrant about 10 to 20 seconds. Now pour in your salsa and let it simmer another 2 minutes. Taste and adjust the seasoning with a little salt if needed.

3. **Turn off heat:** Stir in crispy tortillas from the baking sheets and give everything a good mix. Cover skillet and let it sit about 2 to 5 minutes. The tortillas will soften up a little but won't turn mushy—that's the perfect texture we're going for.

4. **Cheese it up:** Spoon on the sour cream in small dollops and sprinkle with crumbled queso fresco. Put the whole skillet back in the oven (still at 425°F / 220°C)) for about 5 minutes, until everything is heated through and cheese starts to melt.

5. **Add the finishing touches:** While the chilaquiles are in the oven, fry up an egg or two—this step is totally optional, but trust me, it's worth it. Once chilaquiles are done, take them out and top with the fried egg(s). Garnish with fresh cilantro for a little pop of color and flavor.

6. **Serve up hot and fresh:** And, don't forget to pass around extra salsa for those who like an extra kick!

# Eggs in Purgatory

Eggs in Purgatory gets its name either from the fiery kick of red pepper flakes or the bubbling red sauce the eggs gently poach in. This Southern Italian dish, built from simple pantry staples, is proof that humble ingredients can feel indulgent. I first made it when our hens were laying more eggs than we could keep up with, and it quickly became a favorite. Served with garlic-rubbed bread for scooping, it's an easy, soulful meal any time of day.

**What you need:**

- 4 tablespoons extra-virgin olive oil, divided
- 2 large garlic cloves (1 thinly sliced, 1 halved)
- 2 tablespoons grated onion (using the large holes on a box grater)
- 1½ teaspoons tomato paste
- ½ teaspoon red pepper flakes, more to taste and for serving
- ¼ teaspoon fine sea salt, more to taste
- ⅛ teaspoon black pepper
- 1 (14.5-ounce / 411 g) can diced tomatoes
- 1 large sprig fresh basil or rosemary (or a pinch of dried rosemary)
- 1 tablespoon finely grated Parmesan, plus more for serving
- 1½ teaspoons unsalted butter, more to taste
- 4 large eggs
- 2 to 4 slices crusty bread, for serving
- Small handful chopped basil or parsley, for garnish

**NOTES FOR NEXT TIME:**

1. **Toast the bread:** Adjust oven rack to middle position and heat the broiler. Arrange bread slices on a baking sheet and drizzle the first side with 1 tablespoon olive oil. Flip the slices and drizzle with another tablespoon of oil. Broil until deep golden brown, about 3 minutes per side. While still warm, rub the toast with the halved garlic clove and sprinkle with salt. Set aside and reduce oven temperature to 400°F (200°C).

2. **Sauté garlic and onion:** In a 10-inch skillet with a lid, heat 2 tablespoons olive oil over medium heat. Add sliced garlic and red pepper flakes, cooking just until garlic turns golden at the edges, about 1 minute. Stir in grated onion, tomato paste, salt, and black pepper. Cook, stirring occasionally, until the tomato paste deepens in color, about 4 minutes.

3. **Make it a sauce:** Add diced tomatoes and sprig of basil (or rosemary), then reduce the heat to medium-low. Simmer, gently mashing the tomatoes with a wooden spoon or potato masher, until the sauce thickens, about 20 to 25 minutes. Stir in the Parmesan, butter, and additional red pepper flakes, if desired.

4. **Add the eggs:** Remove skillet from the heat and let it cool for 2 minutes. Crack one egg into a small bowl. Using a rubber spatula, clear a 2-inch-diameter well in the sauce, exposing the bottom of the skillet. Carefully pour in the egg, using the spatula to hold the well open if needed. Repeat with remaining eggs, evenly spacing 3 eggs in total around perimeter of skillet and 1 in center.

5. **Cook eggs:** Season eggs with a pinch of salt and pepper. Cover skillet and cook over medium heat until egg whites begin to set but remain slightly translucent with some watery patches, about 3 minutes.

6. **Bake:** Uncover skillet and transfer it to the oven. Bake until the whites are fully set, 4 to 5 minutes for slightly runny yolks or 6 minutes for soft-cooked yolks. Rotate skillet halfway through for even cooking.

7. **Finish and serve:** Sprinkle with more Parmesan, chopped basil or parsley, and an extra drizzle of olive oil. Serve immediately with the toasted bread.

# Easy Sausage and Spinach Egg Bake

Egg bakes started popping up in community cookbooks and magazines like Better Homes and Gardens decades ago, becoming a staple of church potlucks and family brunches. To me, they've always felt like good old-fashioned farm kitchen cooking—the kind my grandmothers and aunts would serve when family gathered. This version, with sausage, spinach, and a little heat from your favorite hot sauce, is my nod to that tradition. I've adapted it for two, though it still carries the spirit of the holiday mornings and homecomings when I first enjoyed it.

**What you need:**

*1 tablespoon olive oil*

*⅓ pound (150 g) pork breakfast sausage*

*1 large shallot, finely chopped*

*1 cup (30 g) fresh baby spinach*

*½ red bell pepper, chopped*

*4 large eggs*

*¼ teaspoon kosher salt or Tuscan salt (pg. 225)*

*⅛ teaspoon freshly ground black pepper*

*½ cup (120 ml) sour cream*

*½ cup (120 ml) milk*

*6 ounces (170 g) shredded sharp cheddar cheese, divided*

*1½ cups (225 g / 8 ounces) frozen hash browns, thawed (I like to use Simply Potatoes® hash browns found in the refrigerated section)*

**TABLE TALK TIPS:** Baked egg dishes keep surprisingly well! Store leftovers tightly covered in the refrigerator up to 3 days. To reheat, cover with foil and warm in a 325°F (163°C) oven until heated through, or microwave individual portions gently so the eggs don't overcook.

1. **Getting started:** Preheat oven to 350°F (175°C) Grab two to three large 16-ounce (480 mL) ramekins or a 8½ × 4½ inches (21.5 × 11.5 cm) loaf pan, spray with PAM® vegetable oil, set aside.

2. **Brown sausage:** Heat a medium non-stick skillet over medium-high heat. Heat oil and toss in the sausage and shallot. Use a wooden spoon to break up the sausage as it cooks. Keep stirring until the sausage is no longer pink and shallot is soft and fragrant.

3. **Sauté vegetables:** Add spinach and chopped red bell pepper, cooking just until spinach wilts—this only takes about a minute. Drain off any excess grease and set mixture aside to cool. (Make ahead tip: You can do this step a day ahead. Just cool the mixture completely, pop it in an airtight container, and store it in the fridge.)

4. **Whisk eggs:** In a large bowl, whisk eggs together with a generous ¼ teaspoon salt and ⅛ teaspoon pepper. Add sour cream and milk, whisk again until the mixture is smooth and creamy. Stir ¾ of shredded cheese into the egg mixture, followed by the hash browns and cooled sausage-spinach mixture. Mix everything together until well combined. If the mixture seems too dry, whisk in more milk, about 2 tablespoons at a time, until you reach your desired liquid consistency. You want enough liquid to moisten the filling and bubble up gently wherever there's a little room.

5. **Bake:** Divide the mixture evenly between your prepared ramekins or pour into loaf pan. Use a spatula to smooth the tops, then sprinkle the remaining cheese over each. Cover the ramekins with foil. Place the ramekins on a baking sheet (just in case of spills) and bake for about 45 minutes. You'll know they're ready when a knife inserted into the center comes out clean. Remove foil and let the egg bakes cook for another 5 minutes to get that cheesy golden-brown top.

6. **Serve:** Take the ramekins out of the oven and let them rest for 5 minutes. Serve warm.

Acai Bowls | 186    187 | Good Morning Smoothies - blueberry

Maple Granola | 188    187 | Good Morning Smoothies - mango lassi

# Acai Bowls

Superfoods may sound trendy, but açaí (pronounced ah-sigh-EE) has earned a permanent spot in my kitchen. This deep purple fruit blends into a thick, refreshing smoothie bowl that feels just as good for an afternoon pick-me-up as it does for breakfast. With frozen açaí puree now easy to find at natural grocery stores and co-ops, it's simple to bring a little café-style treat to your own table. The fun part? Piling on your favorite toppings—think fruit, nuts, and crunchy granola—for a bowl that's as colorful as it is nourishing.

**What you need:**

*1 banana, sliced and frozen*

*½ cup (75 g) blueberries, frozen*

*½ cup (75 g) strawberries, frozen*

*¾ cup (180 ml) milk or juice (dairy milk, soy, almond, apple, or orange)*

*½ cup (120 g) plain yogurt (or substitute with additional milk or juice)*

*1 to 2 tablespoons honey (optional)*

*200 g (2 packets) frozen açaí puree, broken into pieces*

*Assorted toppings: nuts, seeds, fresh fruit, granola, coconut, etc.*

**NOTES FOR NEXT TIME:**

1. **Prepare the fruit:** Slice banana and transfer it to a small baking sheet or plate lined with parchment paper. Add blueberries and strawberries to the same plate. If you're short on time, store-bought frozen fruit works just as well. Freeze until completely solid.

2. **Blend the base:** In a high-speed blender with a tamper, combine the milk and yogurt. Add frozen banana slices, blueberries, strawberries, honey, if using, and broken-up açaí puree. Blend on low speed, using tamper to push the frozen fruit down and mix evenly. Continue blending until smooth, adding additional liquid as needed to achieve your desired consistency.

3. **Assemble the bowls:** Divide smoothie mixture into two bowls. Decorate with your favorite toppings. Popular choices include sliced banana, granola, nuts, seeds, coconut flakes, and fresh berries.

4. **Serve immediately:** Enjoy your açaí bowls fresh for best texture and flavor.

**TABLE TALK TIPS:** I slice ripe bananas into ½-inch pieces and pop them into a zip-top freezer bag, then into freezer—the same with my strawberries. You can even pre-measure fruit into individual freezer zip-top bags to make it easy to whip up one of these bowls in the morning.

If your blender doesn't have a tamper, pulse the ingredients to start breaking them down, then blend on low, stopping frequently to scrape down the sides and stir. Add liquid gradually to prevent a watery consistency.

# Good Morning Smoothies

Smoothies are one of my favorite ways to start the day, and these three—Blueberry Yogurt, Mango Lassi, and Mango Green Tea—each bring their own little boost of sunshine to the morning. I like to pick up ingredients like chia seeds and turmeric from the grocery store bulk section so I only buy what I need and keep everything fresh. The best part? These smoothies are delicious on their own but even better topped with a sprinkle of my homemade granola (pg. 188) on top for a little crunch.

### Blueberry Yogurt

*1½ cups (225 g) frozen blueberries*

*1¼ cups (300 mL) whole milk, Greek plain yogurt, or coconut-flavored yogurt (*

*½ cup (75 g) frozen raspberries 1 frozen banana, sliced into ½-inch (1.25 cm) pieces*

*2 tablespoons almond butter or peanut butter (optional)*

*1 teaspoon vanilla extract*

*1 tablespoon maple syrup or honey — usually not needed if using vanilla (optional)*

*½ cup (120 mL) milk or almond milk, if needed*

### Mango Lassi

*1 cup (150 g) frozen mango chunks*

*1 cup (240 mL) plain Greek yogurt or whole milk yogurt*

*2 tablespoons almond butter or peanut butter (optional)*

*1 teaspoon vanilla extract*

*1 tablespoon maple syrup or honey — usually not needed if using vanilla (optional)*

*½ cup milk (120 mL), if needed*

### Mango Green Tea

*2 ripe mangoes, peeled and diced, about 3 cups / 450 g*

*1 teaspoon turmeric*

*1 tablespoon minced fresh ginger*

*1 cup (240 mL) brewed green tea — or a single-serve bottle of your favorite ready-to-drink green tea*

*1 cup (240 g) ice cubes*

*¼ cup (40 g) chia seeds, soaked in water for at least 1 hour, up to overnight*

*Matcha powder, for garnish or extra flavor (optional)*

1. **For the Blueberry Yogurt or Mango Lassi:** Blend all ingredients on low until the blender gains traction, then ramp up to the highest speed as soon as possible (or if your blender has a smoothie function, that will work great). Stop to scrape down the sides or add milk for a thinner consistency.

2. **Finishing touches:** Once smoothie is completely smooth and creamy, taste it and blend in maple syrup if you'd like a sweeter smoothie. Divide smoothie into 2 glasses. Serve immediately!

3. **For Mango Green Tea:** In a blender, combine mango, turmeric, ginger, green tea, and ice. Blend until smooth. Add chia seeds and pulse just to combine. Serve garnished with matcha powder, if using.

 **NOTES FOR NEXT TIME:**

# Maple Granola
## with Cranberries, Cherries and Blueberries

I still remember the thank-you gift that sparked this recipe—a beautiful bag of maple granola with Michigan-dried cherries tucked in among other local treasures. The blend was so flavorful and just the right amount of sweet; it quickly disappeared. I knew I had to recreate it. So I started experimenting, and over the years, I have perfected this small-batch granola with old-fashioned rolled oats, maple syrup, and a trio of dried fruits: cranberries, tart cherries, and wild blueberries. It's now a staple in my kitchen, and I love to share it with friends as a holiday or hostess gift. Sprinkle it over yogurt, top off your smoothie, or enjoy it straight from the pan—it's a little gift of cozy in every bite.

**What you need:**

- 4 cups (360 g) old-fashioned rolled oats
- 1 cup (120 g) raw slivered almonds
- ½ cup (60 g) raw pepitas (hulled pumpkin seeds)
- 1 teaspoon fine sea salt
- 1 teaspoon ground cinnamon
- 1 teaspoon ground cardamom
- ⅓ cup (80 mL) melted coconut oil or extra-virgin olive oil
- ½ cup (120 mL) maple syrup
- 1 teaspoon vanilla extract
- ¼ cup (30 g) dried cranberries
- ¼ cup (30 g) dried tart cherries
- ⅛ cup (20 g) dried wild blueberries

 **NOTES FOR NEXT TIME:**

1. **Mix together dry ingredients:** Adjust oven rack to center position and preheat oven to 350°F (175°C). Line a large rimmed baking sheet with parchment paper. In a large bowl, combine oats, almonds, pepitas, salt, cardamom, and cinnamon. Stir with a wooden spoon until combined.

2. **Add liquids:** Pour in coconut oil, maple syrup, and vanilla. Give it a good mix until every oat and almond is lightly coated. Using large spoon, spread the granola in an even layer. Bake until golden, about 21-23 minutes. If you have a convection oven, use it for the first 13 minutes at 350°F (175°C). After 13 minutes, give the granola a stir. Continue to bake (without convection at 350°F (175°C)) for another 10 – 12 minutes. Don't worry- the granola will continue to crisp up as it cools.

3. **Cool and store:** Let granola cool completely, undisturbed, before breaking it into pieces and stirring in dried cranberries, cherries and blueberries. Store the granola in an air tight container at room temperature for 1 to 2 weeks, or seal in a freezer bag and freeze up to 3 months.

**TABLE TALK TIPS:** This recipe makes about 6 cups of granola.

When you're cooking for two, the bulk aisle is your best friend. I buy dried fruits for granola there, along with nuts, seeds, and spices. The beauty is you can scoop just what you need.

# Citrus-Cured Gravlax
## with Tarragon Crème Fraîche

I'll admit, making gravlax once felt intimidating, at least until my dear friend Mia coached me through her family's method. She learned it from her mother, Myrna, an accomplished cook who was even featured in Bon Appétit for her Scandinavian family Christmas. For Mia, gravlax isn't just a recipe, it's a tradition that connects her to her mother. Each time she checks the cure, she can almost hear Myrna's voice guiding her along. Thanks to Mia, I've learned that gravlax is surprisingly approachable—and the citrus-cured version here, paired with a bright tarragon crème fraîche, feels both classic and fresh.

### Gravlax

*1 tablespoon Cointreau or other orange liqueur*

*½ to ¾ pound (225–340 g) salmon fillet, skin on*

*1 tablespoon light brown sugar*

*1 tablespoon + 1 teaspoon coarse salt*

*1 teaspoon fennel seeds, toasted and crushed*

*Zest of ½ lemon*

*Zest of ½ lime*

*Zest of ½ orange*

*Leaves from 1 thyme sprig, crushed*

*1 dried bay leaf, crumbled*

*½ cup (15 g) chopped fresh dill (optional)*

### Tarragon crème fraîche

*⅓ cup (80 mL) crème fraîche or sour cream*

*Zest of ½ lemon*

*Zest of ½ lime*

*Zest of ½ orange*

*½ tablespoon freshly squeezed orange juice*

*1 teaspoon fresh tarragon, chopped*

*1 scallion, minced*

*Salt and freshly ground black pepper, to taste*

1. **Prepare the cure:** Grab a small bowl and mix together brown sugar, salt, and crushed fennel seeds. Stir in lemon, lime, and orange zest, along with thyme leaves and crumbled bay leaf. If you're using dill, hold off—we'll add it later.

2. **Prep the salmon:** Remove all bones from salmon. Sprinkle 1 teaspoon sugar-salt mixture in a 13 × 9-inch (33 × 23 cm) glass baking dish. If using dill, spread half in a layer. Top with salmon, skin-side down. Drizzle Cointreau evenly over the flesh, making sure you cover the entire surface.

# Citrus-cured Gravlox *(continued)*

Press remaining cure mixture firmly onto the salmon. You want an even layer covering every inch—this is what will draw out moisture and infuse all that bright citrus and herb flavor. If using dill, press it on top of the cure now, patting it down so it adheres.

1. **Weight and cure:** Loosely cover the salmon with plastic wrap (so it is touching the fish), then place a smaller baking dish or a pie plate on top. Add a few large cans or something heavy to weigh it down—this helps press out moisture and results in a firmer texture. Now, into the fridge it goes! Let the salmon cure for about 3 days, basting once a day with liquid that pools in the dish. This speeds up the process and keeps the fish from drying out.

2. **Finishing touches:** Once salmon feels firm to the touch, it's ready! Unwrap, gently scrape off excess cure mixture (and dill, if used). Pat fillet dry with paper towels. At this point, gravlax can be tightly wrapped and refrigerated up to a week, but don't slice it just ye it's best sliced fresh before serving.

3. **Slice and serve:** Using a sharp knife, slice gravlax paper-thin on a diagonal. Arrange on crackers or buttered and toasted rye bread and top with a dollop of citrusy tarragon crème fraîche for the perfect bite.

4. **Tarragon crème fraîche:** In small bowl, stir together crème fraîche, lemon zest, lime zest, orange zest, and orange juice. Fold in the chopped tarragon and minced scallion. Season with salt and freshly ground pepper to taste. Cover and refrigerate until ready to serve.

**TABLE TALK TIPS:** I like to use skin-on salmon because it makes slicing easier, and a splash of Cointreau not only adds a subtle citrusy depth, but also helps the cure adhere and preserves the fish. Most recipes use granulated sugar, but I prefer brown sugar because its caramel notes complement the salmon beautifully. Pressing the fillet under a few heavy cans encourages it to release moisture, resulting in a firmer, more sliceable texture. Basting the salmon once a day with its own briny juices speeds up the curing process and keeps it from drying out.

 **NOTES FOR NEXT TIME:**

# Parsnip and Potato Latke

While you can make these latkes potatoes-only, I like the little bit of added sweet and earthiness provided by parsnips. We served ours with homemade jam, but you can use any jam or the traditional apple sauce. These are great served with gravlox on page 189. Makes 8 latkes.

### The latkes

- ½ lb (225 g) parsnips, peeled and shredded using the large holes on a box grater
- ½ lb (225 g) russet potatoes, peeled and shredded using the large holes on a box grater
- ½ cup (75 g) medium yellow onion, shredded using the large holes on a box grater
- 1 teaspoon kosher salt, divided
- 1 fresh garlic clove, finely grated (use a microplane zester)
- ½ teaspoon black pepper
- 3 tablespoons potato starch (found in the baking aisle or bulk section) or corn starch
- Vegetable oil or schmaltz - this is a chicken fat (or a combination), as needed for frying

1. **Release excess potato moisture:** Preheat oven to 250°F (120°C). Toss parsnips, potatoes, onion and ¾ teaspoon salt in a bowl. Let rest for about 5 minutes; we are trying to let the starch water release to the bottom of the bowl. Water is the enemy when it comes to frying, make sure that your spuds are as dry as possible. Place half of potato mixture in the center of a clean cotton dish towel. Gather ends together and twist tightly to drain as much liquid as possible. Transfer drained potato mixture to second bowl and repeat process with remaining potato mixture. Add garlic, ¼ teaspoon salt and pepper and potato starch, stirring to coat.

2. **Set up frying station:** Set a wire rack in clean rimmed baking sheet and line with a triple layer of paper towels. Heat ¼ inch depth of oil in a 12-inch skillet over medium-high heat until shimmering but not smoking (350°F (175°C)). Place rounded ¼ cup potato mixture in oil and press with nonstick spatula into ⅓-inch-thick disk. Repeat until 4 latkes are in the pan. Cook, adjusting heat so fat bubbles around latke edges, until golden brown on bottom, about 3 minutes. Turn and continue cooking until golden brown on second side, about 3 minutes longer. Drain on paper towels and transfer to baking sheet in oven. Repeat with remaining potato mixture, adding oil to maintain ¼-inch depth and returning oil to 350°F (175°C) between batches. Season with salt and pepper to taste, and serve. Garnish with rhubarb jam, sour cream and caviar, if desired. Serve immediately.

**TO MAKE AHEAD:** Cover cooled latkes loosely with plastic wrap and hold at room temperature up to 4 hours. Alternatively, freeze on baking sheet until firm, transfer to zipper-lock bag, freeze up to 1 month. Reheat latkes in 375°F (190°C) oven until crisp and hot, 3 minutes per side for room-temperature latkes and 6 minutes per side for frozen latkes.

# Avocado Toast
## with Sweet & Spicy Tomatoes

Growing up, my dad always had a bumper crop of tomatoes, which meant we were never short on BLTs, deli sandwiches, or steaming bowls of tomato soup. But the fun came when I started experimenting—immersing the tomatoes in a thick, herby, chile-spiked marinade that turned them into a tangy, sweet-and-spicy treat. The hardest part is waiting three days for the flavors to settle in—though more than once I've caught family sneaking an early taste, or sipping the leftover pickling liquid once the tomatoes were gone.

These vibrant tomatoes quickly became the star of one of my favorite breakfasts: avocado toast. Creamy avocado spread over crisp toast gets a burst of flavor from the marinated tomatoes, a combination that's as bold as it is satisfying. Top it with a poached egg, and suddenly this simple dish feels indulgent and elevated.

### Sweet and spicy tomatoes

- 1 pound (450 g) cherry tomatoes, quartered, or small red tomatoes (such as Campari or Pearl), halved and then each half cut into quarters
- ½ green bell pepper, seeded and roughly chopped
- ½ medium fresh jalapeño chile, ribs and seeds removed
- 2 garlic cloves
- ¾ cup (30 g) chopped mixed fresh herbs (such as ¼ cup dill, ¼ cup flat-leaf parsley, and ¼ cup cilantro)
- 2 tablespoons olive oil
- 3 tablespoons distilled white vinegar
- 1 Tablespoon granulated sugar
- ½ teaspoon salt

### For the poached eggs

- 1 tablespoon vinegar
- ½ teaspoon salt
- 2 eggs

### For the toast

- 2 slices of bread (I like thick-sliced whole-grain bread best)
- 1 ripe avocado
- 1 to 2 tablespoons cream cheese (optional)
- ⅓ cup (80 g) Sweet and Spicy Tomatoes plus 2 to 3 tablespoons of the tomato marinade (or more to your liking)
- Drizzle of balsamic vinegar glaze (optional)
- Pinch of flaked salt

1. **Start 3 days before:** Pack tomatoes into a clean, wide-mouthed 2-quart glass jar with a tight-fitting lid.

2. **Make the marinade:** In a food processor or the beaker of an immersion blender, combine bell pepper, jalapeño, garlic, herbs, olive oil, vinegar, sugar, and salt. Pulse until a thick, slightly chunky mixture forms, about 30 seconds or 10–15 pulses. Pour marinade over the tomatoes. Screw lid onto the jar and give it a good shake to coat the tomatoes evenly.

3. **Refrigerate:** Let tomatoes marinate for at least 3 days before serving. They will keep in the refrigerator up to 1 month. Over time, the acidity will brighten, and the flavors will deepen, developing a lightly fermented tang.

4. **Season poaching water:** Fill an 8-inch skillet with water to the rim. Add vinegar and salt, then bring the to a rolling boil. The vinegar helps the egg whites set up with fewer wispy bits floating in the skillet.

5. **Poach the eggs:** Crack two eggs into a shallow teacup. Then, gently pour the eggs into the skillet. Cover skillet, remove from heat, and let eggs gently steam until the whites are set but yolks are still slightly runny, about 3 to 4 minutes. If you prefer firmer yolks, let them sit for an additional 1 to 2 minutes. Using a slotted spoon, transfer the eggs to a paper towel-lined plate to drain excess moisture.

6. **Prepare the toast:** Meanwhile, toast the bread until golden and firm. Remove the pits from the avocados and scoop the flesh into a bowl. Mash with a fork until smooth or chunky, depending on your preference. Season with ¼ to ½ teaspoon salt, adjusting to taste.

7. **Finishing touches:** If using, spread a thin layer of cream cheese over each slice of toast. Then spread the mashed avocado on top. Layer 2 to 3 tablespoons of Sweet and Spicy Tomatoes onto each slice, followed by a poached egg. Drizzle with 1 to 2 tablespoons of the tomato marinade and some balsamic glaze, if desired. Finish with a pinch of flaked salt.

**TABLE TALK TIPS:** To make transferring poached eggs easier, place each egg on an individual square of paper towel. Lift corners and gently roll the egg onto the toast.

**SERVING SUGGESTIONS:** Enjoy these sweet and spicy tomatoes as a topping for toast, tucked into sandwiches, on a cheese board or straight from the jar with a fork!

 **NOTES FOR NEXT TIME:**

**Salted Shortbread Chocolate Chip Cookies** Pg.202

**Panna Cotta Dessert Cups** Pg.199

**Chocolate Mousse** Pg.204

# Two Spoons, Please

*"Seize the moment. Remember all those women on the Titanic who waved off the dessert cart."*

— Erma Bombeck

# Lemon-Blackberry Fool

This blackberry fool is bright, creamy, and surprisingly simple to make. I learned a version of this recipe during a week-long farm-to-table boot camp at the Culinary Institute of America. We spent hours cooking each day, learning new techniques and bonding over food. This particular recipe came from a mother-daughter duo who whipped it up so effortlessly that I knew I had to adapt it for two. Picture this: luscious lemon curd, tangy blackberries, and fluffy whipped cream swirled together into a dreamy dessert.

**What you need:**

¼ cup plus 1½ teaspoons (55 g) sugar, divided

3 large egg yolks

¼ cup plus ½ teaspoon (65 ml) fresh lemon juice, from 3–4 lemons, divided

1 teaspoon lemon zest, finely grated

2½ tablespoons unsalted butter, softened

½ cup (70 g) fresh blackberries, plus extra for garnish

½ cup (120 ml) chilled heavy cream

2 tablespoons Greek-style yogurt or crème fraîche

 **NOTES FOR NEXT TIME:**

1. **Make the lemon curd:** Whisking ¼ cup sugar and egg yolks in a small saucepan until smooth and combined. Place the pan over medium heat, whisking constantly to prevent eggs from curdling, until the curd thickens and bubbles just start to rise to the surface, about 5 to 6 minutes.

2. **Make it smooth:** Once thickened, strain the lemon curd through a fine-mesh sieve into a clean bowl. Using a rubber spatula to press every last bit of velvety goodness through the strainer. Whisk in ¼ cup fresh lemon juice, finely grated lemon zest, and unsalted butter until smooth. Cover the curd with plastic wrap pressed directly onto the surface (to prevent a skin from forming) and chill for about an hour or until completely cold. The curd will thicken more as it cools.

3. **Make the blackberry compote:** In a small saucepan, combine a cup of fresh or frozen blackberries with 1½ teaspoons of sugar. Cook over medium heat, gently mashing the berries as they soften, until the mixture thickens slightly—about 8 minutes. Remove from heat, stir in ½ teaspoon lemon juice, and cool completely.

4. **Whip It all together:** In a chilled mixing bowl, whip ½ cup heavy cream until soft peaks form. Fold in yogurt or crème fraîche, along with half the chilled lemon curd. The goal is creamy perfection with a hint of lemony brightness.

5. **Assemble the fools:** Now the fun part: spoon a layer of lemon cream into two dessert glasses, followed by a dollop of blackberry compote and a drizzle of the reserved lemon curd. Repeat layers, then use a skewer or chopstick to swirl everything together just slightly—think marbled, not mixed.

6. **Garnish and chill:** Top each fool with a few fresh blackberries for that finishing touch. Chill the glasses for at least 30 minutes before serving—if you can wait that long!

Panna Cotta Dessert Cups | 199

200 | Molten Lava Cakes

Tiramisu Icebox Cake | 201

202 | Salted Shortbread Chocolate Chip Cookie

# Panna Cotta Dessert Cups

When strawberries start appearing at the farmers' market or co-op, it's hard to resist creating a dessert that celebrates their vibrant sweetness. These panna cotta dessert cups are a riff on a classic Italian panna cotta pie, complete with silky custard base, a sprinkle of toasted graham cracker crumbs, and fresh berries. We also add a drizzle of really good aged balsamic vinegar—its complexity elevates the fruit and brings the whole dessert together. This pint-sized version is our tribute—a no-bake dessert that's perfect for days when it's simply too hot to turn on the oven. It's quick, cool, and simply a keeper. This recipe makes four - 4 ounce ramekin desserts.

### Panna cotta

3 tablespoons milk, (skim, low-fat, or whole)

1 teaspoon powdered gelatin

1 to 1½ cups (120–180 ml) heavy cream, divided

¼ cup sugar + 2 tablespoons (50 g + 25 g) sugar, divided

1 teaspoon vanilla extract

### Strawberries and raspberries

½ pint (450 g) strawberries, rinsed, hulled, and sliced, or raspberries, rinsed

1 teaspoon balsamic vinegar

Freshly ground black pepper, as needed (optional)

### Graham cracker crumb topping

1 graham cracker (honey-flavored or gluten-free)

½ tablespoon unsalted butter, melted

**NOTES FOR NEXT TIME:**

1. **Bloom gelatin:** Place milk in a small bowl or glass measuring cup. Sprinkle the surface evenly with gelatin. Whisk to combine. Set aside to bloom the gelatin, about 10 minutes.

2. **Heat the cream:** In small saucepan, combine ¾ cup heavy cream and "bloomed" gelatin, stirring continuously over medium heat until gelatin is dissolved and mixture registers 135°F (57°C) on instant-read thermometer. Off heat, add ¼ cup sugar and vanilla, stirring until sugar is dissolved. Set aside.

3. **Strain and chill:** Place remaining ¾ cup cream in a medium stainless-steel bowl. Add warm cream mixture and stir to combine. Allow mixture to cool until it registers 85 to 90°F (29 to 32°C) on an instant-read thermometer. Strain mixture into large measuring cup or pitcher, then distribute evenly among wine glasses or ramekins. Cover with plastic wrap, making sure that plastic does not mar the surface of cream; refrigerate until set (mixture should wobble when shaken gently), 4 hours.

4. **Season berries:** In a large bowl, combine berries, the remaining 2 tablespoons sugar, and the vinegar. Season with pepper, if desired, and toss to combine.

5. **Toast graham cracker topping:** Place the graham cracker in a large zipper-lock plastic bag. Press out as much air as possible from the bag and seal the bag. Use a rolling pin to gently crush graham crackers into crumbs . In a small microwave-safe bowl, combine graham cracker crumbs and butter. Microwave until crumbs are toasted, about 1 minute. Stir with rubber spatula to combine. Set aside.

6. **Serve cold:** When ready to serve, top the dessert with berries and graham cracker topping.

# Molten Lava Cakes

Molten lava cakes were one of the first desserts I learned to make, and over the years I've refined this small-batch, microwave-friendly version. Inspired by my time in the Betty Crocker Kitchens developing single-serve desserts, these little cakes are baked right in a coffee mug for an almost-instant indulgence. Microwave baking has its quirks, but with a few smart tricks—like swapping some chocolate for cocoa powder, cooking at 50% power, and stirring halfway through—you'll end up with a perfectly tender cake every time. And of course, we finish with a couple of chocolate pieces tucked inside for that irresistible molten center.

**What you need:**

- 4 tablespoons unsalted butter
- 1 ounce (28 g) bittersweet chocolate, chopped, plus 1 ounce (28 g) broken into 4 equal pieces
- ¼ cup (50 g) sugar
- 2 large eggs
- 2 tablespoons unsweetened cocoa powder
- 1 teaspoon vanilla extract
- ¼ teaspoon salt
- ¼ cup (35 g) all-purpose flour
- ½ teaspoon baking powder

NOTES FOR NEXT TIME:

1. **Melt the chocolate and butter:** In large microwave-safe bowl, combine butter and chopped chocolate. Microwave at 50 percent power in 15-second intervals, stirring after each, until smooth—this should take about 1 minute total.

2. **Mix up the batter:** Whisk in sugar, eggs, cocoa powder, vanilla, and salt until smooth. In a separate bowl, whisk together flour and baking powder, then fold into the chocolate mixture. Divide batter evenly between two 11-ounce (325 ml) coffee mugs.

3. **Start cooking:** Place mugs on opposite sides of microwave turntable. Microwave at 50 percent power for 45 seconds. Remove, give the batter a good stir, then microwave again at 50 percent power for another 45 seconds. By now, the cakes should have puffed up just below the rim of the mugs.

4. **Make it molten:** Gently press two pieces of chocolate into center of each cake, just until they're flush with the surface. Microwave one final time at 50 percent power for 35 seconds. Cakes should look slightly wet around the edges and a little drier in the center.

5. **Let them rest:** Patience, my friend! Let the cakes sit for 2 minutes so heat can finish working its magic. Then grab a spoon and dive into warm, molten chocolate bliss.

**TABLE TALK TIPS:** This recipe was developed in a full-size, 1200-watt microwave. If yours is 800 watts or less, increase the cooking time to 90 seconds for each interval. No matter what, always cook at 50 percent power—it's the key to a perfectly tender cake.

Use a coffee mug that holds at least 11 ounces, or your batter might overflow. And remember, we're adding the bittersweet chocolate in two stages—some melts into the batter, and some goes in at the end to create that dreamy molten center.

# Tiramisu Icebox Cake

I'm bringing back one of my favorite retro desserts: the icebox cake. With its no-bake ease and creamy layers, it's a classic that feels like a sweet hug from the past. Traditionally made with chocolate wafers and whipped cream, the real beauty of an icebox cake is how the refrigerator transforms crisp cookies into a soft, cake-like delight. In this version, I swap in my favorite store-bought chocolate chip cookies—Tate's thin and crisp perfection—and add cocoa powder, shaved chocolate, and a dash of instant espresso powder for rich mocha depth. Remember to use instant espresso, not ground, so it melts seamlessly into the cream.

**What you need:**

- 1⅓ cups (320 ml) cold heavy cream
- 8 ounces (225 g) Italian mascarpone cheese
- ⅓ cup + 1 tablespoon (75 g) sugar
- 2 tablespoons + 2 teaspoons Kahlúa® liqueur
- 1⅔ tablespoons unsweetened cocoa powder, such as Droste®
- ½ rounded teaspoon of instant espresso powder like Medaglia D'Oro®, found coffee aisle
- Generous ½ teaspoon pure vanilla extract
- 2 (8-ounce) packages Tate's Bake Shop chocolate chip cookies (450 g total)
- Shaved semisweet chocolate, for garnish

 **NOTES FOR NEXT TIME:**

1. **Prepare cake pan:** We will use a 6-inch (15 cm) cake pan for a scaled down version of this classic icebox cake. Line the bottom of cake pan with parchment paper. To make a parchment paper round, take a square piece of parchment paper, fold in half twice to create a triangle, then fold the triangle in half again; place the point of the triangle in the center of your round pan and cut along the edge to create a perfect circle when unfolded; this method essentially "folds" the paper into a shape that can be easily cut to fit your pan's circumference.

2. **Make the "batter":** In the bowl of electric mixer fitted with whisk attachment, combine heavy cream, mascarpone, sugar, Kahlúa, cocoa powder, espresso powder, and vanilla. Mix on low speed to combine, then slowly raise the speed, until it firm peaks form.

3. **Assemble cake:** Spread a fifth of the mocha whipped cream evenly over the parchment paper in a 6-inch cake pan. Arrange chocolate chip cookies on top, covering as much cream as possible (I break some cookies to fill in the spaces.) Spread a fifth of the mocha whipped cream evenly over cookies. Place another layer of cookies on top, lying flat and touching, followed by another fifth of the cream. Continue layering cookies and cream until there are 5 layers of each, ending with a cookie layer. Cover with plastic wrap, and refrigerate overnight.

4. **To serve:** Run a small sharp knife around the outside of the cake, Carefully flip the cake onto a platter and remove parchment. Use any left-over cream to smooth out the top and sides. Sprinkle top with the chocolate, cut in wedges. Serve cold.

**TABLE TALK TIPS:** I reserve a couple of tablespoons of whipped cream to smooth out the sides and top before serving. Refrigerate cake and any reserved whipped cream in an airtight container.

# Salted Shortbread Chocolate Chip Cookies

Growing up, my aunts filled their Nebraska farmhouse kitchens with the very best cookies and my mother-in-law "Annie" swore by the Toll House recipe on the back of the bag. I could never quite capture their magic, so I turned to something new. This salted chocolate chip shortbread is inspired by Alison Roman's genius recipe—crisp, buttery, and flecked with sea salt. With a few small tweaks to make a small batch, it's become my new favorite.

**What you need (makes 12 cookies):**

- ½ cup + 1 tablespoon (125 g) salted butter, cold (room temperature if using a hand mixer), cut into ½-inch (1.25 cm) pieces
- ¼ cup (50 g) granulated sugar
- 2 tablespoons (25 g) light brown sugar, packed
- ½ teaspoon vanilla extract
- 1¼ cups (160 g) all-purpose flour
- 3 ounces (85 g) semi-sweet or bittersweet dark chocolate, chopped into chunks
- 1 large egg, beaten
- Demerara sugar, for rolling
- Flaky sea salt, for sprinkling

NOTES FOR NEXT TIME:

1. **Prep the pans and mix the dough:** Line a baking sheet with parchment paper. In a stand mixer with paddle attachment (or using a hand mixer), beat butter, both sugars, and vanilla on medium-high until light and fluffy, about 2-3 minutes (double the time for a hand mixer). Scrape down the sides of the bowl. On low speed, slowly mix in the flour until well combined, then fold in the chocolate chunks. If needed, knead the dough gently with your hands to ensure flour is fully incorporated. The dough should feel smooth, like Play-Doh. We do not want to see any evidence of flour pockets.

2. **Shape and chill the dough:** Place dough on a piece of plastic wrap and shape it into a 6-inch log about 2 inches in diameter. My handy trick is to roll the wrapped dough on the counter to smooth it out. Chill in the fridge until firm, about 2 hours.

3. **Coat and slice the cookies:** Preheat oven to 350°F (175°C). Brush the outside of the log with the beaten egg and roll in demerara sugar. Using a serrated knife, slice the logs into ½-inch-thick rounds. If a slice crumbles-simply, press it back together. It's easier if you score the log halfway in, then score 5 cuts on each side of the center to make 12 even slices. Place cookies 1-inch apart on prepared baking sheet. Sprinkle with flaky sea salt.

4. **Bake:** Bake until the edges are lightly golden, 12-14 minutes. Let cookies cool slightly before digging in (or eating them all).

**TABLE TALK TIPS:** The dough can be made ahead and stored in the fridge up to 1 week or frozen for up to 1 month. Store baked cookies in an airtight container up to 5 days—if they last that long!

Reprinted with permission from Alison Roman, whose original recipe appeared in the Minneapolis Star Tribune and in her cookbook *Dining In: Highly Cookable Recipes*.

Chocolate Mousse | 204    205 | Vanilla's Ice
Upside Down Peach Cake | 206    207 | Stout Chocolate Bundt Cake

# Chocolate Mousse
## with Roasted Rhubarb Agrodolce

Some recipes become instant classics—the kind you make once and never forget. This chocolate mousse is one of those: foolproof, elegant, and made with just one ounce of chocolate and one egg per person. Over the years, I've dressed it up with a tangy-sweet roasted rhubarb agrodolce (see page 223), which balances the richness beautifully. Plan ahead for chilling time—the mousse is worth the wait.

**For the Mousse**

*2 ounces (55 g) dark chocolate (70% cocoa)*

*2 large eggs, pasteurized*

**Topping (optional)**

*Crème fraîche or sweetened whipped cream*

*Roasted Rhubarb Agrodolce (pg. 223)*

*Flaked sea salt*

 NOTES FOR NEXT TIME:

1. **Melt the chocolate:** Break chocolate into pieces and place in a heatproof bowl with 2 tablespoons water. Set bowl over a pot of gently simmering water (double boiler) and let the chocolate melt slowly without stirring. Once fully melted, stir until smooth. If the mixture is too thick, add another tablespoon water and mix until silky.

2. **Separate egg yolks and whites:** Place whites in a large mixing bowl.

3. **Add eggs yolks:** Once chocolate has cooled slightly, stir in egg yolks until well combined. If the mixture appears grainy or splits, add one tablespoon water at a time, stirring vigorously until smooth.

4. **Whisk egg whites:** Whisk by hand until they form stiff peaks. Using an electric mixer is fine, but be careful not to over-whip, which can lead to a grainy texture (I prefer to whisk by hand). The whites should form a peak with a slight curve when whisk is lifted.

5. **Fold in egg whites:** Fold a third of whipped egg whites into the chocolate mixture using a gentle figure-eight motion, making sure there are no flecks. Gently fold in remaining egg whites, being careful not to deflate the mixture. Spoon the mousse into individual ramekins or a single serving bowl. Cover and refrigerate at least a few hours, until set.

6. **Finishg touches:** Add about ¼ cup roasted rhubarb alongside the mousse and a generous drizzle of rhubarb juices. Top with a dollop of crème fraîche or sweetened whipped cream and finish with a pinch of flaky sea salt.

# Grandma's 4th of July Ice Cream

Some of my fondest summer memories are of 4th of July gatherings at my grandparents' farm in Nebraska, where making ice cream was an all-day tradition. Fresh cream came straight from a local farm and the muscle came from my dad and uncles, who took turns churning the old-fashioned ice cream maker. My brother and I had the all-important job of sitting on top of the machine to keep it steady as the handle cranked round and round. By the time the ice cream was ready, we were all sun-kissed, sticky, and eager for that first cold, creamy bite. This recipe is a modern twist on that cherished tradition—no churning required. It still delivers that rich, velvety texture, but without the need for hand-cranking. And to elevate it even more, drizzle with homemade fudge sauce (pg.223) or serve with my brownie recipe— pure summer nostalgia in a bowl.

### What you need (makes about 1 quart):

*2 cups (480 ml) heavy cream, chilled*

*1 cup (240 ml) sweetened condensed milk*

*¼ cup (60 ml) whole milk*

*¼ cup (60 ml) light corn syrup*

*2 tablespoons sugar*

*1 tablespoon vanilla extract*

*¼ teaspoon table salt*

 **NOTES FOR NEXT TIME:**

1. **Set up the pan:** Use an 8½ x 4½-inch (22 x 12 cm) loaf pan—this shallow shape helps the cream freeze faster. (No loaf pan? An 8-inch square baking dish will do just fine). Pop this into the freezer to make sure it is good and cold.

2. **Whip the cream:** Pour cold cream into a heavy-duty blender. Process until it looks soft and billowy, about 20 to 30 seconds. Stop and scrape down the sides, then blend about 10 seconds more, just until stiff peaks hold their shape. (When the peaks stand tall, you're there.

3. **Add milks:** With a rubber spatula, stir in sweetened condensed milk, whole milk, corn syrup, sugar, vanilla, and ¼ teaspoon salt. Let the blender run on high, about 20 seconds, scraping the sides if anything clings.

4. **Freeze:** Pour the mixture into the chilled loaf pan. Smooth the top, then press plastic wrap directly onto the surface so it's snug, to avoid ice crystals forming. Slide the pan into the freezer and let it rest until firm, at least 6 hours.

**TABLE TALK TIPS:** If you happen to have a kitchen counter ice cream maker, you can transfer your mixture to the ice cream machine after step 3. Churn the ice cream for about 30 minutes until it resembles thick soft-serve ice cream. Then, continue to Step 4. This helps expedite the freeze.

# Upside Down Peach Cake
## with St. Cecilia Sauce

Oh, this cake is a beauty—juicy peaches, caramel, and a fluffy golden top (or bottom, depending on how you slice it). Inspired by my friend Mia's showstopping pineapple upside-down cake, I couldn't resist swapping in ripe summer peaches from the farmers' market. The result is pure delight, especially when paired with creamy St. Cecilia sauce for drizzling or spooning alongside. It's a simple bake with a wow-factor finish.

**Cake**

4 tablespoons unsalted butter, melted

½ cup (100 g) light brown sugar

2 eggs, separated

½ cup (100 g) granulated sugar

½ cup (65 g) all-purpose flour

½ teaspoon baking powder

Fresh peaches (enough to slice and cover the pan)

**St. Cecilia Sauce**

1 egg yolk

½ cup (60 g) powdered sugar

A pinch of salt

½ cup (120 ml) heavy whipping cream

1 teaspoon vanilla extract

1. **Getting started:** We will use a 6-inch (15 cm) round cake pan for a scaled down version of this classic upside down cake. Line the bottom of cake pan with parchment paper. To make a parchment paper round, take a square piece of parchment paper, fold it in half twice to create a triangle, then fold the triangle in half again. Place the point of the triangle in the center of your round pan and cut along the edge to create a perfect circle when unfolded. This method essentially "folds" the paper into a shape that can be easily cut to fit your pan's circumference. Butter or grease the 6-inch pan, line with parchment paper, and grease the parchment for good measure. Flour the pans too, just to be safe. Preheat oven to 350°F (175°C) and slide the oven rack to the middle.

2. **Arrange peaches:** Peel, pit and slice the peaches into neat ½-inch wedges. Lay them down in a pretty pattern on the bottom of pan on top of the parchment paper.

3. **Make the caramel:** Melt the butter in a small saucepan. Add brown sugar and cook over medium heat until it starts bubbling and the sugar dissolves. (Don't walk away—it's quick!) Pour this mixture over the peaches.

4. **For the batter:** In medium bowl, sift together flour and baking powder. Set aside. In a bigger bowl, beat egg yolks and granulated sugar with an electric mixer on medium-high speed until it looks pale and fluffy—about 3 minutes. Lower the speed and mix in the flour mixture just until combined.

5. **Whip the whites:** In a separate clean bowl (and with clean beaters!), whip egg whites until soft peaks form—another 3 minutes or so. Take a scoop of those fluffy whites and gently stir it into your batter to loosen things up. Then fold in the rest, ever so gently, until no streaks remain.

6. **Bake:** Pour batter over your peaches and caramel, spreading it out evenly. Pop the pan into the oven and bake for 30–35 minutes. The top should be golden brown and the cake should feel set. Let cool on a baking rack for about 5 minutes. Run a knife around the edges, place a platter on top, and flip it over. If any peaches stick to the pan, simply nudge them back into place.

7. **Make St. Cecilia sauce:** While cake cools, whip up the sauce. Beat egg yolk, powdered sugar and salt on medium-high until smooth. Add cream and vanilla, beating until soft peaks form. Chill the sauce in the fridge for at least an hour—it gets better with time. Drizzle over the cake and pass extra sauce.

# Stout Chocolate Bundt Cake
## with Irish Cream Filling

If you love the bold flavors of Irish spirits wrapped in a rich chocolate cake, this little 6-inch bundt is for you. Filled with Irish Cream and topped with a silky whiskey ganache, it's like a grown-up chocolate Twinkie—playful, decadent, and just the right size for two (with a slice or two left to share). Perfect for celebrating or simply indulging in a little chocolate heaven together.

**Stout chocolate cake**

½ cup + 1 tablespoon (75 g) all-purpose flour

¼ cup (25 g) high-quality Dutch-processed cocoa powder, sifted to remove lumps

Scant ½ teaspoon baking powder

¼ teaspoon fine sea salt

2 tablespoons (30 ml) whole milk, 2% milk, or heavy cream, room temperature

Scant ½ teaspoon freshly squeezed lemon juice or distilled white vinegar

3 ounces (90 ml) Guinness stout beer (about ¼ bottle), or your favorite stout, room temperature

¼ cup (57 g) unsalted butter, softened

½ cup + 1 tablespoon (115 g) packed light brown sugar

1 large egg, room temperature

1 tablespoon mayonnaise, room temperature

Scant ½ teaspoon baking soda

½ teaspoon apple cider vinegar

**Irish cream filling**

½ of a 3.4-ounce (96 g) box instant vanilla pudding

1 cup (240 ml) heavy cream or whipping cream

2 tablespoons (30 ml) Irish Cream (such as Bailey's® of Brady's®), or more to taste

**Irish whiskey ganache**

2 ounces (57 g) bittersweet or semisweet chocolate, chopped

2 tablespoons (30 ml) heavy cream

½ teaspoon light corn syrup

¾ teaspoon unsalted butter

1 teaspoon Irish whiskey (such as Jameson®)

Pinch of fine sea salt

1. **Getting started:** Preheat oven to 350°F (175°C) and slide the oven rack to the middle. Grease 6-inch (15 cm) round bundt pan with vegetable spray. In a medium bowl, whisk together flour, sifted cocoa powder (to avoid lumps), baking powder, and salt in a measuring cup, combine the milk, lemon juice and stout, whisking until smooth. Set aside.

2. **Cream butter and sugar:** In stand mixer fitted with paddle attachment, cream softened butter and brown sugar on medium speed until light and fluffy (about 6-8 minutes). Add the room temperature egg, mixing just until incorporated. Scrape sides and bottom of the bowl.

3. **Make the batter:** Add one-third of the dry ingredients to the butter mixture and mix on low speed until just combined. Pour in half of beer mixture and mix until just combined. Using a rubber spatula, scrape the bowl to make sure ingredients are incorporated. The mixture might look curdled at this point, but it will come back together. Repeat the process by adding another third of the dry ingredients, then the remaining beer mixture, mixing after each addition.

4. **Add mayo for moistness:** Scrape sides and bottom of the bowl to ensure all ingredients are well incorporated. Add the final third of the dry ingredients and mix until just combined. Add mayonnaise, mixing on low for 10 seconds.

5. **Add cider vinegar:** In a small bowl, mix the baking soda and cider vinegar. Pour into the batter and mix on low for another 10 seconds.

# Stout Chocolate Bundt Cake *(continued)*

1. **Bake:** Dollop batter evenly into prepared pan. You want the bundt pan about ¾ full - you might have some batter left. Place on baking sheet to catch any drips and bake on center rack 40-45 minutes, or until a toothpick inserted in the center comes out with just a few moist crumbs. Let cool in pan on a wire rack for 10 minutes, then invert onto rack, lift pan to remove cake, and let cool completely. If cake sticks to the pan, use a butter knife to go around the edges to loosen the cake. You can hasten the cooling process by placing the cake in the fridge; it will take about 45 minutes.

2. **Make Baileys Irish Cream filling:** Chill a mixing bowl and beaters in the fridge for 10–15 minutes to speed up mixing time. In chilled bowl, sift in dry pudding mix and pour in heavy cream, and Baileys Irish Cream. Start mixing on low speed until combined, increase to high and beat until thick. If whisking by hand, whisk rapidly for about 2 minutes until thickened. Refrigerate until ready to use. It is important that the filling is cold when you begin filling the cake.

3. **Make a tunnel for filling:** When the cake is completely cool, invert it again onto a sheet pan to capture all the crumbs. I like to put it back into the bundt pan to keep the cake sturdy while you scooping out a tunnel for filling. Using a melon baller, small spoon or paring knife, scoop out several mounds of cake through the underside, being sure not to cut through the top or sides of the cake. I scoop out 6 to 7 holes around the center of the cake. Once the holes are made, use the best kitchen tools you've got: your hands! Burrow your fingers into the holes and create a tunnel from hole to hole. Be careful not to split the cake. Carefully flip the cake over to clear the holes; using a wire rack is handy. Flip back over again and get ready to fill.

4. **Fill the cake:** Scoop filling into a large piping bag fitted with a large, round tip or plastic bag with the corner cut off. Fill the indentations of the cake. Center your cake platter over the cake and invert your filled cake back onto it.

5. **Make the Irish Whiskey Ganache Drip:** Place chocolate in a microwave-safe bowl and pour heavy cream over it. Microwave for 1 minute, then stir. Microwave for another 30 seconds, then let sit for 1 minute before stirring again until smooth. If the chocolate isn't fully melted, microwave in 10–15 second increments, stirring in between, until smooth.

6. **Give it structure:** Stir in corn syrup, butter and Irish whiskey until fully incorporated. Let the ganache cool until it reaches a good dripping consistency. To test, drizzle a little inside the bowl—if it runs too quickly, let it thicken slightly before using.

7. **Pour on the ganache:** Once ganache is cool, pour into a squeeze bottle or piping bag. No piping bag? Use a plastic food storage bag and snip the corner. Pipe drips around the cake, then spread additional ganache on top - it's okay if some goes into the inside wall of the bundt! Slice into pieces and serve.

 **NOTES FOR NEXT TIME:**

# Fudgy Brownies

Some recipes are worth their weight in gold, and my friend Kate's brownies are one of those. Her family recipe, guarded like a treasure, has raised serious funds for our public school foundation and countless other causes—it's that good! Inspired by her baking magic, I set out to create my own ultimate brownie recipe, and this is the result. These brownies are rich, fudgy, and designed to make boxed mixes a distant memory. They've become a family favorite in our house, making appearances in care packages sent to the boys during finals week or just as a sweet reminder to come home.

**What you need:**

⅓ cup (28 g) Dutch-processed cocoa, my favorite cocoa is a brand from Holland called Droste®. You can find it in most specialty grocery stores.

½ cup + 2 tablespoons (148 ml) boiling water

2 ounces (57 g) unsweetened chocolate, finely chopped, I use 70% cacao

4 tablespoons unsalted butter, melted

½ cup plus 2 tablespoons (140 g) vegetable oil

2 large eggs

2 egg yolks

2 teaspoons vanilla extract

2½ cups (496 g) granulated sugar

1¾ cups (248 g) all-purpose flour

¾ teaspoon salt

1 cup (170 g) semisweet chocolate chips

1 cup (50 g) miniature marshmallows

1. **Getting started:** Adjust your oven rack to the lowest position and preheat it to 350°F (175°C). Grab a 8x8-inch (20 x 20 cm) baking pan and line it with foil, leaving a bit of an overhang on all sides. Spray it generously with baking spray (I use PAM® baking spray).

2. **Melt chocolate:** In a big mixing bowl, whisk together cocoa powder and boiling water until it's smooth and glossy. Add unsweetened chocolate and keep whisking until it melts into the mix. Whisk in melted butter and oil. Don't panic if it looks a little weird and curdled—it's totally normal and will smooth out soon!

3. **Add wet ingredients:** Crack in eggs and egg yolks, pour in vanilla, and whisk until mixture looks silky and uniform. Stir in sugar until it's fully dissolved and everything is smooth.

4. **Fold in flour:** Switch to a rubber spatula and gently fold in flour and salt, mixing just until combined. Finally, stir in the chopped chocolate and mini marshmallows—they'll make these brownies next-level delicious.

5. **Bake:** Scrape the batter into your prepared pan and spread out evenly. Slide into the oven and bake 30–35 minutes. Keep an eye on it toward the end—poke a toothpick into the middle (but not near edges). If it comes out with a few moist crumbs clinging on, they are done.

6. **Let them cool (seriously):** This is the hardest part—let the brownies cool in the pan on a wire rack for about 1½ hours. Then, use that handy foil overhang to lift the whole brownie slab out of the pan. Let it cool completely on the rack for another hour before cutting.

7. **Slice and serve:** Cut your brownies into 2-inch squares (or

**TABLE TALK TIPS:** The secret to these fudgy brownies? Chopped chocolate for depth and, wait for it—mini marshmallows! I know, it's not exactly farm-to-table, but sometimes, pure joy on a plate is all the reason you need. These brownies are my love letter to decadent, homemade indulgence, and I hope they'll bring a little extra sweetness to your table, too. Reynolds® non stick aluminum foil is a game changer. No need to spray or grease.

# Layered Pumpkin Cake
## with Browned Butter Cream Cheese Frosting and Caramel

Okay, so here's the deal—this cake has been declared the best cake I've ever made and I'm not exaggerating. It's a bit of a process, sure—there are a few steps, a few bowls to dirty, and a couple of things to watch carefully (caramel sauce, I'm looking at you), but trust me, it's all worth it. So much so that it has completely replaced the pumpkin pie we used to serve during the holidays. Yup, you read that right. People now expect this showstopper on the dessert table, and I'm more than happy to deliver.

**Cake (2 or 4 layer 6-inch cake)**

1 ⅔ cups plus 2 teaspoons (210 g) cake flour

1¾ teaspoon baking powder

¾ teaspoon baking soda

¾ teaspoon kosher salt

1 ½ teaspoons ground cinnamon

¾ teaspoon ground cardamom

¼ teaspoon freshly grated nutmeg

⅛ teaspoon ground allspice

¾ cup canola or vegetable oil

¾ cup (165 g) brown sugar

⅓ cup (65 g) granulated sugar

1 ½ teaspoons vanilla extract

1 (15 ounce/425g) canned pumpkin, at room temperature

3 large eggs, at room temperature

**Caramel sauce**

1 cup (200 g) granulated sugar

2 tablespoons unsalted butter, softened

¾ cup (180 ml) heavy cream, at room temperature

1 tablespoon whiskey or 2 teaspoons vanilla extract

½ teaspoon kosher salt

**Browned butter cream cheese frosting**

1 ½ sticks (170 g) unsalted butter

12 ounces (340 g) cream cheese

2 teaspoons vanilla extract

¼ teaspoon kosher salt

3 ½ cups (420 g) confectioners' sugar, sifted if very lumpy

**You will need two 6-inch round cake pans for this recipe**

1. **Before you begin:** Bring eggs, cream cheese and butter to room temperature.

2. **Grease pans:** Preheat oven to 350°F (175°C) and slide the rack to the middle. Butter or grease two 6-inch (15 cm) round cake pans, line them with parchment paper and grease the parchment for good measure. Flour the pans too, just to be safe.

3. **Sift dry ingredients:** Sift flour, baking powder, baking soda, cinnamon, cardamom, nutmeg, all spice and salt into a big bowl and set aside.

4. **Whisk together wet ingredients:** Using stand mixer, mix oil, sugar, brown sugar, and granulated sugar on medium-high. Let it beat away until everything is completely combined. Don't forget to stop and scrape the bowl every now and then.

5. **Add the eggs:** Add eggs one at a time, mixing for about 20 seconds between each one. When eggs are fully combined, add vanilla and pumpkin purée and mix well (it might look a little curdled, but trust me, that's normal).

## Layered Pumpkin Cake *(continued)*

1. **Add dry ingredients:** Turn mixer down to low, and add dry ingredients all at once. Stir until a few flour bits are still visible, then take the bowl off the mixer. Grab a rubber spatula and finish folding everything together, scraping bottom and sides so no dry bits are left behind. The batter will be thick.

2. **Bake:** Divide batter among the pans, smooth out the tops, and give each pan a little tap on the counter to release any trapped air. Wipe off any stray batter on the sides of the pans, then pop them in the oven and bake for 40-45 minutes, rotating halfway through. You'll know they're done when they're golden and puffy, and a toothpick inserted in center comes out with just a few moist crumbs. Cool in the pans for 10 minutes, then loosen the edges with a knife, flip them onto a rack, and let them cool completely, about 60 minutes.

3. **Caramel sauce:** While cakes cool, make the caramel sauce. Place sugar in a clean and dry heavy-bottomed medium saucepan over medium heat. Swirl it around frequently until the sugar dissolves ***(don't stir - unless you think it is burning)***. The sugar will begin to melt and turn a deep amber color—this happens fast, so don't walk away and keep swirling! When it's ready, remove from heat and whisk in softened butter and room temperature cream (it will expand and sputter before turning into a smooth sauce - just keep on whisking). Add whiskey and salt, then pour the caramel into a heat-safe container to cool to room temperature. You'll have about 1½ cups of liquid gold, plenty for another use.

4. **Make browned butter:** Melt butter in a small saucepan and cook, stirring constantly, 8-10 minutes until it turns golden brown with little browned bits (that's the good stuff). Pour butter into a bowl and set it over an ice bath to cool, stirring occasionally until it solidifies a bit—about 13-15 minutes. You're aiming for room-temperature consistency, so don't let it get too hard.

5. **Make frosting:** In stand mixer, beat cream cheese and the cooled browned butter on medium-high until smooth (about 2 minutes). Add vanilla and salt, mix it in, then slowly add powdered sugar. Start on low to avoid making a mess, increasing the speed after each addition. Once all the sugar is in, beat on medium-high for 1-2 minutes until smooth and fluffy. If it's too soft, throw it in the fridge for 20 minutes to firm up a bit.

6. **Trim cakes:** When the cakes are completely cool, gently peel off the parchment and trim any uneven edges (use a serrated knife if needed).

7. **Make it a 4 layer cake (see Table Talk Tips):** Set your baked and cooled cake on a flat parchment paper lined surface, such as a cake stand or cutting board. Using six to eight toothpicks mark around the sides of the entire cake so you can easily see the middle of the cake.

8. **Separate cakes:** Once you've marked the center with toothpicks, cut a strand of dental floss that's long enough to wrap around the cake. Wrap floss just above or below the toothpicks. Pull the floss toward the middle of the cake to make a quarter-inch incision around the entire cake. This action will help mark and guide your final cut. Using the dental floss or a long serrated knife, carefully slice the cake along the marked line, using a gentle sawing motion.

9. **Transfer to parchment paper:** Once you've sliced the cake in half, carefully remove the top layer

with a long cake spatula and the support of your non-dominant hand. Transfer the cake layer to a piece of parchment paper for easy moving.

10. **To decorate:** Add a small spoonful of buttercream onto the serving plate. Place your first cake layer on a serving plate, flat side up. Spread ¾ cup frosting on top, right to the edges. Drizzle 1 tablespoon caramel sauce over frosting, but don't go too crazy—it's all about balance. Place the second cake layer on top, then spread ¾ cup frosting and drizzle with another tablespoon of caramel. Repeat with a third layer if you are making a four layer cake. For the final cake layer, spread remaining 1 cup of frosting over top and sides. Smooth it out with an offset spatula for that sleek finish. Pop the cake in the fridge for 30 minutes to firm up the frosting.

11. **For the caramel drizzle:** Because who doesn't want more?: Spread ⅓ cup of room-temperature caramel sauce over the top and gently coax it toward the edges so it drips down the sides in a beautiful, messy cascade. Serve cake at room temperature, and store any leftovers in the fridge—but don't forget to bring it back to room temp before you dive in!

**TABLE TALK TIPS:** This makes a 4 layered 6 inch cake, for those who like a bit more frosting. Or keep it a 2 layer cake (more cake than frosting ratio). Trust me, this one's a keeper.

• Making this cake has become a bit of a family event. Everyone loves getting involved—especially when it comes to decorating (and by decorating, I mean licking the frosting bowl). Honestly, I think that's what they're really after, but who's judging? The frosting is just that good! Plus, you'll have some leftover caramel sauce, which—don't worry—it won't go to waste. Drizzle it on ice cream or just eat it straight with a spoon.

**NOTES FOR NEXT TIME:**

**Tuscan Salt**
Pg. 225

**Garlic Confit**
Pg. 229

**Mediterranean Relish**
Pg. 218

# Little Extras

"Sometimes the smallest things take up the most room in your heart."

— A.A. Milne (Winnie the Pooh)

# Mediterranean Relish

This relish is a game-changer. I first made a version of it during a week-long farm-to-table cooking class at the Culinary Institute of America, where we explored how simple ingredients can transform into something extraordinary. This is one of those recipes. The secret? Oven-dried roma tomatoes (pg.227)—a little planning ahead is worth the deep, concentrated tomato flavor they bring. Once you've got those on hand, this relish comes together easily and is so versatile.

**What you need (makes about 3 cups):**

- 1 cup (100 g) eggplant, peeled and cut into ½-inch (1.25 cm) cubes
- ¼ cup (60 ml) extra-virgin olive oil
- ½ red bell pepper, chopped
- ½ yellow bell pepper, chopped
- Generous pinch of salt
- ½ rounded cup (90 g) oven-dried Roma tomatoes (pg.227)
- 2 tablespoons Italian parsley, chopped
- 2 tablespoons green olives, pitted and chopped
- 2 tablespoons Niçoise olives, pitted and chopped
- 1 tablespoon garlic, peeled and chopped
- 3 tablespoons balsamic vinegar

1. **Roast the vegetables:** Preheat oven to 450°F (240°C). Line a rimmed baking sheet with parchment paper—this keeps the delicious caramelized bits from sticking to the pan. In a large bowl, toss eggplant and bell peppers with the olive oil, a generous pinch of salt, and a few grinds of black pepper. Spread out on the baking sheet in a single layer. Roast 20 minutes, give them a good turn, then roast another 10 minutes. You're looking for lightly charred edges and a soft, tender interior—perfectly roasted, but not shriveled.

2. **Prep the remaining ingredients:** While the vegetables roast, chop up oven-dried tomatoes, parsley, olives, and garlic. This is when the flavors start to come together.

3. **Combine and serve:** When roasted vegetables are out of the oven and still warm, transfer them to a serving bowl. Add the chopped ingredients and drizzle everything with balsamic vinegar. Give it a gentle toss, taste and adjust seasoning if needed.

NOTES FOR NEXT TIME:

**TABLE TALK TIPS:** Serve warm or at room temperature. It's amazing on toasted baguette slices, spooned over pasta, layered into sandwiches, or as a topping for grilled portobello mushrooms (pg. 84).

# Fruit Compote

**What you need:**

*2 tablespoons unsalted butter, divided*

*1 tablespoon olive oil*

*¼ cup (30 g) shallots, minced*

*2 cups coarsely chopped stone fruit, such as peaches and cherries, about 340 g / ¾ pound total*

*2 tablespoons honey*

*Coarse salt and pepper, to taste*

*¼ teaspoon ancho chili powder*

*¼ cup (60 ml) balsamic vinegar – I like to use a good-quality aged balsamic from Modena, Italy.*

1. **Sauté shallots:** In a large sauce pan over medium heat, melt one tablespoon butter with the olive oil. Add shallots and saute 2 minutes.

2. **Cook to thicken:** Add honey, salt, pepper and, stone fruit. Cook over medium-low heat, stirring occasionally, until fruit is soft, 8 to 12 minutes. Stir in balsamic vinegar and chili powder. Reduce heat to low and simmer until sauce begins to thicken, about 2 minutes. Add remaining one tablespoon of butter and cook for another 1 to 2 minutes.

3. **Cool and store:** Remove from heat and let cool. Refrigerate in air tight container if not using immediately; the compote will keep for up to one week. Serve on grilled or roasted meats like prime rib (pg. 120)

# Horseradish Sauce

**What you need:**

*¼ cup (60 ml) crème fraîche, sour cream, or heavy whipping cream*

*1 tablespoon prepared horseradish*

*¾ tablespoon freshly ground pink peppercorns*

*Salt, to taste*

1. **Whipping cream:** If using whipped cream, place in a mixing bowl and whisk until soft peaks form. If using crème fraîche or sour cream, place in a mixing bowl and give a good stir.

2. **Mix it all together:** Gently fold in horseradish and ground pink peppercorns. Season with salt to taste.

 **NOTES FOR NEXT TIME:**

# My "keeper" Risotto

**What you need:**

0.25 ounces (7 g) Arborio rice

¼ cup (40 g) yellow onion, diced

4 tablespoons butter, divided

1 cup (240 ml) white wine

3 to 4 cups (720–960 ml) vegetable or chicken stock

¼ cup (25 g) Parmesan cheese, grated

2 heaping tablespoons mascarpone cheese

salt and pepper, to taste

olive oil or walnut oil, for garnish

**Sachet / Bouquet Garni**

1 sprig thyme

1 sprig rosemary

1 clove garlic, peeled and cracked

1. **Getting started:** Warm stock in a saucepan. Using a cheese cloth, make a bundle with rosemary, thyme, and garlic. In a heavy bottomed pan, melt 2 tablespoons butter over medium heat  Add onion and cook 3 minutes until translucent. Add rice and cook, stirring constantly, 1 minute. Pour wine into the pan and continue stirring. When wine is reduced, add a ladle of hot stock and the sashet/bouquet garni. Give it a quick stir. When stock is absorbed add more stock until it begins to puddle. Give another stir then wait for the stock to be absorbed. Repeat this process until rice is cooked al dente, then add the rest of the butter, giving it a good stir.

2. **Make it cheesy:** Stir in mascarpone cheese and Parmesan cheeses, until a creamy consistency is achieved. Add more cheese if needed. Season with salt and pepper. Taste and adjust seasoning. Transfer to a serving bowl and drizzle with olive oil or walnut oil.

**TABLE TALK TIPS:** Other garnish ideas:  ½ cup oven-dried tomatoes (pg.227) or sun dried tomatoes, 1 cup medley of mushrooms, sauteed (Oyster, Shiitake, etc), ½ cup diced roasted butternut squash. This risotto pairs beautifully with wine braised short ribs (pg.119)  Start the risotto after the short ribs have braised for the first 2 hours.

# Homemade Gravy

1/4 pound (1 stick / 113 g) unsalted butter

1 1/2 cups (225 g) chopped yellow onion , about 2 medium onions

1/4 cup (30 g) all-purpose flour

1 teaspoon kosher salt

1/2 teaspoon freshly ground black pepper

2 cups (480 ml) chicken stock, heated — Note: you can use Better Than Bouillon® chicken or Turkey  bouillon base

1 tablespoon cognac or brandy

1 tablespoon white wine (optional)

1 tablespoon heavy cream (optional)

1. **Sauté onions:** Melt butter in a large sauté pan (around 10 to 12 inches) over medium-low heat. Add onions and let them cook slowly, about 12 to 15 minutes. You're looking for them to turn a light golden brown. Once onions are soft and caramel-colored, sprinkle flour over the top. Whisk it in so it coats onions evenly, then season with salt and pepper. Cook for 2 to 3 minutes. This step is key; This helps cook off the raw flour flavor.

2. **Add stock:** Pour in the hot chicken stock and cognac. Stir well and let it simmer, uncovered, 4 to 5 minutes, until it starts to thicken and looks glossy and luscious. If you're feeling fancy, stir in a splash of wine and a little cream at the end for extra depth.

3. **Taste and adjust seasoning:** Serve warm—maybe over roasted turkey or chicken, mashed potatoes, or whatever calls for a generous drizzle of gravy.

# Homemade Chicken Stock

**What you need:**

*4 bone-in chicken thighs or 2 bone-in chicken breasts (6–8 ounces / 170–227 g each)*

*2 quarts (1.9 liters) water or chicken stock for richer flavor*

*1 small leek, white and light-green parts only, roughly chopped*

*1/2 fennel bulb, including fonds, roughly chopped*

*3 garlic cloves, smashed*

*1 sprig fresh thyme or 1 teaspoon dried thyme*

*5 sprigs fresh parsley*

1. **Gather all your ingredients:** Combine all ingredients in a stockpot. Make sure you have enough water or stock to cover the chicken and most of the vegetables and herbs, about 2 to 3 quarts. Cover and bring stock to a boil.

2. **Simmer:** Uncover and reduce heat to simmer for about 1-½ hours.

3. **Remove from heat:** Remove chicken from the pot and reserve for another use.

4. **Strain liquid:** Strain into another pot or large measuring cup, discarding the solids.

**TABLE TALK TIPS:** How to use leftover chicken meat from the stock? Once chicken from the stock is cool enough to handle, shred the meat from the bones using your hands and reserve for another use. The breast meat is best when diced with a knife to make equal 1-inch pieces. Stock can be refrigerated up to 4 days or frozen up to 6 months.

# Mint Mojo Sauce

**What you need:**

*1 cup (30 g) fresh-picked mint leaves*

*½ cup (15 g) fresh-picked parsley leaves*

*2 medium garlic cloves, minced, about 1 teaspoon / 5 g*

*¼ cup (40 g) capers, rinsed and drained*

*1 ½ tablespoons lemon juice and 1 teaspoon grated lemon zest from 1 lemon*

*2 tablespoons freshly squeezed orange juice*

*1 small shallot, minced, about 2 tablespoons / 15 g*

*Pinch of red pepper flakes*

*¾ cup (180 ml) extra-virgin olive oil*

*Kosher salt and freshly ground black pepper, to taste*

1. **Blend into chunky puree:** Combine mint, parsley, garlic, capers, lemon juice, orange juice, shallot, pepper flakes, and olive oil in the bowl of a food processor or blender and process until a chunky puree is formed. Transfer to a small bowl, stir in zest and season to taste with salt and pepper, and set aside.

**TABLE TALK TIPS:** Fantastic sauce to dollop onto a bowl of chicken noodle soup or spread on your favorite sandwich (like my smashed chicken sandwich (pg.87).

**NOTES FOR NEXT TIME:**

# Roasted Rhubarb Agrodolce

**What you need to make 2 cups:**

*4 cups (about 480 g) rhubarb, cut into 1-inch (2.5 cm) pieces*

*1 to 2 tablespoons white balsamic vinegar*

*⅓ cup (70 g) organic raw turbinado sugar*

*1 teaspoon vanilla paste – note: you can substitute with vanilla extract, though vanilla paste has a more intense flavor*

1. **Getting started:** Preheat oven to 350°F (175°C) and line a baking dish with parchment paper for easy cleanup. In a mixing bowl, combine rhubarb, vinegar, sugar, and vanilla paste. Gently toss until rhubarb is evenly coated.

2. **Bake:** Spread rhubarb in a single layer in your prepared baking dish—try not to crowd the pieces so they roast evenly. Slide dish into the oven and roast for 30 to 40 minutes, or until rhubarb is tender but still holding its shape. You're looking for that perfect balance—soft, but not collapsing.

3. **Cool and store:** Once it's out of the oven, carefully pour rhubarb and all those lovely pan juices into an airtight container. Let cool to room temperature before refrigerating.

**TABLE TALK TIPS:** This roasted rhubarb agrodolce was inspired by a trip to Modena, Italy. After touring a balsamic vinegar loft, I came home determined to put my bottle of white balsamic vinegar to good use—and find a new way to use the armfuls of rhubarb growing in the garden. The result? A tangy-sweet condiment that's wildly versatile. It makes about 2 cups (480 mL) — enough to swirl into yogurt or spoon over a chocolate mousse (pg.204) ice cream (pg.205), fold into crème fraîche, or serve alongside grilled pork tenderloin or chops.

# Hot Fudge

**What you need to make 1 cup:**

*5 ounces (140 g) semisweet chocolate, chopped*

*2 tablespoons plus 2 teaspoons Dutch-processed cocoa powder, sifted*

*1/4 cup plus 2 tablespoons (75mL) light corn syrup or substitute honey*

*2 tablespoons plus 2 teaspoons sugar*

*2 tablespoons plus 2 teaspoons heavy cream*

*2 tablespoons plus 2 teaspoons water*

*Pinch of table salt*

*1 ½ tablespoons unsalted butter, cut into ¼-inch (6.35 mm) pieces*

*½ teaspoon vanilla extract*

1. **Melt chocolate:** Grab a microwave-safe bowl (like a 4-cup (960 mL) or glass pyrex® measuring cup) and pop in the chocolate. Microwave in 30-second bursts, whisking between each round, until totally melted and smooth. This usually takes 1-3 minutes, depending on your microwave.

2. **Add cocoa powder:** Sift cocoa powder into melted chocolate. Whisk until it's fully mixed and with no lumps. Trust me, sifting is worth the little extra step—no one wants lumpy fudge sauce! Set aside.

3. **Cook to thicken:** Grab a medium saucepan. Combine corn syrup, sugar, cream, water, and salt. Set heat to medium and stir often, watching it thicken, about 4 minutes.

4. **Make it smooth:** Once that sauce is thickened, take pan off the heat and whisk in butter and vanilla. Let cool down for about 2 minutes, so it's not boiling hot. Whisk in your melted chocolate mix. Keep whisking until it's all smooth and dreamy.

5. **Now for the best part:** Drizzle that warm, glorious hot fudge sauce over ice cream (pg. 205)!

# Green Salad and Jam Vinaigrette

**Jam vinaigrette**

1 tablespoon sweet and spicy pepper jelly, divided (or another jelly of choice)

1 ½ tablespoons extra virgin olive oil

1 ½ tablespoons apple cider vinegar

1 shallot, minced or thinly sliced, about 1 tablespoon / 15 g

¼ teaspoon table salt

⅛ teaspoon pepper freshly ground black pepper, to taste

**Mixed Greens Salad**

4 ounces (115 g) mixed greens (about 3 cups)

⅓ cup (50 g) red or green seedless grapes, halved

2 tablespoons sunflower seeds, toasted and salted

2 tablespoons golden raisins

2 tablespoons pumpkin seeds, toasted and salted

2 ounces (55 g) manchego cheese, grated

Toasted or caramelized nuts (optional)

1. **Make vinaigrette:** In large salad bowl, whisk together 1 tablespoon jelly, olive oil, vinegar, shallot, ¼ teaspoon salt, and ⅛ teaspoon pepper. Give it a taste—if you want more of that sweet-spicy kick, stir in more jelly.

2. **Assemble salad:** Add mixed greens, grapes, sunflower seeds, raisins, and pumpkin seeds directly into the bowl with the dressing. Using tongs, toss everything together until the greens are well coated and glossy.

3. **Finish and serve:** Add the manchego cheese over the top and sprinkle with nuts, if using. Give it one final gentle toss, then serve immediately.

**TABLE TALK TIPS:** This is an any-season salad, and the best part is that the dressing is homemade using jam or jelly. I love picking up local jams and transforming them into quick, flavorful salad dressings.

 **NOTES FOR NEXT TIME:**

# Tuscan Salt

**What you need:**

¼ cup (12g) chopped fresh rosemary leaves

¼ cup (5g) chopped fresh sage leaves

2 tablespoons chopped fresh parsley leaves

1 tablespoon chopped fresh thyme leaves

1 tablespoon chopped fresh oregano leaves

17-18 ounces (500g) flaked Mediterranean sea salt or right around 2 cups , divided

2 medium garlic cloves

1 teaspoon fine ground black pepper

1. **Getting started:** Preheat oven to 200°F (95°C). While it's warming, grab a 12 × 18-inch (30 × 46 cm) sheet pan and set aside.

2. **Rough chop the herbs:** Give the herbs a quick chop to make the rosemary, sage, parsley, thyme, and oregano manageable. Don't stress about getting them super fine—the food processor is about to be your best friend and do the heavy lifting.

3. **Give them a good blitz:** Toss chopped herbs into bowl of a food processor (a mini one works great here). Add ¼ cup sea salt and pulse until everything is chopped down to the texture of slightly damp sand. Add the garlic and pulse again. Keep going until the garlic disappears into the mix—it should look like wet sand at this point, green and fragrant.

4. **Add more salt:** Scrape every last bit of that herby goodness out of the food processor and onto sheet pan. Add the rest of the sea salt and black pepper, using your hands to mix it all together. Go ahead, get in there—it should look like a gorgeous, green, slightly damp salt blend.

5. **Bake:** Pop the pan into preheated oven for 30 minutes. After that, turn off the oven but leave the pan inside for another 30–60 minutes to cool down and dry out completely.

6. **Cool:** Once the salt is completely cool, rub it between your hands to break up any clumps. For smaller lumps, a spoon works great. Don't skip this step—you want that beautifully textured salt, not a giant herb salt brick.

7. **Store:** Transfer your finished Tuscan Sea Salt to airtight jars. It'll keep practically forever (thanks, salt!) and will be ready to sprinkle on just about anything, any time.

**TABLE TALK TIPS:** This salt makes a fantastic hostess gift! I order these cute jars online including wooden spoons.

# Lemon Tahini Sauce
## The Ultimate Creamy, Tangy Finishing Touch

Let's talk tahini sauce—a creamy, nutty, and slightly tangy condiment that transforms everything it touches. Whether you're serving grilled meats, kebabs, roasted veggies, or even baked fish, this sauce ties it all together with its velvety texture and bright flavor. It's also a go-to for garnishing hummus or drizzling over a chopped salad for that perfect finishing touch.

**What you need:**

*1 clove garlic, minced*

*Fresh squeezed juice of ½ a lemon, adjust to taste*

*2 tablespoons quality tahini*

*2 tablespoons ice-cold water, plus more if needed*

*A pinch of cumin (optional)*

*Pinch of salt*

1. **Combine ingredients:** In a bowl, combine tahini paste, minced garlic, lemon juice, and a pinch of salt.
2. **Add water gradually:** Start adding ice-cold water one tablespoon at a time, whisking vigorously after each addition. At first, it might look like the sauce is splitting—don't panic! Keep going. Slowly, it will emulsify into a smooth, creamy sauce. Continue adding water, a little at a time, until you reach your desired consistency. Want a thicker sauce? Use less water. Looking for a drizzle-friendly version? Add a bit more. Taste and adjust with more lemon, salt, or garlic to suit your preferences. If making the Harissa Baked Fish on pg.139, add a pinch of cumin.
3. **Cover and chill:** Once you've nailed the flavor, cover and refrigerate sauce until you're ready to use it. It thickens slightly as it chills, so give it a quick stir before serving.

**TABLE TALK TIPS:** There are many ways to use your lemon tahini sauce. Drizzle it over grilled meats or kebabs for a nutty, tangy punch. Toss it with roasted vegetables like carrots, sweet potatoes, or cauliflower. Use it as a dressing for chopped salads or grain bowls. Spoon it over baked fish for an elegant, flavorful finish. Swirl it into hummus or use it as a garnish for soups and stews.

**Pro Tip:** When buying tahini, don't worry if it looks separated—just stir it back together. Everyone has their favorite brand, but I'm partial to those with a rich, toasted sesame seed flavor. Once you find one you love, you'll never look back.

 **NOTES FOR NEXT TIME:**

# Creamy Green Peppercorn Sauce

Looking for the perfect sauce to pair with your Beef Wellington, tenderloin or a beef roast? This green peppercorn sauce has just the right amount of savory, creamy, and peppery goodness. A touch of brandy and soy sauce gives it depth, while heavy cream makes it luscious without feeling over-the-top. Plus, it's quick to whip up while your roast or beef wellington rests—or you can make it ahead and simply warm it up when ready to serve.

**What you need:**

1 tablespoon unsalted butter

2 tablespoons jarred green peppercorns (in brine), rinsed and smashed. I have bought these online.

1 tablespoon minced shallot

1 ½ teaspoons all-purpose flour

¾ cup (180 ml) beef broth

2 tablespoons brandy

1 tablespoon soy sauce

½ cup (120 ml) heavy cream

1. **Melt and sizzle:** In a small saucepan, melt butter over medium-low heat. While it's warming, take a moment to rinse and gently smash the green peppercorns—either using a mortar and pestle, or by placing them in a plastic resealable bag and giving them a few firm whacks with a rolling pin or rubber mallet. You don't need to pulverize them—just crack them open a bit to release their flavor. Add the crushed peppercorns and minced shallot to the butter and cook, stirring often, until shallot softens—about 3 to 5 minutes. Stir in flour and cook for 2 minutes, stirring constantly.

2. **Whisk and reduce:** Turn up heat to medium and whisk in beef broth, brandy, and soy sauce. Bring it all to a boil, then let it simmer until mixture reduces to about ¾ cup, which should take around 12 to 15 minutes.

3. **Finish with creamy goodness:** Stir in heavy cream and let the sauce cook down a bit more until reduced to about 1 cup, about 10 minutes. Taste and season with a pinch of salt and pepper if needed.

# Oven-Dried Tomatoes

These homemade "sun-dried" tomatoes are easy to make and bring a deep, rich flavor to anything they touch. Plan ahead, as they take a few hours in the oven, but the payoff is incredible.

1 pint (10–12 ounces / 280–340 g) cherry, grape or Roma tomatoes—see note below)

Fine sea salt

**TABLE TALK TIPS:** If using roma tomatoes, cut them in half lengthwise, scoop out the pulp, and follow the same roasting method. Because of their size, they will take around 5-6 hours to fully dry.
• Freezing tip: Arrange dried tomatoes in a single layer on parchment-lined baking sheet and freeze for 2 hours. Then transfer to a freezer-safe bag, remove any excess air, and freeze up to 3 months

1. **Prepare the tomatoes:** Preheat oven to 250°F (120°C). Line a large baking sheet with parchment paper. Slice tomatoes in half lengthwise and arrange them cut-side up on the baking sheet.

2. **Slow roast:** Bake 2.5 to 3.5 hours, checking occasionally to avoid burning. They should be shriveled and slightly chewy but still tender.

3. **Store or serve:** Use right away, or store them in a jar covered with olive oil. Add a clove of garlic or some herbs if preferred. Keep refrigerated up to 4 days, or freeze for longer storage (see note).

# Garlic Confit

This is more than just garlic—it's a jar of garlic and herb-infused oil. It's a beautifully mellow, flavorful oil that carries subtle garlic and herb notes. It's perfect for adding a mild garlic flavor to your dish without overpowering it.

**What you need:**

*10 garlic cloves, peeled*

*1 cup (240 ml) olive oil (or enough to cover the garlic)*

*1 green chili pepper, for a mild kick (optional)*

*4-5 sprigs fresh thyme (or your favorite herb like rosemary or oregano)*

1. **Prep your ingredients:** Gather peeled garlic cloves, chili pepper (leave it whole or slice for more heat), and thyme.
2. **Combine everything and simmer:** In heavy-bottomed saucepan, add garlic cloves, chili pepper, and thyme. Pour in enough olive oil to mostly cover the garlic—you want those cloves swimming in the oil.
3. **Cover and simmer:** Put lid on the saucepan and place over medium-low heat. Let it gently simmer for about 25 minutes. The key here is low and slow—don't rush it! Once the oil gets hot, turn heat down to keep it from bubbling too hard. You're aiming for soft, golden garlic, not crispy brown.
4. **Cool It down:** When garlic is soft and oil is infused with all that aromatic goodness, remove saucepan from heat and let it cool.
5. **Store:** Pour cooled oil into a clean jar, making sure to include the garlic cloves, chili, and thyme. Seal it up and let it sit on the counter or a pantry shelf. It'll keep for ages.

**TABLE TALK TIPS:** There are many ways to use your Garlic Confit. Drizzle oil over hummus for a gourmet upgrade. Toss it with salads or roasted veggies for instant sophistication. Brush it on sandwiches or use it to finish a steak. Spoon it over fried or scrambled eggs—seriously, try it. Mash the cloves onto bread for an impromptu garlic toast.

**Pro Tip:** The soft garlic cloves and sprigs of thyme make gorgeous garnishes, so don't skip those. They taste as good as they look!

 **NOTES FOR NEXT TIME:**

# Recipe Index

**Açaí**
- Açaí Bowls..........186

**Alcohol Drinks**
- Blackberry Mojito..........39
- Blood Red Orange Margarita..........45
- Dr. Werley Whiskey Sour..........43
- Limoncello Sorbet Spritz..........41
- Minnesota Bootlegger..........39
- Twist on a Dirty Martini..........42

**Apple**
- Apple & Winter Squash Salad...173
- Apple Kohlrabi & Manchego Slaw..........158
- Bookclub Quinoa Chicken Salad..........163
- Lagoon Chicken Wild Rice Salad..........167
- Turkey Breast Stuffing..........149

**Apple Cider**
- Fruitcake Stuffed Pork..........104
- Pear & Prosciutto Stuffed Pork..103

**Apple Juice**
- Lagoon Chicken Wild Rice Salad..........167

**Apricot Preserves & Dried**
- Apricot Harissa-Glazed Chicken..125

**Artichoke**
- Artichoke and Ricotta Flan..........167

**Arugula, Baby Leaves**
- Asian Flat Iron Steak..........112
- Balsamic Pear, Pistachio Pesto Tartine..........28
- Grilled Portobello Burger..........84
- Rosemary Ricotta Toast w/ Figs..32

**Asparagus**
- Asparagus, Leek & Edamame Soup..........62
- Spring Lasagna..........145

**Avocado**
- Adobo Flank Steak..........110
- Avocado Toast w/ Sweet&Spicy Tomatoes..........192
- Tuna Poke Bowl..........136

**Bacon**
- Chicken, Leek & Tarragon Pot-Pie..........142
- Supper Club Wedge Salad..........171

**Baguette (see also Crostini)**
- Asparagus, Leek & Edamame Soup..........62
- Baked Onion Soup..........57
- Heirloom Tomato Gazpacho..........72
- Parmesan-Crusted Salmon Caesar Salad..........155
- Rosemary Ricotta Toast w/ Figs..32

**Balsamic Vinegar of Modena PGI**
- Avocado Toast with Sweet & Spicy Tomatoes..........192
- Baked Salmon..........147
- Balsamic Pear, Pistachio Pesto Tartine..........28
- Chicken Marsala..........146
- Fall Farmer's Market Soup..........54
- Fruit Compote..........220
- Heirloom Tomato Gazpacho..........72
- Mediterranean Relish..........218
- Panna Cotta Dessert Cups..........199
- *white balsamic*, Roasted Rhubarb Agrodolce..........223
- Strawberry Gazpacho..........74

**Banana**
- Açaí Bowls..........186
- Blueberry Yogurt Smoothie..........187

**Beans (see also Cannellini beans)**
- Adobo Flank Steak (black beans)..........110
- Kim's White Chicken Chili..........66
- Soupe au Pistou (green beans)....58

**Beef**
- Adobo Flank Steak..........110
- Asian Flat Iron Steak..........112
- Aunt Sherril's Runza (ground beef)..........80
- Beef Wellington (tenderloin)..........93
- Hachis Parmentier (ground beef)..........116
- Hollace's Bolognese Recipe (ground beef)..........107
- Passover Brisket..........99
- Perfect Pot Roast..........114
- Philly Cheesesteaks (flank)..........79
- Prime Rib Roast..........120
- Short Rib Burger..........82
- Wine-Braised Short Ribs..........119

**Beer**
- California Fish Tacos (light lager..........126
- Stout Chocolate Bundt Cake.....207

**Beets**
- Roasted Beet..........158

**Blackberries**
- Blackberry Mojito..........41
- Lemon-Blackberry Fool..........197

**Blood Oranges**
- Blood Red Orange Margarita..........43

**Blueberries**
- Acai Bowls..........186
- Blueberry Yogurt Smoothie..........187
- Lagoon Chicken Wild Rice Salad..........167
- Lemon Blueberry French Toast..181
- Maple Granola (dried blueberries)..........188

**Bourbon**
- Bourbon-Glazed Salmon Bites.....35
- Fruitcake Stuffed Pork Loin..........104

**Brandy**
- Creamy Green Peppercorn Sauce..........227
- Homemade Gravy..........221

**Bread (see also Baguette and Crostini)**
- Avocado Toast with Sweet & Spicy Tomatoes..........192
- Croque Monsieur Sandwich..........88

Deviled Egg Salad........................168
Eggs in Purgatory....................183
Fall Farmer's Market Soup............54
Grilled Portobella Burger..............84
Heirloom Tomato Gazpacho........72
Lemon Blueberry French Toast.181
Pan con Tomate................................21
Philly Cheesesteaks......................79
Rosemary Ricotta Toast w/ Figs.32
Short Rib Burger..............................82
Smashed Chicken Sandwich.........87
Spiedies.................................................95
Tuna Cheese Melt............................86

### Burrata
Chicken Parmesan Meatballs....132
Pasta Diavola................................127

### Cabbage
Aunt Sherril's Runzas......................80

### Cantaloupe
Cantaloupe Sweet Corn
  Gazpacho.........................................72

### Capers
Mint Mojito Sauce........................222

### Caramelized Onions
Baked Onion Soup...........................57

### Carrots
Chicken, Leek & Tarragon Pot Pie.....
  ....................................................142
Fall Farmer's Market Soup............54
Hachis Parmentier........................116
Hollace's Bolognese Recipe........107
Roasted Chicken Noodle Soup....65
Maple-Roasted Carrots...............170
Roasted Carrot Soup......................53
Roasted Vegetable Platter..........160
Soupe au Pistou...............................58
Sunday Supper Pork Ragu..........115
Tuna Poke Bowl..............................136
Wine-Braised Short Ribs............119

### Celery
Chicken, Leek & Tarragon Pot Pie.....
  ....................................................142
Deviled Egg Salad........................168
Hachis Parmentier........................116

Hollace's Bolognese Recipe........107
Icelandic Fish Stew..........................68
Lagoon Chicken Wild Rice
  Salad.............................................167
Roasted Chicken Noodle Soup....65
Soupe au Pistou...............................58
Sunday Supper Pork Ragu..........115
Tuna Cheese Melt............................86
Turkey Breast Stuffing............... 149
Wine-Braised Short Ribs ............119

### Celery Root
Roasted Celery Root.................. 172

### Chai Seeds
Mango Green Tea..........................187

### Cheese (see also Parmesan Cheese
Apple,Kohlrabi & Manchego Slaw...
  ....................................................158
Asparagus, Leek & Edamame Soup.
  ......................................................62
Aunt Sherril's Runza......................80
Baked Onion Soup..........................57
Balsamic Pear, Pistachio Pesto
  Tartine............................................28
Cheesy Mexican Street Corn
  Dip.....25
Croque Monsieur Sandwich..........88
Easy Sausage & Spinach Egg Bake...
  ....................................................184
Goat cheese in Spring Lasagna.145
Greek Baked Ziti...........................100
Green Salad and Jam
  Vinaigrette................................224
Icelandic Fish Stew..........................68
Kim's White Chicken Chili............66
Mediterranean Crostini.................24
North Shore Taleggio Fondue......23
Philly Cheesesteaks......................79
Roasted Red Pepper Soup............60
Rosemary Ricotta Toast w/ Figs..32
Skillet Scalloped Potatoes........174
Spring Lasagna.............................145
Supper Club Wedge Salad.........171
Supper Club Creamed Spinach
  Casserole..................................157
Tuna Cheese Melt............................86

### Chestnuts
Lagoon Chicken Wild Rice
  Salad.............................................167

### Chicken
Apricot Harissa-Glazed Chicken125
*breast in*, Bookclub Quinoa Chicken
  Salad ..........................................163
   Chicken, Leek & Tarragon
     Pot Pie......................................142
   Chicken Marsala...................146
   Supper Club Cordon Bleu....134
*ground in*, Baked Chicken Parmesan
  Meatballs..................................132
Homemade Chicken Stock.........222
Kim's White Chicken Chili.............66
Lagoon Chicken Wild Rice
  Salad.............................................167
*rotisserie in*, Leftover Roasted
  Chicken Noodle Soup .............65
*thighs in*, Sheet Pan Chicken......128
   Smashed Chicken Sandwich...87
*whole legs*, Can Pepi Fried
  Chicken........................................131

### Chickpeas
Traditional Hummus.....................26

### Chilies
Adobo Flank Steak.......................110
California Fish Tacos....................126
Cantaloupe Sweet Corn
  Gazpacho......................................72
Cheesy Mexican Street Corn Dip.25
Kim's White Chicken Chili.............66
Peach & Cucumber Gazpacho......73

### Chutney
Mango, in Glazed Ham.................97

### Chocolate and Chocolate Chips
Chocolate Mousse......................204
Fudgy Brownies............................210
Hot Fudge.......................................223
Molten Lava Cakes......................200
Salted Shortbread Chocolate Chip
  Cookies......................................202
Slope-Side Hot Chocolate...........46

**Chocolate Chip Cookies**
  Tiramisu Icebox Cake...................201
**Clam Juice**
  Icelandic Fish Stew.........................68
**Cocoa Powder**
  Fudgy Brownies............................210
  Hot Fudge........................................223
  Molten Lava Cakes.......................200
  Slope-Side Hot Chocolate............46
  Stout Chocolate Bundt Cake.....207
  Tiramisu Icebox Cake...................201
**Coconut Milk and Coconut Cream**
  Roasted Beets..............................158
  Roasted Carrot Soup......................53
  Roasted Red Pepper Soup..................60
**Compote**
  Prime Rib Roast............................120
**Coconut Milk and Coconut Cream**
  Roasted Beets..............................158
  Roasted Carrot Soup......................53
  Roasted Red Pepper Soup............60
**Compote**
  Prime Rib Roast............................120
**Corn**
  Adobo Flank Steak......................110
  Cantaloupe Sweet Corn Gazpacho......................................72
  Cheesy Mexican Street Corn Dip.25
  Low Country Boil..........................130
**Couscous**
  Apricot Harissa-Glazed Chicken.......................................125
**Cranberries**
  Apple & Winter Squash Salad..173
  Lagoon Chicken Wild Rice Salad.............................................167
  Maple Granola...............................188
**Cream Cheese**
  Avocado Toast w/ Sweet & Spicy Tomatoes....................................192

Cheesy Mexican Street Corn Dip.25
Layered Pumpkin Cake...............213
Mediterranean Crostini................24
**Crème Fraîche**
  Chocolate Mousse.......................204
  Citrus-Cured Gravlax...................189
  Heirloom Tomato Gazpacho........72
  Horseradish Sauce.......................220
  Lemon-Blackberry Fool...............197
  Roasted Carrot Soup.....................53
  Spicy Cucumber Salad................165
**Crostini**
  Asparagus, Leek & Edamame Soup.
  ...........................................................62
  Mediterranean Crostini................24
**Croutons**
  Baked Onion Soup..........................57
  North Shore Taleggio Fondue...233
**Cucumbers**
  Crispy Lamb Pita............................83
  Heirloom Tomato Gazpacho........72
  Peach & Cucumber Gazpacho......73
  Strawberry Gazpacho....................74
  Tuna Poke Bowl.............................136
**Curry Paste**
  Green, Can Pepi Fried Chicken...131
**Currants**
  Apricot Harissa-Glazed Chicken.......................................125
**Ciabatta (see also Bread and Baguette)**
  Balsamic Pear, Pistachio Pesto Tartine...........................................28
  Turkey Breast Stuffing.................149
**Dips**
  Baba Ghanoush...............................31
  Cheesy Mexican Street Corn Dip.25
  Traditional Hummus.......................26
**Edamame**
  Asparagus, Leek & Edamame Soup.
  ...........................................................62
**Eggplant**
  Baba Ghanoush...............................31

Greek Baked Ziti............................100
Mediterranean Relish...................218
Soupe au Pistou..............................58
**Espresso**
  Tiramisu Icebox Cake...................201
**Farro**
  Apple Winter Squash Salad.....173
**Fennel**
  Harissa Baked Fish.......................139
  Roasted Vegetable Platter.........160
  Sausage and Fennel Rigatoni...113
  Sunday Supper Pork Ragu.........115
  Tomato and Fennel Soup..............50
**Feta (see also Whipped Feta)**
  Greek Baked Ziti............................100
**Figs**
  Pear and Prosciutto Pork Loin...103
  Rosemary Ricotta Toast w/ Figs..32
**Fruit Cake**
  Fruitcake Stuffed Pork Loin........104
**Furikake Rice Seasoning**
  Tuna Poke Bowl.............................136
**Garlic Confit**
  Traditional Hummus.......................26
  Rosemary Ricotta Toast.w/ Figs..32
**Gouda Cheese**
  Croque Monsieur Sandwich..........88
  Icelandic Fish Stew.........................68
  Roasted Red Pepper Soup............60
**Graham Crackers**
  Panna Cotta Dessert Cups..........199
**Grapes**
  Bookclub Quinoa Chicken Salad.............................................163
  Green Salad and Jam Vinaigrette...............................224
  Lagoon Chicken Wild Rice Salad.............................................167
**Gruyère Cheese**
  Baked Onion Soup..........................57
  Hachis Parmentier........................116
  Herb-Pot & Gruyère Soufflé.......179

Supper Club Cordon Bleu.................134
Tuna Cheese Melt................................86

## Halibut
Baked Halibut ben Papillote............140
California Fish Tacos........................126
Harissa Baked Fish.............................139
Icelandic Fish Stew...............................68

## Ham (see also Prosciutto)
Croque Monsieur Sandwich..............88
Glazed Ham............................................97

## Horseradish
Horseradish Sauce............................220
Low Country Boil..............................130

## Hot Honey
Can Pepi Fried Chicken......................131

## Hummus
with Garlic Confit and Tahini Sauce...26

## Iceberg Lettuce
Supper Club Wedge Salad...............157

## Irish Crème
Stout Chocolate Bundt Cake..........207
Tiramisu Icebox Cake........................201

## Jam
Green Salad and Jam Vinaigrette...224
Lemon Blueberry French Toast.......181

## Kahlúa Liqueur
Tiramisu Icebox Cake........................201

## Kohlrabi
Apple, Kohlrabi & Manchego Slaw.158

## Lamb
Crispy Lamb Pita..................................83
Greek Baked Ziti................................100
Hachis Parmentier..............................116
Spiedies..................................................95

## Leeks
Asparagus, Leek & Edamame Soup .62
Chicken, Leek & Tarragon Pot Pie ..142
Homemade Chicken Stock...............222
Icelandic Fish Stew...............................68
Roasted Chicken Noodle Soup..........65
Soupe au Pistou....................................58
Supper Club Cordon Bleu................134

Wine-Braised Short Ribs..................119

## Lemon Curd
Lemon Blueberry French Toast.......181

## Lemonade Concentrate
Dr. Werley Whiskey Sour.....................43
Minnesota Bootlegger.........................39

## Limoncello
Limoncello Sorbet Spritz....................41

## Limeade Concentrate
Minnesota Bootlegger.........................39

## Madeira
Beef Wellington....................................93

## Mango
Mango Green Tea................................187
Mango Lassi Smoothie......................187

## Marsala
Chicken Marsala.................................146

## Mascarpone Cheese
My "Keeper" Risotto.........................221
Tiramisu Icebox Cake........................201

## Marshmallows
Fudgy Brownies.................................210

## Mint
Blackberry Mojito................................41
Roasted Chicken Noodle Soup..........65
Limoncello Sorbet Spritz....................41
Minnesota Bootlegger.........................39
Mint Mojo Sauce.................................222
Peach and Cucumber Gazpacho......73
Roasted Beets.....................................158
Smashed Chicken Sandwich..............87

## Miso
Roasted Beets.....................................158
Roasted Celery Root..........................172
Short Rib Burger..................................82

## Mocktails
Blackberry Mo.......................................41
Watermelon Lime Mocktail.....42

## Mushrooms
Beef Wellington....................................93
Chilaquiles with Mushrooms182

Chicken Marsala.................................146
Fall Farmer's Market Soup.54
Grilled Portobella Burger...84
Supper Club Cordon Bleu134

## Mustard
Apple Winter Squash Salad.173
Apple, Kohlrabi & Manchego Slaw.................................158
Beef Wellington....................................93
Chicken Marsala.................................146
Chicken, Leek & Tarragon Pot Pie...142
Croque Monsieur Sandwich.....88
Deviled Egg Salad..................168
Glazed Ham............................................97
Herb-Pot and Gruyère Soufflés..........................................179
Low Country Boil..............................130
Parmesan-Crusted Salmon Caesar Salad...................................155
Sheet Pan Chicken Thighs ....128
Tuna Cheese Melt................................86

## Nuts
*Almonds in*, Artichoke and Ricotta Flan........................166
Bookclub Quinoa Chicken Salad..................................163
Maple Granola..................188
Lagoon Chicken Wild Rice Salad..................................167
*Hazelnuts in*, Apple and Winter Squash Salad................... 173
*Pine nuts in*, Greek Baked Ziti................................................100
Balsamic Pear, Pistachio Pesto Tartine.................................28
*Peanuts in*, Spicy Cucumber Salad..................................165

## Oats
Maple Granola.........................188

## Olives
Mediterranean Relish............218

## Onion Soup Mix
Passover Brisket........................99

**Oranges and Orange Liqueur**
   Apricot Harissa-Glazed Chicken...125
   Blood Red Orange Margarita.......45
   Citrus-Cured Gravlax..................189
   Glazed Ham......................97

**Pancetta**
   Chicken Marsala..........................146

**Panko Bread Crumbs**
   Artichoke and Ricotta Flan .......166
   Chicken Parmesan Meatballs....132
   Pear and Prosciutto Pork Loin...103
   Supper Club Cordon Bleu...........134
   Supperclub Creamed Spinach Casserole................................157
   Tuna Poke Bowl............................136

**Parmesan Cheese, see also Cheese**
   Apple ..Winter Squash Salad.....173
   Baked Halibut en Pappillote .....140
   Balsamic Pear, Pistachio Pesto Tartine..................................28
   Chicken Parmesan  Meatballs..132
   Eggs in Purgatory........................183
   Hachis Parmentier......................116
   Herb-Pot & Gruyere Soufflés....179
   My "Keeper" Risotto....................221
   Parmesan-Crusted Salmon Caesar Salad................................155
   Pear and Prosciutto Pork Loin...103
   Philly Cheesesteaks......................79
   Sausage and Fennel Rigatoni....113
   Skillet Scalloped Potatoes........174
   Soupe Au Pistou.............................58
   Spring Lasagna............................145
   Sunday Supper Pork Ragu.........115

**Parsnips**
   Fall Farmer's Market Soup...........54
   Roasted Chicken Noodle Soup....65
   Parsnip and Potato Latke...........191

**Pasta, in**
   Soupe Au Pistou............................58
   Baked Halibut en Pappillote......140
   Hollace's Bolognese Recipe......107
   Leftover Bolognese Lasagna.....108
   Roasted Chicken Noodle Soup....65
   Pasta Diavola................................127
   Sausage and Fennel Rigatoni... 113
   Spring Lasagna............................145
   Sunday Supper Pork Ragu.........115

**Peaches**
   Peach and Cucumber Gazpacho..73
   Fruit Compote..............................220
   Upside Down Peach Cake...........206

**Pecorino Romano, in**
   Artichoke and Ricotta Flan........166

**Peas**
   Baked Halibut en Pappillote......140
   Fall Farmer's Market Soup...........54
   Spring Lasagna............................145

**Pepitas**
   Maple Roasted Carrots..............170
   Maple Granola..............................188

**Peppercorns**
   Creamy Green Peppercorn Sauce......................................227

**Peppers**
   *banana, in* Rhode Island–Style Calamari...............................133
   *red, in* Adobo Flank Steak.........110
   Bookclub Quinoa Chicken Salad...................................163
   Cantaloupe Sweet Corn Gazpacho...................................72
   Easy Sausage & Spinach Egg-Bake......................................184
   Kim's White Chicken Chili...........66
   Mediterranean Relish..............218
   Philly Cheesesteaks...................79
   Roasted Celery Root...............172
   Roasted Red Pepper Soup..........................................60
   Roasted Vegetable Platter.....160
   green, in Aunt Sherril's  Runza 80

**Pernod**
   Tomato and Fennel Soup........50

**Pesto**
   Balsamic Pear, Pistachio Pesto Tartine..................................28
   Soupe Au Pistou............................58

**Pears**
   Balsamic Pear, Pistachio Pesto Tartine..................................28
   Pear and Prosciutto Pork Loin...103

**Pickles**
   *cucumber in*, Tuna Cheese Melt..86
   *red onion in*, California Fish Tacos.....................................126

**Pistachio, see also Nuts**
   Apricot Harissa-Glazed Chicken....................................125
   Balsamic Pear, Pistachio Pesto Tartine..................................28

**Pitas**
   Crispy Lamb Pita............................83
   Traditional Hummus.....................26

**Pomegranate Seeds and Syrup**
   Maple Roasted Carrots..............170
   Roasted Vegetable Platter........160

**Pork**
   *breakfast sausage in,*  Easy Sausage and Spinach Egg Bake..................................184
   *kielbasa in,* Low Country Boil....130
   Pear and Prosciutto Pork Loin ..103
   *sausage in,* Hachis Parmentier .116
   Hollace's Bolognese Recipe...107
   Sausage and Fennel Rigatoni113
   Spring Lasagna.........................145
   *roast in,*Sunday Supper Pork Ragu..............................................115

**Potatoes, in**
   *hashbrowns in,* Easy Sausage and Spinach Egg Bake...................184
   Fall Farmer's Market Soup ..........54
   Hachis Parmentier........................116

Icelandic Fish Stew..........................68
Low Country Boil.........................130
Parsnip and Potato Latke............191
Roasted Carrot Soup......................53
Skillet Scalloped Potatoes.........174
Soupe Au Pistou.............................58
*sweet potatoes in*, Roasted Vegetable Platter....................160

## Proscuitto
Balsamic Pear, Pistachio Pesto Tartine................................. 28
Beef Wellington...............................93
Croque Monsieur Sandwich..........88
Pear and Prosciutto Pork Loin...103
Rosemary Ricotta Toast w/ Figs. 32
Supper Club Cordon Bleu...........134

## Prosecco
Limoncello Sorbet Spritz.............. 41

## Pudding, in
Stout Chocolate BundtCake......207

## Pumpkin
Layered Pumpkin Cake............213

## Quinoa
Bookclub Quinoa Chicken Salad.........................................163

## Queso Fresco, in
Chilaquiles with Mushrooms......182

## Raisins
Green Salad and Jam Vinaigrette...............................224

## Rice
Asparagus, Leek & Edamame Soup. .......................................................62
Arborio rice in My "Keeper" Risotto......................................221
Tuna Poke Bowl............................136
*wild rice in* Lagoon Chicken Wild Rice Salad................................167

## Rice Vinegar, in
Peach & Cucumber Gazpacho......73

## Ricotta, in
Balsamic Pear, Pistachio Pesto Tartine................................. 28
Artichoke and Ricotta Flan ........166
Rosemary Ricotta Toast Figs.......32

## Rhubarb
Roasted Rhubarb Agrodolce.....223

## Ritz Crackers
Chicken Parmesan Meatballs....132

## Romaine Lettuce
Parmesan-Crusted Salmon Caesar Salad........................................ 155
Smashed Chicken Sandwich........87

## Rose Harissa
Apricot Harissa-Glazed Chicken....................................125
Harissa Baked Fish .....................139
Roasted Red Pepper Soup ...........60
Roasted Vegetable Platter .......160

## Rosemary
Rosemary Ricotta Toast w/ Figs..32

## Rutabaga
Perfect Pot Roast....................... 114

## Salmon
Bourbon-Glazed Salmon Bites.....35
Baked Salmon...............................147
Citrus-Cured Gravlax..................189
Parmesan-Crusted Salmon Caesar Salad ........................................155

## Sauces
*Alfredo sauce in* Baked Halibut en Papillote.................................140
*Bechamel sauce in* Croque Monsieur Sandwich..........................88
Greek Baked Ziti......................100
Spring Lasagna.........................145
*Bolognese sauce in* Leftover Bolognese Lasagna...............108
*Creole remoulade in* Low Country Boil............................................130
*Green peppercorn sauce in* Beef Wellington..................................93
*Horseradish sauce in* Perfect Pot Roast..........................................114
*Mint mojo sauce in* Leftover Roasted Chicken Noodle Soup.........65
Smashed Chicken Sandwich....87
*Romesco sauce in* Roasted Celery Root...........................................172
*Soubise sauce in* Supper Club Cordon Bleu...........................134
*Spicy mayo in* Rhode Island-Style Calamari...................................133
*St. Cecilia Sauce in* Upside-Down Peach Cake.............................206

## Scallions
Bourbon-Glazed Salmon Bites.....35
Cheesy Mexican Street Corn Dip.25

## Seafood
*Shrimp, in* Low Country Boil......130
*Squid, in* Rhode Island-Style Calamari...................................133

## Sesame Oil & Seeds
Asian Flat Iron Steak...................112
Tuna Poke Bowl............................136
Six-Minute Seared Ahi Tuna Steaks........................................148

## Sherry
Roasted Red Pepper Soup............60
Baked Onion Soup..........................57
Asian Flat Iron Steak...................112

## Spinach (baby)
Lagoon Chicken Wild Rice Salad.........................................167
Easy Sausage & Spinach Egg Bake... ......................................................184
Fall Farmer's Market Soup...........54
Smashed Chicken Sandwich.........87
Spring Lasagna.............................145
Supper Club Creamed Spinach Casserole................................157

## Squash
Apple Winter Squash Salad......173

## Sriracha
Low Country Boil.........................130
Rhode Island-Style Calamari ....133
Tuna Poke Bowl............................136

## Strawberries
Panna Cotta Dessert Cups.........199
Strawberry Gazpacho................74

### Sumac
Strawberry Gazpacho..........
### Sweetened Condensed Milk
Aunt Sherril's Runza......................80

Grandma's July 4th Ice Cream..205
### Tahini
Baba Ghanoush..............................31

Harissa Baked Fish .....................139

Lemon Tahini Sauce....................226

Roasted Beets................................158

Roasted Celery Root....................172

Traditional Hummus.....................26
### Tajín
Cheesy Mexican Street Corn Dip.25
### Tea
Mango Green Tea Smoothie..187
### Tequila
Blood Red Orange Margarita.......45
### Tofu
Roasted Beets...............................158
### Tomato
Adobo Flank Steak......................110

Asian Flat Iron Steak...................112

Avocado Toast with Sweet & Spicy Tomatoes....................................192

Chicken Parmesan Meatballs....132

Cantaloupe & Sweet Corn Gazpcho......................................72

Crispy Lamb Pita...........................83

Eggs in Purgatory........................183

Harissa Baked Fish......................139

Hollace's Bolognese Recipe......107

Mediterranean Relish..................218

Oven-Dried Tomatoes.................227

Pan Con Tomate..............................21

Pasta Diavola...............................127

Roasted Red Pepper Soup...........60

Sausage and Fennel Rigatoni....113

Smashed Chicken Sandwich........87

Strawberry Gazpacho....................74

Sunday Supper Pork Ragu.........115

Supper Club Wedge Salad.........171

Tomato and Fennel Soup..............50
### Tortillas and Tortilla Chips
California Fish Tacos...................126

Cheesy Mexican Street Corn Dip.25

Chilaquiles w/ Mushrooms........182
### Tuna
Tuna Cheese Melt..........................86
### Turkey
Turkey Breast..............................149

Bookclub Quinoa Chicken Salad..............................................163
### Vinegar also see Balsamic
Avocado Toast with Sweet & Spicy Tomatoes....................................192

Stout Chocolate Bundt Cake ....207

*apple cider vinegar,* in Adobo Flank Steak...........................................110

Apple Kohlrabi and Manchego Slaw......................158

Apple Winter Squash Salad..............................................173

Green Salad and Jam Vinaigrette................................224

*red wine vinegar,* in Bourbon-Glazed Salmon Bites........35

Crispy Lamb Pita........................83

Grilled Portobello Burger.........84

Low Country Boil....................130

Roasted Celery Root............172

Spiedies..................................95

Supper Club Wedge Salad...171

*rice vinegar,* in Deviled Egg Salad........................................168

Peach & Cucumber Gazpacho..................................73

Roasted Vegetable Platter...160

Short Rib Burger......................82

Spicy Cucumber Salad..........165

Tuna Poke Bowl.....................136

*white wine,* in California Fish Tacos......................................126

Strawberry Gazpacho..............74
### Vodka
Minnesota Bootlegger..................39

Twist on a Dirty Martini................42
### Vermouth
Chicken, Leek & Tarragon Pot Pie.......................................................142

Twist on a Dirty Martini................42
### Wasabi
Bourbon-Glazed Salmon Bites.....35

Tuna Poke Bowl...........................136
### Watermelon
Watermelon Lime Mocktail.........42
### Whipped Feta
Grilled Portobello Burger.............84

Mediterranean Crostini..................24
### Whiskey
Dr. Werley Whiskey Sour..............43

Layered Pumpkin Cake...............213

Stout Chocolate Bundt Cake ....207
### Wine
*red wine,* in Perfect Pot Roast..114

Sunday Supper Pork Ragu......115

Wine-Braised Short Ribs........119

*white wine,* in Baked Halibut en Pappillote...............................140

Baked Onion Soup...................57

Baked Salmon........................147

Chicken, Leek & Tarragon Pot Pie........................................142

Hollace's Bolognese Recipe.107

Homemade Gravy..................221

Icelandic Fish Stew..................68

Low Country Boil...................130

My "Keeper" Risotto...............221

Passover Brisket......................99

Pear & Prosciutto Pork Loin..103

Sausage & Fennel Rigatoni..113

Sheet Pan Chicken Thighs ....128

Spiedies...................................95

Turkey Breast..........................149

**Yeast**
- Aunt Sherril's Runza……………80

**Yogurt**
- Açaí Bowls…………………………186
- Blueberry Yogurt Smoothie……187
- Crispy Lamb Pita…………………83
- Lemon-Blackberry Fool…………197
- Peach & Cucumber Gazpacho……73
- Roasted Vegetable Platter………160

**Zucchini**
- Roasted Vegetable Platter………160
- Soupe au Pistou……………………58

*"I have loved to cook since I was a child in my mother's kitchen. If I don't have time to cook, I'll just read a cookbook.*
— ***Kamala Harris***

# Gratitude Around the Table

This cookbook began with thirty loyal followers—friends and family—who cheered me on when I launched ourtable42.com (read as our table for two) back in 2022. You told your friends, shared my recipes, and believed in my new adventure. I am still humbled by that early support and by everyone who has joined this community since.

To all my readers and followers across every platform: your kind messages, recipe comments, and words of encouragement over the years have meant more than you know. You've inspired me to keep cooking, creating, and sharing. Truly—you made this book happen.

To my husband, Mark—thank you for your endless patience as I "take one more photo" before we eat, and for your quiet support every step of the way.

To the 18 recipe testers who gave honest feedback, helped me refine, and even nudged me to let go of a few recipes (for now)—this book is stronger because of you.

To my dear friend and project manager extraordinaire, Diane Tigner—there would be no Around Our Table For Two without you. You've been my coach, videographer, organizer, and cheerleader, helping me grow from thirty newsletter subscribers to nearly a thousand loyal readers each week. From long kitchen days filming for community education classes to formatting class booklets and learning new platforms together, you've given countless hours with endless enthusiasm. Thank you for believing in me.

To Kurt, thank you for helping me create the look and feel of Our Table 4 2 and Around Our Table for Two. You helped make this vision a reality.

To my aunts, thank you for digging through Grandma's recipe box and sharing stories of Grandma Lois—her way of turning simple farm ingredients into feasts that brought everyone together. Your memories kept her spirit alive in these pages.

To my proofreaders—Juli, Kim, Camie, and Laura—thank you for your time, attention to detail, and thoughtful insights. My favorite line from you all: "This is the first time I've read every word in a cookbook." That made me smile and kept me pushing to the finish line.

To Pam, Kim, Sherril, Hollace, and Alison—thank you for letting me bring your cherished family recipes into this collection and for trusting me to adapt them for a table of two.

To my boys, Michael and Zach—thank you for always wanting to talk food and for your own adventures in the kitchen that continue to inspire me. From helping name this cookbook to sharing it proudly with your friends, you've grown our community and my confidence.

To my book club, thank you for being willing taste testers, enthusiastic supporters, and the best company around a table. We read, eat, and drink wine very well.

Finally, to everyone who has ever cooked one of my recipes, sent a note, shared a photo, or told a friend about Around Our Table 4 2 (for two)—thank you. You've helped turn my kitchen stories into something far bigger than I ever imagined.

With deep gratitude,

Pam

# About the Author

Pam is the creator of ourtable42.com (read as "our table for two"), where she celebrates an enduring love of heirloom recipes and turns them into thoughtful meals for two. Her summers in the warm, bustling kitchens of her grandmothers taught her that cooking is more than nourishment—it's connection, care and heritage. Now working and cooking in Minnesota, Pam champions locally sourced ingredients and supports small producers, believing that food tastes better when you know the people who brought it to the table.

With Around Our Table 4 2: Heirloom Cooking, Time-Honored Techniques, Local Flair, Pam brings together recipes rooted in childhood memories and scaled for today's dinner for two. Whether adapting her aunts' farm-style Runzas or re-imagining a Sicilian family Bolognese, she honors the past while embracing wherever life has led her. She's guided by the belief that:

*"A recipe has no soul. You, as the cook, must bring soul to the recipe."*
– **Thomas Keller**

www.ingramcontent.com/pod-product-compliance
Lightning Source LLC
Chambersburg PA
CBHW051514110526
44582CB00008B/157